EXCALIBUR
THE·SEARCH·FOR·ARTHUR

li rois escui uos en uoient deus auram̃e
part ausi com il afet espee. Lors regardeñ
uers la riue ꝺ̃ trcual et uoit uenir ausi
come abeloing une dumoiselle monte
seur un palefroi blãc et uenoit uers
aus g̃nt aleure.

EXCALIBUR

THE·SEARCH·FOR·ARTHUR

Gwyn A. Williams

BBC BOOKS

•*Frontispiece* Watched by King Arthur and Queen Guinevere,
Galahad sheaths the sword, having drawn it from the stone; from the
Romance of Lancelot du Lac, 1385–90.
•*Pages 6 and 7* Lancelot jousting before Arthur and Guinevere,
from the *Romance of Lancelot du Lac*, 1344.

© Gwyn A. Williams 1994
The moral right of the author has been asserted

ISBN 0 563 37020 3

Picture research by Deirdre O'Day
Published by BBC Books, a division of BBC Enterprises Ltd
Woodlands, 80 Wood Lane, London W12 0TT

First published 1994

Set in Berling by Ace Filmsetting Ltd, Frome, Somerset
Printed by Cambus Litho Ltd, East Kilbride and bound by
Hunter & Foulis Ltd, Edinburgh
Jacket printed by Belmont Press Ltd, Northampton

Contents

for SIÂN

·

'Four white trefoils sprang up behind her
wherever she went . . .'

Culhwch ac Olwen, c. 1080

PREFACE

In the summer of 1993, I was sitting on a beach in Amroth, Pembrokeshire, when I heard a strange, rhythmic sound. I turned to see a man who was obviously a Traveller, his arms outstretched, intoning a hymn to King Arthur, directed at Caldey Island of the monks.

I cite this to make it clear that, in this book, I have rigorously avoided all kinds of speculation (though I may sometimes have failed!). I have tried to detect the moment when Arthur may have emerged in the Britain which was struggling free of the disintegrating Roman Empire, to confront pagan enemies known generally as Saxons. I have assessed the sparse evidence which suggests his historical existance, before embarking on that odyssey through romance and legend which begins in Welsh oral literature and goes on, over centuries, to embrace the whole of Europe and beyond. At every stage, I have tried to relate legend to its social, political and religious context. I am a historian and I suppose this is a historian's book. I can do no other.

It has been a memorable and rewarding experience. A particular pleasure has been the discovery that Welsh Arthuriana, obviously prominent at the beginning, in fact keeps cropping up throughout. I still find stunning the discovery that the story of Perceval which I thought I 'knew' – he of the first encounter with the Fisher King, one of the Three Elect of the Grail – was, in the actual texts of the romances from Chrétien de Troyes through to the German Wolfram von Eschenbach and beyond, the story of Perceval the Welshman whose nationality his distraught mother, in a familiar exercise, tried to disguise!

For further pleasures, I am indebted to Martha Caute and her staff at BBC Books, who even made proof-reading enjoyable, and I thank my friends and colleagues of Teliesyn TV Co-operative who laboured hard and ingeniously to produce the film series for BBC and S4C under the same title: Colin Thomas, Ray Orton, Alan Jones, Non Hughes, Alwyn Hughes, Maurice Hunter, Pauline Williams, Dafydd Rowlands, Mali Evans, Hayden Pearce and the rest, who jousted with sundry demons under the eye of our lady of the unfathomable lake, Carmel Gahan.

Did someone mention the *Auteur* of a film?!

Gwyn A. Williams, Drefach Felindre, 1994

CHAPTER ONE
ARTHUR·THE·BRITON: THE·MYSTERY

King Arthur is the greatest of British literary heroes and one of the greatest heroes of France and Europe. He reigned over European and British minds from the eleventh century, at the latest, to the twentieth. Yet his beginnings, and those of his knights, are singularly obscure.

He seems to have emerged as Britain struggled into independence as the Roman Empire collapsed and he entered almost immediately into the imaginative literature of the Welsh, who considered themselves heirs to the independent Britons. After the Normans encountered the Welsh in the eleventh to twelfth centuries, the stories and legends about Arthur began almost at once to commandeer the minds of story-tellers throughout French-speaking Europe, to be given substance by Geoffrey of Monmouth's *History of the Kings of Britain* (*c.*1138), which made the 'Matter of Britain', as the story of Arthur was known, a best-seller in Europe and the Crusader states, rivalling the 'Matter of France' with its riveting heroes, Charlemagne and Roland. Chrétien de Troyes, the first major French writer to embrace the stories in the twelfth century, started the process which made Arthur and his knights the very stuff of the European imagination until the fifteenth century.

As he began to fade in Europe, he took off anew in England, to climax in Sir Thomas Malory's *Le Morte d'Arthur* of the fifteenth century and the period of the Tudor dynasty, before falling silent for two hundred years, until his near-incredible renaissance in modern times, in Blake and Tennyson, the paintings of the House of Lords . . . and so into the present day. In every generation, people have made him and his knights a vehicle for their own values. Few legend cycles can have been so potent.

• The Round Table in Winchester Great Hall, possibly dating from the thirteenth century; the portrait of Arthur and the names of his knights were probably added during the reign of Henry VIII.

Given how slender the evidence is for Arthur's historical existence, the more miraculous the endurance of this epic seems. But before embarking on this odyssey, there is another set of problems whose solution seems to stretch the historian's mind to the limit. In the Arthurian legends, almost from their first appearance, there figure men and women who were once gods, and knightly rituals which were once divine. Unexpected but riveting is the relationship between the world of Arthur and that of two thousand years and more earlier, the world of that mighty and unequalled memorial to the shadowy people of the Bronze Age – Stonehenge.

Around 330 BC Hecateus of Abdera, a Greek, wrote an account of the Hyperboreans, the people long rumoured to dwell beyond the north wind. It is an account which has a golden age nostalgia about it and is known only from another author, Diodorus Siculus, writing about 50–30 BC. In book five of the *History* of Diodorus Siculus, Hecateus is quoted as saying that opposite the land of the Celts (Gaul) 'there is an island not smaller than Sicily, situated under the constellation of the Bear, which is inhabited by the Hyperboreans'. Even earlier, and similarly known only from later sources, a Greek writer in the mid-sixth century BC reported that the inhabitants of present-day Brittany traded with the people of two large islands to the north, Albion and Ierne. These, the first recorded names of Britain and Ireland, seem to be Greek versions of Irish Celtic names, themselves probably derived from an earlier, now lost language. It was about the same time as Hecateus wrote that Pytheas of Massilia (Marseilles) made a journey on the western sea-route and called the islands Pretanic – *Prydain* in Welsh – undoubtedly a Celtic name from a form of speech which became Brittonic, the language of the Britons.

Those pre-historians and archaeologists who mention the text of Hecateus hasten to add that there is no proof that the island to which he refers is Britain and that the text cannot be used as evidence. True enough, but it seems to me they protest too much; a little controlled speculation seems not only justifiable but, in this case, necessary. What island – 'of a happy temperature, rich in soil and fruitful', producing two harvests every year – do they imagine it could have been, particularly since the same author is credited with a few kind words about the inhabitants of present-day Cornwall on the metal-route to Ireland? The constellation of the Bear even plays an odd role in the very name of Arthur himself, as will be seen.

The author goes on in what is no doubt a disconcerting manner to some scholars:

Tradition says that Latona, the mother of Apollo, was born there, and for that reason the inhabitants venerate Apollo more that any other God . . . In this island, there is a magnificent precinct of Apollo and a remarkable temple, of a round form, adorned with many consecrated gifts. There is also a city, sacred to the same God, where most of the inhabitants are harpists and play continually on their harps and sing hymns to the God . . . The Hyperboreans use a peculiar dialect and have a remarkable attachment to the Greeks . . . It is related that some Greeks formerly visited the Hyperboreans, with whom they left consecrated gifts of great value.

He adds that from the island the moon seems close, with promontories just like the earth, and every nineteen years, in which period the stars complete their revolutions, the god appears, to play and dance every night from the spring equinox until the rising of the Pleiades.

How un-British! But if the island is indeed Britain, Hecateus must be referring to Stonehenge, Avebury and the whole complex of settlement and memorial on Salisbury Plain, hub of the chalk uplands which, until the coming of the Romans, was the 'capital' of prehistoric Britain.

Stonehenge, that mighty structure, was without parallel in prehistoric Europe. With its great circles and avenues of bluestones and massive sarsen stones, its various calculated alignments on the moon and the sun, its hints of human sacrifice and ritual (its most sober archaeologist can outline the possibility of 'sinuous dances'), its carved symbols – which include a dagger whose only parallel is Mycenean, with other suggestions of Mycenean and Minoan contacts – Stonehenge was vastly impressive. It underwent many changes in its two- to three-thousand-year history; it fell into disuse and was revived, must have taken enormous human resources to build and rebuild, and testifies to the formative significance of the Bronze Age, when the Wessex civilization had such a wide-ranging influence and when the human matrix of Britain took shape.

Stonehenge with its servitor city was dedicated to Apollo the sun god and his mother, according to the ancient Greek writers, who would have given the god and his mother names familiar to them. In Roman or Romano-Celtic Britain, maybe five or six hundred years later, evidence from Hadrian's Wall indicates the existence of a strong British cult of a god called Apollo-Maponos. Later still, in the first Arthurian romance to survive, the Welsh *Culhwch ac Olwen*, there appears a famous prisoner, Mabon mab (son of) Modron, who appears to have been imprisoned since the beginning of time,

+————

- *Overleaf* Stonehenge, the awesome prehistoric stone circle once dedicated to the sun god Apollo and his mother, and later associated with many Arthurian mysteries.

since Arthur has to consult the 'Oldest Animals in the World' to find him. Once released, he becomes one of Arthur's men, plunging into the River Severn with him to wrestle with a huge wild boar who was once a king.

He goes on to become an established character in French Arthurian romances. Scholars identify him with a Celtic god, Maponos, son of Matrona, a goddess who gave her name to the River Marne in France. Matrona is the Welsh Modron, the Earth Mother. Mabon mab Modron literally means 'Son son of Mother', the Apollo-Maponos of the Romans – and the Apollo of Hecateus? He and his mother may have been given Celtic names but they seem to be much older.

It is known that an Earth Mother of some kind was characteristic of the culture of Neolithic and Mesolithic peoples of the Stone Ages; the transition to the Bronze Age is believed to have turned religion skywards, but fusion rather than displacement seems to have been the theme. A 'Son son of an Earth Mother' who was a sun god was natural. That he should turn up in Arthurian romance and the medieval Welsh stories incorporated in the later collection, *The Mabinogion*, indicates a remarkable persistence, transmitted and distorted orally through time.

Mabon is only one of a legion of old Welsh and Irish gods – Math, Pelles, Beli, Bran, the dynasty of Don, Bors and Ban, Balin and Balan, Morgan la Fay (the list can seem endless) – who in various forms inhabit the romances of the Arthurian cycle in Britain and Europe. They are called Celtic. Many probably were, but many others seem older, reaching back to the time when Britain assumed its basic human character in the Bronze Age. In their oral transmission over centuries into the Arthurian cycle, they lost their nature as gods and became human beings with supernatural attributes.

Other Arthurian mysteries cluster around Stonehenge. According to Hecateus, there was a city nearby sacred to Apollo. In the Arthurian romances, particularly their French forms, as in the enormous collection known as the *Vulgate Cycle*, and in the English Sir Thomas Malory's work, a holy city called Sarras, with its people the Sarrasens, figures largely. It was once chief city of the pagans. Sir Galahad himself reigned there, though he was first imprisoned by its pagan king for proclaiming the Grail; he and the other Grail knight, Sir Perceval, die there. The climax of the Grail quest is reached in Sarras, not the more familiar Camelot.

But many of the romances confuse the Sarrasens with the Saracens, the Arab Muslims against whom the Crusades were fought. So much so that Sarras is transferred to the East. And a similar confusion may explain the incredible sequence in Geoffrey of Monmouth's *History* where, after Arthur, Britain is overrun and practically destroyed by 'the inhuman tyrant' Gormund and an army of 160 000 non-Christian Africans who ultimately hand the realm over to the Saxons. But in Malory, where

Saxons figure not at all, armies of Sarrasens from the holy city, forty-thousand-strong, do battle for the Christian Arthur.

French Arthurian romances refer to the gods of the pagan Sarrasens, who exacted human sacrifice, as 'Tervagant, Mahomme, Apolin and Jupiter'. Mahommed is an obvious intruder, derived from the same confusion with the Saracens, but the other names seem apt. Jupiter is equated in inscriptions with Taranis, a Celtic thunder god, Apollo is Mabon mab Modron and Tervagant or Terican is a god described as having a fountain, shaded by three pines, from which water flowed through a silver pipe on to a stone or peron of marble and thence into a vessel of lead – a version of which is very familiar from the Arthurian tales of Challenge and Combat.

It seems clear that Sarras was originally in Britain. The name of the massive sarsen stones of Stonehenge is said by dictionaries to derive from Saracen, but this, too, seems a much later confusion with those Arabs who stood in Western minds for pagans; maybe original memories had been lost. The sarsen stones may point to an original and pagan Sarrasen 'city dedicated to Apollo' in the vicinity of Stonehenge. In the Arthurian romances Sarras represents a vague, confused and corrupted memory of such a place, which resurfaces in the myriad stories that accumulated around Arthur.

But Geoffrey of Monmouth in his *History* tells a much more striking story, from the Arthurian period itself, which deals with the very existence of Stonehenge. The story is set in the fifth century AD when Britain is at grips with the invading and pagan Saxons. In restoring the kingdom during an interval of success, the king of the Britons, Aurelius (based on a historical figure who was a precursor of the historical Arthur), comes to Salisbury and is overwhelmed by the memory of the 'Treason of the Long Knives' – the Saxon massacre by treachery of 460 British leaders – and seeks a suitable memorial for them. Carpenters and stonemasons came from all over the kingdom, racked their brains but could think of nothing suitable. The archbishop of the City of the Legions (Caerleon) advised him to send for Merlin from his haunts in the Welsh borderlands. Merlin, then little more than a boy, had already distinguished himself as a prophet. Aurelius pressed him on the memorial.

Merlin said, 'Send for the Giants' Ring which is on Mount Killaraus in Ireland. In that place there is a stone construction which no man of this period could ever erect, unless he combined great skill and artistry. The stones are enormous and there is no one alive strong enough to move them.'

At these words of Merlin's Aurelius burst out laughing. 'How can such large stones be moved from so far-distant a country?' he asked. 'It is hardly as if Britain itself is lacking in stones big enough for the job!' 'Try not to laugh in a foolish way, your Majesty,' answered Merlin. 'What I am suggesting has nothing ludicrous about it.'

He explained that the stones, transported from Africa by giants many years ago, were connected with certain secret religious rites and had various medicinal properties – the giants used to run water over the stones and take baths to cure their illnesses.

The Britons were convinced and an army crossed over the sea, led by the king's brother, Uther (the father of Arthur). The Irish king also burst out laughing when he heard their mission, but he and his army were defeated by the British army. When the British stonemasons made their way to Mount Killaraus, they stared at the structure with wonder.

Merlin came up to them as they stood round in a group. 'Try your strength, young men,' said he, 'and see whether skill can do more than brute strength, or strength more than skill, when it comes to dismantling these stones!'

At his bidding, they set to with every conceivable kind of mechanism and strove their hardest to take the Ring down. They rigged up hawsers and ropes and they propped up scaling-ladders, each preparing what he thought most useful, but none of these things advanced them an inch. When he saw what a mess they were making of it, Merlin burst out laughing. He placed in position all the gear which he considered necessary and dismantled the stones more easily than you could ever believe. Once he had pulled them down, he had them carried to the ships and stored on board, and they set sail once more for Britain.

When he got the stones to the monastery at Mount Ambrius on Salisbury Plain (probably Avebury or Amesbury), Aurelius summoned a national assembly; he filled vacant sees and gave Dubricius (Dyfrig, first of the Welsh 'saints') the see of Caerleon. He then ordered Merlin to erect the stones in exactly the manner of Ireland around the burial place of the martyrs, which was to serve henceforth as a sepulchre for the kings of Britain, including Arthur's father. Merlin did so, 'thus proving his artistry was worth more than any brute strength'.

This entertaining story, in which Merlin figures less as a magician than as a superlative engineer, is clearly ludicrous in placing the erection of Stonehenge in the

• Merlin erects Stonehenge; an illustration from a
fourteenth-century French manuscript.

rathe; vous dit qverhi eu dus
A par folie ne fere; plus
congre; ongnie z senou
enfe; de puth de cornaffler

fifth century AD. Geoffrey of Monmouth obviously derived it from stories already in circulation, for there are other tales of stones floating in the Severn down to Caerleon or Camelot, which could represent 'memories' of a time when miraculous Stonehenge was thought to have been brought by sea from Ireland or the 'Ireland' represented by the Irish kingdoms of west Wales which were established at the end of Roman rule.

Just such a possibility became very real from 1923 when it was apparently proved that the bluestones of Stonehenge came from one place and one place only – the far-off Preseli mountains of Pembrokeshire in south-west Wales. Considerable research and a practical project to try the several routes the stones might have taken backed up the theory. It became the standard opinion, still held by many. The link with the Preseli mountains had considerable justification. The area was a recognized station on the metal trade route with Ireland; it had small stone circles of its own; glacial action within Wales had uprooted many of the stones there; and transport by sea was proved feasible. The feeling was reinforced that much of southern Britain in the Bronze Age enjoyed a unity which could enable such a project to be conceived and executed – a major archaeologist of Stonehenge, R. J. C. Atkinson, could speculate on a Bronze Age proto-Arthur and proto-Merlin. And, of course, the theory strengthened the belief that Geoffrey's story, however misplaced in time, enshrined what had become popular memories.

But in the 1970s a counter-theory was developed that the stones were moved not by human agency but by an ice-sheet: the bluestones on Salisbury Plain were 'erratics' carried there by glacial action. No other stone circle in Britain has stones which were dragged more than five to six miles and it is believed that the bluestones were already present, ready to be worked up. This theory, too, has resulted in massive research and it seems the profession is divided. There are furious battles over one stone, not a bluestone, which is apparently from the Snowdon area; was it carried to the bluestones at Preseli by natural glacial action within Wales or directly to Salisbury Plain? Are the stray bluestone artefacts and chippings in the area evidence that the stones were available on the Plain already or were they the result of ceremonial work on stones brought by sea? The idea of 'erratics' being carried by glacial drift of the type proposed has been discounted; river gravels in the area, it is claimed, show no sign of glaciation. The argument is between geologists and geomorphologists. Challenges have flown both ways; an Open University discussion of the theme has been denounced and a recent volume on Stonehenge (1993) dismisses the glacial theory. A historian can make only marginal observations.

One tendency which I have already noted in my work on the myth of Madoc, a Welsh medieval prince who was alleged to have discovered America in 1170, is that some historians take a narrow view: it is enough for them to show that a legend has no foundation. In doing so they throw out several babies with the bath water. Given the advance of scientific technique, any fool can demolish a legend; it takes a special kind of fool to try to answer the question of why a legend took the form it did; there is usually some ember under the smoke.

If the glacial theory carries the day, as it well might, this would remove a valuable prop from proponents of both the unity of much of southern Bronze Age Britain and the popular memory interpretation of Geoffrey of Monmouth's Merlin story. Personally, I do not think it would make much difference one way or another. There is already sufficient evidence to convey a strong idea of an underlying unity in southern Britain in the Bronze Age. And, whether misguided or not, I think Geoffrey's story points to some kind of popular belief about the origins of Stonehenge.

There is abundant material, then, hinting at a Bronze Age provenance for many of the characters in Arthurian romance, who emerge much later from former gods and their environments, filtered through the Celtic and Roman experience. But when Arthur himself rises to visibility, he does so in a very different context, that of a Christian warrior who emerges at the end of Roman rule over a Britain which was essentially Celtic.

Celts seem to have appeared in Britain in the first millennium BC when the island's people dissolved into warring tribal groups which shared a common culture but had little political coherence. The old view that they came in a series of invasions from their European heartland has largely been discarded; archaeologists stress independent regional development of similar ideas. Celtic refers to a language group, rather than an ethnic community. Celts themselves, by every European witness, were described as big, fair and well built, and although there are large, fair, well-built people among the Welsh, they are hardly representative of our gallant little nation. Whenever Celts appeared in this island, my ancestors, certainly, were on the beach to meet them! The Welsh were physically similar to many of the Britons – what used to be called Mediterranean in physiognomy.

What made the island part of a Europe-wide entity called Celtic was the superior technology and brilliant, flamboyant culture of the Celts. There is a theory that people managed to 'grow into' this culture and language. (The Bronze Age Beaker Folk, so called after their distinctive flat-based pottery and sometimes credited with a key rebuilding of Stonehenge, have been called 'proto-Celts'.) But I do not know of any people who have grown into another language without an initial compulsion of some kind. The late Raymond Williams, who worked hard on pre-history for his last book

People of the Black Mountains, once rebuked me for not having made clear that Celtic hill forts played the same role as Norman castles. Certainly the old language was completely blotted out except in the North, where people called Picts still spoke it. Everywhere else, people spoke a version of the Celtic language called Brittonic, the British mother-tongue of Welsh, Cornish and Breton.

Celtic civilization – probably spread by small, technologically superior, ruling groups – engulfed most of Britain and in the lowlands coinage and something like proto-cities had developed by the eve of the Roman invasion. Britain and Gaul operated as virtually one civilization. Anglesey was a centre of the Druidic religion, attracting acolytes from all over the Celtic world. That religion, with its fixed calendar of festivals (many later Christianized), had hundreds of deities, many no doubt taken over from earlier gods and associated with natural objects, particularly springs and sacred groves. The great god was a tribal god and a horrific character, a grotesque male giant carrying a huge club with which he clobbered his people with various disasters, though he could also reward them from his Cauldron of Rebirth. His goddess was less tribal, more concerned with the land itself. She worked in harmony with the tribal kings. As the rule of the king waxed and waned, so she turned into a hag who presided, in early days at least, at the king's ritual execution. There was an interesting goddess of panic and a universal sort of craftsman god called Lludd, who was said to have built London and given it his name – Caerludd (still remembered in Ludgate). Shape-shifting was frequent, particularly among goddesses; the Celtic triad appears, the greatest deity of them all being a mother and a triple mother. There were many other gods and large numbers of them were to appear in British–Welsh and Irish mythology and ultimately to lodge in the Arthurian stories.

The central controllers of both religion and intellectual life in general were the Druids. They were to exercise such power over later minds that it is necessary to stress that we know very little about them. They were dedicated to magic and among them or dependent on them were shadowy orders of poets who were remembrancers and celebrants of tribal kings, givers and interpreters of the law, soothsayers, astronomers and regulators of the seasonal life rhythms who cultivated medicine and a form of science. They helped shape the culture of the Welsh and Irish as those peoples emerged. Though Stonehenge had nothing to do with the Druids, they may have taken its ruins over for particular purposes – or perhaps the Romans thought they did and tried to demolish it, for the Romans were horrified when they encountered Druids in Anglesey. Not only were there the wild women, whom they called Furies – all flowing hair, curses and rent robes – but the Druids, in their services conducted in sacred woods and enclosures, appeased their gods with human sacrifices, of maidens, babies and kings.

• 'Lord of the Animals', the Celtic stag-god of the forests,
depicted on the Gundestrup Cauldron in the
National Museum, Copenhagen.

The sacrifices were perhaps being commuted to animal sacrifices as the Romans arrived, but the latter were determined to blot the Druids out, as foci of resistance.

Along with the religious traditions went the secular traditions of battle – often as much theatre as slaughter – poem-chanting and mead-drinking around the great fire in the central hall, when the boasting and word-play, the kindred pride, were of an intensity peculiar to Celts. Warriors sat around their king in a circle to make sure no-one took precedence; precious hoards, including swords, were thrown into sacred lakes dedicated to local gods; there was a cult of the severed head, considered the repository of a man's spirit.

The memory of all this, with whatever Bronze Age inheritance it carried with it, was to survive four hundred years of Roman rule; the code of a warrior elite emerged still enshrined in the Brittonic language, to inform the Heroic Age of the Britons and their Arthurian stories. Nevertheless, it is striking how swiftly Celtic deities succumbed to the world religions of Rome, with their single gods like Mithras or Jehovah, and were transmuted into folk heroes. For the Britons emerged from Roman rule with an entirely new set of memories.

After a reconnaissance by Julius Caesar in 55–54 BC, the Roman conquest began in earnest from AD 43 and took nearly a century in the face of fierce resistance in the West and North. The hero Caradoc (Caratacus), who made a last stand with the Silures of south-east Wales, was shipped to Rome and made a speech reported by Tacitus that echoes down the centuries. Four hundred years later, a resurgent king of the same Silures was called by the same name – and would figure later as an Arthurian hero commemorated in Britain, Brittany, Italy and France.

But once the conquest was effective, south of Hadrian's Wall, Britain settled remarkably easily into a two-hundred-year Roman peace. Under the imperial bureaucracy, power passed to about twenty *civitates* – the city state form imposed on former tribal groupings. The Silures, for example, were moved out of their hill fort into the highly fashionable little town of Caerwent, with its sophisticated Mediterranean-style houses. It had its guild of merchants, a patron of high rank and its *ordo* of a hundred councillors who exercised self-government under the imperial bureaucracy. With its upper-class *decurions* it proudly bore the title of a *respublica* – a republic – and was the capital of the commonwealth of the Silures. And the same happened, to a greater degree, in many more favoured places.

Lowland Britain was laced with superb roads, cities and towns, which carried the full panoply of commerce, currency, civilization, more and more deeply into the highlands. It is evident that the degree of Romanization, which varied with the topography, has been underestimated. Even with the later decline in imperial commerce which crippled the cities, life flowed to country estates and villas. In 212–14, every freeman in the empire was given the full rights of a Roman citizen; a hundred years later this discrimination had yielded to the more realistic distinction between upper and lower classes. The Britons, or their directive classes, became Romans, and the memory long outlived the reality.

Many people acquired some literacy in Latin, though, unlike Gaul where the native language disappeared, Brittonic persisted as a major language. Religion tended to go the same way. Druids soon seem to have vanished, though other religions were tolerated, provided they offered no threat to the imperial cult. Possibly the last of the pagan gods was celebrated in a temple to Nodens (who, as the Welsh Nudd, figured later as an Arthurian hero in France and Italy) built at Lydney, across the way from Caerwent, in 367. Christianity had made itself felt by 300. Persecution provided two martyrs in Julius and Aaron at Caerleon, but they were allowed to worship without hindrance from 313, and in 337 Christianity became the official religion of the empire; all other religions had been outlawed by 400. British bishops were present at Church councils in 313 and 359.

By the end of the Roman period much of Britain must have been at least nominally Christian, though it seems to have required the new impulse of Celtic missionaries in post-Roman times to root it. Britain even produced its own heresy – that of the British monk Pelagius – which stressed the doctrine of grace, interwoven with the practice of patronage. It seems to have appealed in particular to local elites increasingly restive at the exacting rule of Rome and its orthodox Christians by the late fourth century.

In these circumstance, while the old British inheritance evidently remained vivid in the native language, newer elements appeared. Nearly two centuries after the end of Roman rule a man in north Wales could still call himself a *cives* – a citizen – and for a century after Roman authority had gone Britons retained a vivid sense of *Romanitas*, which may well have influenced Arthur himself. The central British myth which emerged was that the race had been founded by the classical hero, Brutus of Troy, a myth that seems likely to have struck root in the late Romano-British period. More persistent still was a sense of the unity of Britain and its strength – manifest in the Dark Age preoccupation with *Ynys y Cewri*, the Island of the Mighty, and its inalienable sovereignty. Whatever Celtic and pre-Celtic memories this enshrined, it was Rome which had made the Island Mighty.

From the fourth century, order in this mighty island began to break down. Sufficiently strong to support a succession of military attempts to seize power at Rome itself, Britain as a wealthy and exposed sector suffered from barbarian incursions which became more and more serious. In 367 an organized conspiracy of Picts to the north, Irish to the west and probably people known generically as Saxons to the east, allied with disaffected serfs and slaves within, overran the island and even forced the secession of a province from the empire. Theodosius gradually restored order, but the history of Britain suddenly became one of insecurity. Saxons and other Germans were settled as what the Romans called 'federates', mercenaries hired to strengthen the over-stretched army and rewarded with land. This did not stop the ever increasing attacks. Britain's defences were reorganized to face the sea.

In 383 a general Magnus Maximus was raised on their shields by the army in Britain as yet another usurper and their chosen emperor. With massive British support he crossed to the continent and extinguished a rival emperor, but met death himself in 387. He was to figure very largely in the mythology of Wales and Brittany as a founding father. The ultimate Saxon triumph was said to date from his 'withdrawal of the legions', while the many minor kings who emerged as Rome collapsed nearly all came from the ranks of the aristocracy of Roman Britain, many to claim descent from Magnus, or Macsen Wledig as the Welsh called him.

Stilicho, under the emperor Honorius, had great difficulty restoring imperial power from 402. The imperial court moved to Ravenna and the flow of silver coinage into Britain abruptly stopped, dislocating the civil and military establishment. The landowning magnates continued to enjoy prosperity but authority began to disperse. In 405 there was a massive raid from Ireland, the disaffected army raised yet another soldier to claim the empire even as, at the end of 406, a great horde of Christian German barbarians burst across the Rhine, swept through Gaul and broke into Spain. The army crossed the Channel but became enmeshed in the chaos that Gaul was becoming. In 410 Alaric the Goth sacked Rome itself and as part of this assault, pagan Saxons descended on Britain.

The Britons, led, it seems, by heretic Pelagian magnates, organized their own defence and beat them off. They had had enough. During 408–10 they broke with Rome, bloodily purged the imperial civil service and took power themselves. Honorius was compelled to recognize the coup. Britons embarked on a four-hundred-year adventure of independence out of which came both the historical and the legendary Arthur as the greatest hero of those Britons.

CHAPTER TWO

ISLAND
IN·THE·MISTS

Britain broke free from the Roman Empire in AD 409 and for nearly four hundred years, uniquely in western Europe, fought for its life against the barbarians. It also plunged into some of the most tumult-ridden and obscure centuries in its history, and for the historian the period 400–800 is marked by its intractability as much as the sheer scarcity of evidence.

Language itself is a problem. In a time of rapid change, the Brittonic spoken in the island disintegrated. An inflected tongue like Latin, it lost those inflections, before giving way to its successor tongues of which the most important was Welsh (*Cymraeg*). Attempts, usually by clerics, to write histories of the period foundered in these conditions. As one preface to a surviving ninth-century attempt put it: 'Many learned scholars and copyists have tried to write, but somehow they have left the subject more obscure, whether through repeated pestilence or frequent military disasters.'

The few written sources which survive are all the more precious. The most influential is the sixth-century *Concerning the Fall of Britain* (*De Excidio Britanniae*) by the British monk Gildas. An irate cleric, he directed a ferocious blast at his compatriots, whom he denounced for abandoning Latinity – to which his own verbose opacity offers ample testimony! Historical evidence comes as an afterthought, though he is the source of the traditional story of the coming of the mixed Germanic peoples known to the Britons as the Saxons (*Saeson* in Welsh), whose ultimate triumph he ascribes – like all the clerics, though not the lay writers – to God's punishment of the Britons for their sins.

He can be supplemented on the Saxon side by the magnificent *Ecclesiastical History of the English Nation* (*c*.730) by the Saxon monk, the Venerable Bede, though it is marred by anti-Welsh prejudice, and by the *Anglo-Saxon Chronicle* (*c*.890). On the British side, a collection was made about 960, probably at St David's in Wales, of pedigrees, annals and documents; two of the most important are the *Annals of Wales* (*Annales Cambriae*) and a narrative *History of the Britons* (*Historia Brittonum*), the core of which was probably assembled about 828–30. The latter was the first account to make Brutus the Trojan and his immigrants the founders of the British race. This, with a few European chronicles, the first properly Welsh poets, Aneirin and Taliesin, about 600, and a scatter of archaeological finds and inscribed stones, form the sum total of the evidence.

So difficult is this material, so profound and sustained the arguments among scholars over the very nature of their evidence, that a prudent historian might opt for a pregnant silence. The period has become, as one historian of Wales (aptly in our case) put it, 'a tournament for scholars, with each successive contributor to the debate eager to unhorse his predecessor'. The most anyone can do is offer what seems a believable account.

One thing is certain. At the beginning of the period, around 410, Britain was still one, still largely Romano-British in style, still the single dominion of the Island of the Mighty. Threatened by Picts to the north and Irish to the west, it was holding out. By the end of the period, around 800, Britain had been lost. The great bulk of it had become the *England* of the Saxons. Britain had shrivelled to Wales, Cornwall and Strathclyde in what was becoming Scotland – and a vivid memory of the time when the Old North had been home to Britons. It was a four-hundred-year chronicle of plague, defeat, heroic last stands, dreadful betrayals and catastrophe. There was one exception – the years around 500, when Britons under a great leader won fifty years of triumphant peace. That leader, according to tradition, was Arthur.

Twenty years after British independence, in 429, St Germanus of Auxerre came to the island to combat the Pelagian heresy prevalent there and to ignite the 'Age of Saints' – when the monkish 'saints' of the Celts ranged all over the western seas from Scotland to far Galicia in Spain, establishing their own, distinctive brand of Christianity. Germanus led the Britons in a hallelujah victory over a Pictish-Saxon raid and found the island still governed by the landed aristocracy of the commonwealths. But power was passing to other hands – to Vortigern (Gwrtheyrn), whom Gildas calls a 'proud tyrant', a man without legal authority. Drawn from the western areas, where kingship must have been rapidly advancing in a disturbed age, Vortigern apparently hailed from what had been the commonwealth of the Cornovii and was becoming the kingdom of Powys, which stretched from Wales deep into what became the English Midlands. He was evidently a military commander, appointed by the councils to counter the barbarian threat. He soon towered over them.

Vortigern was apparently a Pelagian and Germanus may have turned to Catholic supporters, such as Ambrosius Aurelianus (Emrys), member of a family, says Gildas, which had 'worn the purple'. The notables contained the threat from Germanus, but within fifteen years they were done for. Around 452 a chronicler in Gaul identified the year 441–2 as that in which Britain, long disturbed, 'passed under the dominion of the Saxons'. Taken literally, this is a gross exaggeration, but it reflects a reality. In the middle of the fifth century Britain suffered a disaster which left tracts of the east under Saxon control. Gildas, supplemented by the *History of the Britons*, the Saxon origin-legend of Hengist from Bede and the *Anglo-Saxon Chronicle*, is the source of the traditional story.

Prosperity in Britain ended in plagues, the renewal of Pictish attacks and civil war. Vortigern countered this by hiring Saxon mercenaries. There were already Germans in Britain, planted there by the Romans as 'federates'. They were fairly strong in the Thames valley and there are persistent reports of an early Saxon settlement to the north, near Hadrian's Wall. Vortigern, threatened by 'the Picts and the Irish, by a Roman invasion and not least by fear of Ambrosius', says the *History of the Britons*, welcomed Hengist and his pagan Saxon raiders. He was also besotted with Hengist's daughter, Rowena, whom he married, pagan or no, and gave the Saxons Kent as a bride-price.

Affronted, Britons under Vortigern's son Vortimer (Gwrthefyr) fought back, winning victories until the latter was poisoned by Rowena. Hengist brought in yet more of his unspeakable kin and, at a peace conference, staged the 'Treason of the Long Knives' (*Brad y Cyllyll Hirion* to the Welsh, who nursed an undying memory of it) in which over nine hundred (by this source) of the British leaders were massacred. In a Britain thus decapitated, the Saxons ravaged without mercy:

> All the greater towns fell to the enemy's battering rams; all their inhabitants, bishops, priests, people, were mown down together . . . Horrible was it to see the foundation stones of towers and high walls thrown down bottom upwards in the squares, mixing with holy altars and fragments of human bodies, as though they were covered with a purple crust of clotted blood, as in some fantastic wine-press.

The rhetoric of Gildas finds a chilling echo in a report he cites, the appeal of the Britons to Aetius, Roman consul in Gaul, between 446 and 454: 'the barbarians drive us to the sea and the sea drives us back to the barbarians'.

Disaster was compounded by repeated outbreaks of plague, which seem to have afflicted the population of the more Romanized tracts in western Europe and to have decimated the 'Welsh' – as the Germans called the Romanized natives they encountered all over Europe. Fleeing plagues and Saxons, large groups of Britons were crossing into Gaul. Many seem to have moved in organized communities; in 461 one of their bishops attended a conference at Tours. The moves grew into a mass migration which continued for a century and more, another of those 'migrations of the peoples' which characterized the times. Most of them settled in Armorica which became Brittany and may already have nurtured Britons since the time of Maximus. Its people were called Britons and they spoke Brittonic, which in time produced Breton, close cousin to Welsh. This Little Britain was to become central. Churchmen crossed endlessly between Brittany, Wales and Cornwall, lives of Welsh and Cornish saints were produced there and the earliest known canon laws of the Welsh came out of it. The connection remained intimate for centuries.

But the whole process must have ripped the heart out of that Britain which the revolt of 409 had created, for underneath Gildas's rhetoric there seems to have been a reality. From the middle of the fifth century, much of a Britain that was still in important senses Roman ceases to be archaeologically recognizable.

It was in that period, with Vortigern a client king, that the *History of the Britons* sets a strange story which became important in the legends of Arthur. Vortigern, trying to build a great tower as a refuge, saw its foundations repeatedly sink. He was advised by his 'magicians' to find a fatherless boy, kill him and sprinkle his blood on the stones, and a youth called Ambrosius from Glamorgan who fitted the bill was tracked down. But confronted with the magicians, the youth overthrew them and revealed that the foundations concealed two dragons, the Red of the Britons, the White of the Saxons, who would battle for dominion over the Island of Britain until the Red would prevail. Vortigern is then said to have given Ambrosius all the kingdoms of the western part of Britain, since the father (of this fatherless boy!) had been a consul of the Roman people.

This fantastic story seems to confuse the boy with Ambrosius Aurelianus, the enemy of Vortigern! Its importance lies in the fact that seven centuries later Geoffrey of Monmouth made it the foundation for his story of Merlin. Not that the incident did Vortigern any good. Shortly afterwards, pursued by Germanus and the British clergy all over Wales, he was burned to death 'with all his wives' in his castle on the River Teifi in the south. Though, the author adds, 'others have different versions'.

What is true, however, is that the late fifth century saw a remarkable reversal of fortune. In Gaul, in the 460s, Roman power revived under Anthemius, an able commander. And central to the force which Anthemius led against the Visigoths in 467 was a powerful army of Britons under Riothamus, king of the Armoricans – the Bretons.

• Merlin (Ambrosius) reads a list of his prophecies to
King Vortigern above the foundations of the great tower
containing the dragons of the Britons and the Saxons;
from a thirteenth-century manuscript.

Sedentis est deliberare. Sedente itaqe eo .i. delibante ⁊ disponente
de edificanda turre qñ magi csulerant in psidium sibi cstruere:
egressi sũt duo dracones. ¶ Coniuncto annectit narracōem
⁊ ordinat ut sic ctinuatio ad hystoriam. ¶ Iñfecto cstantino

At about the same time, according to Gildas, Ambrosius Aurelianus in Britain began to win victories over the Saxons. It was a long process under different leaders, with varying fortunes, until a great three-day siege of Mount Badon (*Mons Badonicus*). No one knows where this was, but one plausible guess would be somewhere near Bath. It saw a total British victory. This happened, said Gildas, writing about 540, in the year of his own birth – possibly around 490 or later. During his lifetime, he added, there had been peace and prosperity.

Mount Badon, then, seems to have inaugurated a period of British victory which lasted for some fifty years. Archaeological evidence from the Saxon settlements in the Thames valley and from the Low Countries and the mouth of the Elbe bears out statements in Frankish chronicles – that in the late fifth century the Saxon advance in Britain suffered a serious check and there was a reverse migration to the continent. And these years, of course, were Arthur's.

But after Gildas, the curtain comes down. The Saxon advance was resumed. It was a slow business; some of the advances may not represent conquests and there is evidence of the transient existence of peoples who were literally mixed. But the advance was remorseless. After a battle near Bristol in 577, Bath, Cirencester and Gloucester were gone and the Saxons reached the Severn Sea. Somerset was not theirs until after 650, and there was a British king in Devon until 710. Cornwall, which remained essentially Celtic in speech and culture, was not absorbed into Wessex until 950.

In the North, there were British attempts to destroy the English kingdom of Bernicia from Rheged in 577 and twenty years later there was another assault from Edinburgh on English Deira. These northern British kingdoms were to play a central role in the history and literature of the Welsh as British survivors. They comprised Strathclyde, with its centre at Dumbarton Rock in the Clyde; Rheged, which stretched from Solway through Carlisle; and the kingdom of the Votadini with its centre at Edinburgh; while to the south lay Elmet, a British kingdom west of York. The sixth and seventh centuries were years of great battles which involved the northern Welsh kingdoms of Gwynedd and Powys. Indeed, the dynasty which ruled Gwynedd was said to have migrated there from Edinburgh. The first Welsh poets, Aneirin and Taliesin, were located there, though the latter may have migrated through all the British lands like any 'saint'. The first poem in recognizable Welsh is Aneirin's *Gododdin*, which is a lament for the heroes from Edinburgh who fell at Catterick (Catraeth) in present-day Yorkshire around 600. Much northern material was transferred wholesale to Wales by the ninth century to form a crucial element in its cultural formation.

The crumbling of these northern regions was slow. After the union of Bernicia and Deira, it was Northumberland which absorbed most of them. Elmet was taken in 617,

Rheged in 635, perhaps by marriage; Carlisle was English by 685. Edinburgh fell about 638. Strathclyde alone survived for another four hundred years; as Northumberland succumbed to the Danes, Strathclyde expanded to include Rheged, where for a century and more after 900, British influence revived. It was not absorbed into the kingdom of the Scots until 1018.

Further south there were great, triangular battles involving Mercians, Northumbrians and West Britons before the Saxons settled on the northern shores of the Irish Sea. It took another century to establish the power of Mercia in the Midlands. Perhaps the last stand of the Britons came with the campaigns of Cadwallon of Gwynedd, who threatened Northumberland with annihilation and was credited by Bede with the intention of exterminating the English race. When his son Cadwaladr died late in the seventh century, a Welsh chronicle declared: 'And from that time onwards the Britons lost the crown of the kingdom and the Saxons won it.'

East of a line from Scarborough to Southampton, there is precious little evidence of any British survival, even in river names. West of that line, however, there is much. Place names remain Celtic. There was provision for a whole, finely graded if inferior British hierarchy with its own language within Wessex society. Beyond this, up to the rooted British lands of north-west Britain, Wales and Cornwall, British survival under Saxon control was extensive; there may have been almost as much fusion as conquest.

Wales was marked off at the end of the eighth century by Offa's Dyke, an agreed frontier from sea to sea and a line that was to survive, more or less, until the Normans. Behind it, the Welsh called the Britons who were left Cymry – fellow countrymen, comrades. They went on calling themselves that even when there was no-one else left to be called fellow countrymen except their cousins the Cornish. It took centuries for these 'Welsh' to conceive of themselves as Welsh. Only in the tenth-century Laws of Hywel Dda is there the first glimmering of a specifically Welsh consciousness and even then, *Armes Prydein*, a polemical poem, was calling on an old alliance of everyone in Britain who was not English to expel the Saxons from the island they had stolen.

These Welsh, regarding themselves as heirs of the Britons and cherishing memories of the time when the Cymry of Wales, Cornwall and the North shared an allegiance to the single crown of the Island of the Mighty, could find one shining exception to a four-hundred-year span of continuous retreat. The fifty years or so around 500 had been years of victory and they made them the years of the greatest hero of the Britons, Arthur. What warrant is there for this identification?

First of all, his very name was Roman. Like Ambrosius, it carried a certain resonance, a certain 'memory' of the Romano-British: he would have been a Christian, with some sense of the life of late Romano-British times, not very remote in the late fifth century, and perhaps of its military organization. Later, his name was sometimes written Arcturus. This, as well as referring to the constellation Ursa Major or the Bear, also signified the polar regions and the tempestuous weather associated with the rising and setting of the star Arcturus. Its use could imply that Arthur was a man of bear-like quality – the Arthur the Terrible known to later Welsh writing. But this was a conceit. The original of his name, Artorius, could easily transmute into Arthur in Brittonic and Welsh. Artorius was rare enough as a Latin name in Britain, but not unknown. Would descendants of the Britons in the eighth or ninth centuries, when memories of Rome had become very remote, invent such a man with such a name as their great *British* hero? It seems very unlikely.

On the other hand, there were at least four British royal families who named their sons Arthur around 600 – notably those of Aedan, king of Dalriada, in what is today western Scotland, and Petr in Dyfed, south-west Wales – which suggests widespread homage to a hero who had lived in fairly recent times. In fact the king of Dalriada, who had British connections, seems to have used the name as a talisman, since he headed what was meant to be a massive attempt to drive the English out of Northumbria.

In the Memorabilia or Marvels of the early ninth-century *History of the Britons*, two places are listed which already had Arthur etched into the landscape. At Builth in mid-Wales, one stone on top of a pile bore the footprint of Cafal, 'the warrior Arthur's hound', left there on the great hunt for the boar Twrch Trwyth, which figures prominently in early Welsh stories. Arthur himself put it there, says the *History*, and today men come and take the stone in their hands for a day and a night and on the morrow it is back on the pile. To the south, in the district called Ergyng, on the borderlands of south Wales, a tomb by a spring called Llygad Amr (Amr's Eye) commemorates an otherwise unknown son of Arthur called Amr, whom he is alleged to have killed. The tomb kept changing its measurements, sometimes six feet, sometimes as many as fifteen. Whatever measure it had when you first tested it, you never found it to be the same again – 'and I have tried it myself' said the *History*'s author!

These are obviously myths, if significant ones. They are the first, early hints of what was to follow. In time, Arthur was to be remembered in the landscape of half Britain and Brittany in Arthur's Rocks and Arthur's Chairs innumerable. In Ireland at this period, it took about a century for a hero to become a god or demi-god. How long would a tradition of a warrior hero take to become embedded in a local landscape before 800?

More substantial evidence are the first poems to be written in a recognizable Welsh, notably the earliest, the *Gododdin* by Aneirin, which is a eulogy to the men who fell in the forlorn raid on Catterick (Catraeth) about 600. Celebrating the prowess of the warrior Gwawrddur, the poet says, 'He glutted black ravens on the wall of the fort – though he was no Arthur.' The raven was a symbol of death which recurs frequently in early poems and is a poetic way of saying that Gwawrddur was a great warrior, but could not compare with Arthur – the very embodiment of martial valour.

If we could be sure that this was a genuinely contemporary couplet written around 600, its evidence could well be decisive. However, it seems to stem from a ninth-century copy and may be an interpolation at a time when the reputation of Arthus had grown to mythic proportions. Much the same is true of other early poems. An elegy for Cynddylan, a king of Powys who fell at the hands of the Mercians, probably about 660, described him and his sons as 'whelps of Arthur, a mighty fortress'. A poem celebrating the deeds of Geraint, a sixth-century ruler of Devon, runs:

> *In Longborth I saw Arthur. . .*
> *Emperor, ruler of battle. . .*

It is necessary to indicate that these verses may have been written several centuries later than their subject-matter, but the tone and meaning of the poems are clear. Very striking, too, are the *Stanzas of the Graves*, listing the graves of about two hundred heroes, chiefly from folklore. One stanza reads:

> *A grave for March, a grave for Gwythur,*
> *A grave for Gwgawn of the Red Sword,*
> *The world's wonder a grave for Arthur*

The last line has been retranslated by a distinguished scholar, Dr Thomas Jones, to read 'Concealed till Doomsday the grave of Arthur'. The suggestion – made in the certainty that the audience would know the details – is that there was something mysterious about Arthur's death or his burial, a suggestion which is fully developed later in the stories about his last battle, Camlan, in a tragic civil war which destroyed his achievement and all hope.

The most serious, indeed only, evidence for the historical Arthur comes from the *History of the Britons* (*Historia Brittonum*) of around 828–30 and the *Annals of Wales* (*Annales Cambriae*), compiled from the eighth century and put together in the tenth. The Latin *History* has long been wreathed in controversy, which today centres on whether it was a 'synthetic' history which could embrace legends or a 'synchronistic' history which need not do so. It uses many sources and in the clerical style of the time is obsessed with chronological calculations. Its governing feature is that it was written *after* the conversion of the English to Christianity. The deeds of Vortigern, Hengist or Arthur in the end counted for nothing; it was St Germanus, St Patrick and the progress of Christian conversion which mattered.

So, after an account of British origins in Brutus the Trojan and his descendants, and of the making of the Irish people, the author runs through the Roman occupation of Britain, the doings of Vortigern, his son Vortimer, Germanus the saint and Hengist the Saxon, with an emphasis on Kent, until he reaches the downfall of Vortigern and the ravaging of the British heartland. He then deals with St Patrick and the British conversion of Ireland and at that point he inserts the successful campaigns of Arthur, which, he says, forced the Saxons to import kings from Germany, leading into the last section on the northern kings of the English. With their conversion, God's will is realized and the Welsh, the last of the Britons, will have to come to terms with it.

What concerns us is the section entitled 'The Campaigns of Arthur (de Arturo)'. After the death of Hengist, his son Octha came from the north to start the kingship of Kent. The *Anglo-Saxon Chronicle* dates this in 488: 'Then Arthur fought against them (the Saxons) in those days, together with the kings of the British; but he was the battle-leader (*sed ipse dux erat bellorum*).' A version a century later reads: 'Then the warrior Arthur, with the soldiers and kings of Britain, used to fight against them [the Saxons]. And though there were many of more noble birth than he, he was twelve times leader in war and victor of the battles.'

A list of the twelve battles then follows. Three cannot be identified: those at rivers called Bassas and Tryfrwyd, and on a hill called Agned. The first of the battles was at the mouth of a river Glein, which has been placed conjecturally either in Northumberland or Lincolnshire; there were no fewer than four along a river Dubglas in the Lindsey district of Lincolnshire, or conceivably along a river near Ilchester, further south. Others were at the city of the Legion – either Chester or Caerleon, probably the former – and in Celyddon Forest or Coed Celyddon, which became famous later as Caledon and has been placed in the southern uplands of present-day Scotland.

The intriguing battles are the eighth and the last.

The eighth battle was in Guinnion Fort and in it Arthur carried the image of the Holy Mary, the everlasting Virgin, on his shield and the heathen were put to flight on that day and there was a great slaughter upon them, through the power of Our Lord Jesus Christ and the power of the holy Virgin Mary, his mother. . .

The twelfth battle was on Badon Hill and in it nine hundred and sixty men fell in one day, from a single charge of Arthur's, and no one laid them low save he alone; and he was victorious in all his campaigns.

And the Saxons, defeated in all their struggles, sent in desperation to Germany and brought over their kings.

The *Annals of Wales* are brief. Though the dates cannot be taken literally, they read:

516 The Battle of Badon, in which Arthur carried the Cross of our Lord Jesus Christ for three days and three nights on his shield and the Britons were the victors.
537 The battle of Camlann, in which Arthur and Medraut fell: and there was plague in Britain and Ireland.

Mount Badon is familiar from Gildas – and he mentions no-one as the leader there – although if anyone would know of, or even know, Arthur, it would be he. However, Gildas, obsessed with his denunciations of the Britons, generally avoided naming names. A well-established, later story had Arthur engaged in a merciless feud with Huail, Gildas's brother, in which Huail was killed. Fraternal rage might be an explanation for Gildas's silence about Arthur, since the context of this later story at no time suggests any effort to explain away any awkward silence. Later on, the story-tellers assert, Gildas was reconciled with Arthur, but Gerald the Welshman in the twelfth century claimed that 'when he heard of his brother's death, or so the Britons say, he threw into the sea a number of outstanding books which he had written in their praise and about Arthur's achievements. As a result, you will find no book which gives an authentic account of that great prince.' Plausible though this might seem, it bears the imprint of a later rationalization.

Another explanation suggests that Arthur was so well-known that it would have been ludicrous for Gildas to single him out; as a formidable scholar, Kenneth Jackson, once put it, 'what English bishop, castigating the vices of his compatriots about 1860, would be so clumsy as to allude to the '"battle of Waterloo, which was won by the Duke of Wellington"'. This is entertaining; whether it is anything more depends on one's

‡——————

• *Overleaf* King Arthur destroying the Saxons at the battle of Mount Badon; from a fifteenth-century manuscript.

taste or scepticism. Yet another suggestion is that Arthur was so different from the run of wicked kings which were Gildas's speciality that he preferred to say nothing at all about him. An alternative explanation, apart from an obvious one – that Gildas did not mention Arthur because Arthur did not exist – is that the battle of Mount Badon was not Arthur's victory at all, but was attributed to him later.

We are stuck with Gildas's bloody-minded silence, but the battle of Mount Badon, whoever fought it – and most sources are unanimous that it was Arthur's great and explicitly Christian battle, almost a crusade in itself – was certainly singled out by the Britons as the crucial point when the tide turned and the Saxons were stopped in their tracks, in a three-day siege of a hill broken, according to the chronicler, by an all-conquering charge by Arthur 'alone'.

The list of twelve battles poses many problems. There is what seems a blur over Christian symbolism. The Virgin Mary was on Arthur's shield at the unknown Guinnion Fort and the Holy Cross on it at Badon; possibly the two were confused. Four or even five battles in Lincolnshire seems excessive, unless Arthur was tackling that zone where the Saxons were at their strongest; the same holds good if the site were further south in Wessex. Coed Celyddon was definitely in what is today southern Scotland and several other battles may have been sited there. Mount Badon, the evidence suggests, was in the south on the borders of Wessex, probably near Bath. This geographical spread is perfectly acceptable; later authentic kings of both Britons and Saxons ranged hundreds of miles in their raids and campaigns; warfare was extremely mobile.

An intriguing argument holds that the list, possibly with additions from other sources, was derived from a British/Welsh battle-listing song. Such songs were common at the time and it is possible that the song was sung in commemoration of Arthur and incorporated in the *History*. There is an important point here: the list in the *History* does not mention the battle of Camlan, whereas it is mentioned in the later *Annals*. Camlan was to loom very large in the tradition of Arthur's life and death. It was a terrible civil war fought between Arthur and Mordred (the Medraut of the *Annals*) which destroyed Arthur's achievement and led on to the loss of Britain and its Crown to the Saxons. The fact that this crucial battle is not present in the *History* suggests that, if a battle-listing poem was the source, it may have been sung, not over Arthur's grave, but to his face.

The list also raises the question of just what kind of a war leader Arthur actually was. He was not a king and there were many more noble than he, yet he had military gifts out of the ordinary. He was called a *dux bellorum*, literally a 'duke of battles', presumably at the service of the kings of Britain – not unlike Vortigern himself. This *dux* seems to have been some confused memory of a Roman title. The argument that he had actually revived the Roman use of heavy cavalry seems far-fetched, but it is perfectly plausible that he and his war band were mounted and fought on horseback. The charge at Badon that he made 'alone' may refer to him and his war band, as distinct from the militias of the kings for whom he fought. He and his war band could therefore be an embryo of Arthur and his knights.

The war band, or *teulu* (family in modern Welsh), was absolutely central to the emerging kingdoms of the Britons. Some of the greatest kings were served and the greatest battles fought by men drawn from all corners of the Britain that was left. This privileged elite of footloose young men, attracted by the prestige and generosity any great leader (the 'gold-giver') generated, was crucial in determining the fate of many kingdoms. As Arthur himself put it in a later story: 'We are noble men so long as we are resorted to. The greater the bounty we show, all the greater will be our fame and our glory.' If Arthur proved as successful in his campaigns as the chronicles indicate, he would have attracted the best warriors in the island. Beginning as a general under the orders of the kings of Britain, he would have ended up towering over them all, as a British version of the Saxon *Bretwalda* – a ruler or emperor of Britain.

This is the sum total of the historical evidence available on Arthur, if one discounts the huge corpus of later story and legend, which may, of course, carry its own meaning. In the end, it seems to me, there are only two real alternatives. You can dismiss the whole story as a myth and assert that Arthur was invented in later years, charged with all the yearning of the Britons and Welsh for a hero of the island of Britain. This alternative is perfectly feasible, but leaves an unconscionable amount of explaining away to do.

Or you can, as I do, accept Arthur as a historical figure and, with whatever qualifications seem necessary, take the picture of him in the chronicles as broadly true. He seems to have emerged some time in the late fifth century, give or take forty years or so. Where he emerged from is sheer speculation. A strong school argues for a purely northern provenance, though I find this untenable. Others point to his later identification with Cornwall.

For what it's worth, I favour the explanation, though not the identification, of two recent writers, Graham Phillips and Martin Keatman, who point to what had been the substantial commonwealth of the Cornovii which became the strongly organized and persistent kingdom of Powys. This straddled what became the English–Welsh border, stretching from deep mid-Wales into the English Midlands beyond Shrewsbury and to the south in the borderlands. It had a focus at Viroconium (Wroxeter), which was reoccupied in some strength during these 'dark ages'. It had been Vortigern's stronghold, seems to fit Arthur's battles and in later years its kings were called 'whelps of Arthur' – and when Merlin appears, he haunts the area! But this is mere speculation.

Arthur emerges from the same kind of stable as Ambrosius Aurelianus, as a great war leader, wins explicitly Christian victories over the pagan Saxons, gathers his war band, in the end looms over the kings of Britain as a kind of *Bretwalda*, meets disaster at Camlan and disappears in a mysterious death. And despite heroic struggles, the Island of the Mighty of the Britons disappears with him.

This few and fragile people, the Welsh, took on their shoulders the whole weight of their lost British inheritance. Their poems and sagas echo to the croak of ravens glutting themselves on human blood, groan under the graves of heroes and martyrs. Their chronicles and histories are charged with a sense of anguish and loss. But that solitary time of glory under Arthur, when the idea of Britain was still alive and triumphant, they seized on with joy and lightness of heart. They fixed it in time, like a gossamer dragonfly in amber.

They elaborated Arthur's time as a *Bretwalda* into a suzerainty over the three successor realms of the island of Britain. To him they attributed conquests 'warranted' by the simultaneous recovery of Roman authority in Gaul. Their heroes, from the great battles of the sixth century in the north, from the semi-pagan tales they absorbed from the Bronze Age inheritance of Britain, they enrolled in his war band. The growing complex of stories could attract many peoples. Arthur carried the appeal of a deathless champion of a lost golden age, of a great Christian hero battling pagans on his Crusade, of warriors made knights who met adventures drawn from a half-understood pagan world. He carried the seed of the Grail. And the tale did not end; such as he could never die. The saga of Arthur, this last hero of the Britons and first of the Welsh, Cornish and Bretons, grew into one of the most mighty and attractive cycles of legend that Christendom has ever known.

That process began at home, in the imaginative literature of the Welsh.

CHAPTER THREE
ISLAND
OF·THE·MIGHTY

'No one has a right to this Island except only the nation of the *Cymry*, the remnant of the Britons who came here in former days from Troy,' declares an early text, 'These are the Names of the Island of Britain' bound with the triads in one source. It conjures up a single Crown at London, now lost to the pagan Saxons, who had stolen half the island, and it hails the surviving British 'Coronets' in the North, Wales and Cornwall.

And Arthur is the Chief Prince, *Pen Teyrned*, of these three realms, says an early triad, one of the groupings in threes, on often surprising subjects, which formed an index to oral poems and tales. Collections of them occur in many sources and they were later published as *The Welsh Triads*. In Wales, the locale of his high court varied before it settled at Geoffrey of Monmouth's Caerleon, but in the north it was fixed at Pen Rhionydd, an old and long-lost site in Galloway, the centre of a British North which persisted for some three to four hundred years and embraced north-western England and southern Scotland. And Celli Wig, probably in westernmost Penrith, is singled out as his court in Cornwall; it was to serve Arthur for centuries as his first Camelot.

True to his origins, Arthur is rarely called a 'king' in Welsh, but he is given kingly attributes and weapons – the Old Welsh names for these are the bane of every scholar who is not Welsh, and of many Welsh people, too! He had his great hall, *Ehangwen*, described as fair and roomy, and built by his craftsman, Glwyddyn; his fine horses, Hengroen and Llamrei; and his marvellous dog, Cafal. He had a great ship, *Prydwen*; his mantle of invisibility; his magic spear, *Rhongomyniad*; his shield, *Wynebgwrthucher*; and his deadly dagger, *Carnwennan*. Above all there was his magnificent sword – *Caledfwlch*, the 'Lightning Sword', associated with the old Lightning Gods – later called Excalibur – probably acquired in a raid on the Otherworld. His wife Gwenhwyfar (Guinevere) was, naturally, the fairest woman in Britain. She sometimes assumed triple form, like any Celtic goddess, and was supplemented by three mistresses.

This portrayal of Arthur the Hero, who was already acquiring magical attributes, emerges in the early imaginative literature of the Welsh. The old Brittonic language of the island had become Welsh by the eighth or ninth centuries and its literature was essentially oral, so, to the intense frustration of scholars, most of it has been lost, leaving them only fragments to chew over. The triads provide an index to many stories and jogged the memory of the poets and story-tellers who declaimed in and out of the many royal courts of Wales.

The great advance in Celtic linguistic studies has enabled scholars to place the date of a text, in its earliest written form, as several centuries earlier than the oldest manuscript in which it is preserved. The set of stories which emerged as the Four Branches of the Mabinogi (mabinogi originally implied a 'tale of youth', later simply a 'tale') – and which were ultimately grouped and published in English as *The Mabinogion* – assumed their present form in a written version composed in about 1060 in south Wales; similarly, the earliest Arthurian romance, *Culhwch ac Olwen*, which is included in *The Mabinogion*, took written shape around 1080–1100.

What they and many of the surviving poems celebrate is the sovereignty of Britain, the Island of the Mighty, now reduced to Wales, Cornwall and a vivid recollection of the time when the North was still British. The early triads, some forty to fifty of them, incorporate memories of the sixth and seventh centuries and are often charged with satire, burlesque, even buffoonery. They offer a chance to filter out a fragmented but vivid picture of Arthur as he seemed then to the Welsh and their fellow Britons.

One startling triad names Arthur as one of the 'Three Frivolous Bards' (*ofer-feirdd*) of the Island of Britain. (An *ofer-fardd* was a scurrilous or perhaps amateur poet, outside the tightly knit and secretive guild of 'bards', as several historical Welsh princes were.) He was said to be skilled at the *englyn*, a very difficult three-line verse form which appears from the ninth century. He sang a mocking one at the expense of Cei, his greatest warrior, which provoked a fatal breach between them. Cei, like Bedwyr, his constant friend, was there from the beginning of the stories and in European literature these two men, Arthur's closest companions, were to become famous as Kay and Bedevere. An early poem, 'What man is the gate-keeper? (*Pa gur yw y porthaur?*), runs:

> *What man is the gate-keeper?*
> *Glewlwyd Mighty-Grasp.*
> *What man asks it?*
> *Arthur with Cei the Fair.*
> *What band goes with you?*
> *The best men in the world.*

Cei is singled out as Arthur's leading warrior. He fought and wielded a polished shield against Palug's Cat, a monster sea cat who was one of the 'Three Oppressions of Anglesey' and was to wander over half Europe before he was through. Bedwyr felled hundreds at the battle of Tryfrwyd, one of the twelve listed battles in the *History of the Britons*, and fought alongside Arthur against the dog-heads on the mountains of British Edinburgh. Some pun may have been intended here, for *Gwrgi* (Dog-Man) appears in the triads as one who 'used to slay every day one of the Cymry and two every Saturday, so as not to slay on the Sunday'.

In the French romances and in Geoffrey of Monmouth's *History*, Cei, as Kay, is Arthur's seneschal (steward) and Bedwyr, as Bedevere, his cup-bearer, but in the early Welsh literature Cei was already displaying those curmudgeonly traits which later distinguished Kay, being hostile to young newcomers to Arthur's court and generally bloody-minded. Indeed, in one French romance of the early thirteenth century, *Perlesvaus*, Kay kills by treachery Arthur's son Llachau, who may have been important earlier but who rapidly fades out. An early poem mourning lost heroes runs: 'I have been where Llachau was killed, son of Arthur, marvellous in songs, when the ravens croaked over blood . . . I have been where the warriors of Britain were slain, from the east to the north; I am alive, they in the grave.' The sagas and poems, like this one, wrestle with encroaching Saxon power and echo to the croak of ravens in stark contrast to Arthurian songs, which are usually quite light-hearted, full of battles with witches, giants and monsters.

Another early hero listed in the triads was Gwalchmai, Arthur's nephew and his most faithful warrior, who enjoyed the status of a man's sister's son in a residually matriarchal society. In 1125 his grave was said to have been discovered on the beach at Rhos in Pembrokeshire, west Wales. Nearby a stream runs to the sea from the significantly named Walwayn's Castle or Castell Gwalchmai. In English, Latin and French texts, his name is Walwen/Gualganus/Gauvain, for this man is Gawain of a myriad tales. A paragon of virtue and courtesy in the French texts, so he is in the Welsh from his first appearance – 'he does more with fair words than we with deeds' – and Gawain was to enjoy a long and honoured career in the Arthurian romances of Europe and England.

From the ninth century – and probably from the sixth and seventh – the Arthurian cycle grows through poem, tale and triad. It draws into itself all manner of originally independent stories. Arthur's Court (*Llys Arthur*) displaces the Island of Britain as a conventional title and the old Brittonic gods, transformed into the men and women of *The Mabinogion*, start to figure among Arthur's entourage, as do the heroes of the Old North in the sixth-century battles against Bernicia – in defiance of historical chronology.

There was, for example, Owain mab (son of) Urien, a historical figure, son of a great king of the North, whose Rheged stretched from Solway through Carlisle. Sixth-century battles by both father and son were celebrated in the authentic poems of the contemporary bard Taliesin and Owain soon figures in the triads and the Arthurian literature. With his 'Flight of Ravens' – who may have been his warriors or even his women kin – he was to be prominent in both Welsh and French romances. Indeed, he was the subject of Chrétien de Troyes's best French work, the twelfth-century *Yvain: the Knight with the Lion*.

Another remarkable historical character to be swallowed up by Arthur was Caradoc Freich-Fras (Caradoc Strong-Arm). He may well have emerged from the *decurions*, the social leaders of Roman Caerwent in the south-east of Wales and his very name may commemorate an ancient hero of the Silures' struggle against Rome, Caratacus/Caradoc. He seems to have been a founder-king of the strong kingdom of Gwent. In the stories, he figures in the triad, 'Three Tribal Kingdoms of the Island of Britain', as Arthur's right-hand man in Cornwall and was early transferred, with much primitive material, to Brittany, whence his career in French romance and Italian sculpture dwarfs his Welsh one. Indeed, in later French romances, he was to merit a whole Book of his own.

Perhaps the most amazing independent tale to succumb to the lure of Arthur of the Britons is that of Tristan and his love for Iseult, wife to his uncle, King Mark of Cornwall. This powerful story, which became a European best-seller and remains so into our own day, originated with a Pictish hero who was absorbed into Welsh: Drystan mab Tallwch. He appears in an early triad, 'Three Powerful Swineherds of the Island of Britain', where he is 'tending the swine of March son of Meirchyawn, while the swineherd went with a message to Essyllt. Arthur and March and Cei and Bedwyr went there all four, but they did not succeed in getting so much as one pigling – neither by force nor by deception nor by stealth.' Whatever the nature of Drystan's love for Essyllt, it was not his prowess as a lover which was at issue here! Moreover, this March was a local hero in Glamorgan.

The story switched to Cornwall and its legendary King Mark (March). *March* in Welsh meant horse and this March had a secret – he had horse's ears – and several barbers and a dwarf paid with their lives for betraying it. The influence of Irish stories was paramount and when the story moved to Brittany, new elements were added. The

• Tristan and Iseult embark from Cornwall; illustration by Everard d'Espingues for a three-volume *Roman de Tristan* written for Jean du Cas, seigneur de l'Isle, 1479–80.

Fdit lecompte q̃
cellui chastel esto

Breton version probably supplied the prototype for its remarkable European diffusion, though various Oriental and Arabic influences have also been detected. A story of dedicated passion and unbridled love mocking all restraint, it is only marginally Arthurian: it really belongs to a history of European Arthurian literature. What it serves to illustrate is the way that even so powerful and independent a tale as this could not apparently resist the all-absorbing allure of the legends crystallizing around Arthur of the Britons.

The picture of Arthur which emerges from the text fragments is not entirely pristine. 'Three Red Ravagers of the Island of Britain' lists three names, then adds: 'But there was one who was a Red Ravager greater than all three: Arthur was his name. For a year neither grass nor plants used to spring up, where one of the three would walk; but where Arthur went, not for seven years.' He had a reputation as Arthur the Terrible. And in another triad, a story, also found in *The Mabinogion*, is told that the head of (former god) Brân was hidden in the White Hill in London, with its face towards France. So long as it were there, no oppression would come to this island. 'And Arthur disclosed the Head of Brân the Blessed from the White Hill, because it did not seem right to him that this Island should be defended by the strength of anyone, but by his own.'

The suggestion that it was Arthur's arrogance which brought about his ruin is echoed elsewhere, particularly in the 'Lives of the Saints', which were written by clerics in Latin in the eleventh and twelfth centuries. The Lives were a by-product of the Norman Conquest and its reorganization of Church life, which threatened the very existence of the independent Celtic Church. In a galvanic response, clerics wrote eulogies of their local 'saints' to advance the cause of their establishments in the new order. They had to confront an all-powerful Arthur in the secular tradition, but they reduced him to a greedy and arrogant tyrant repeatedly overthrown by the piety and power of their favourite saint.

Thus, in the 'Life of St Padarn' Arthur covets the saint's tunic and is swallowed up by the earth as far as his chin, only to be released when he accepts the tutelage of the saint. In the 'Life of St Carannog' a stone set floating in the Severn is seized by Arthur, who tries to use it as a table. But anything placed on it is immediately thrown off (an anticipation of the Round Table with its Perilous Seat which killed anyone unworthy who sat in it?). Arthur duly submits. In the 'Life of St Cadoc' Arthur lusts after a woman fleeing with her consort and only desists when Cei and Bedwyr cry, in effect, 'You can't do that! You're Arthur!' All of these tales are reminiscent of an early poem, 'Dialogue of Arthur and the Eagle', in which Arthur, a self-confessed poet, is given some elementary Christian instruction by a magic eagle. Though a great Christian hero, he evidently needs it.

The most interesting of the Lives is the 'Life of St Gildas', which Caradoc of Llancarfan wrote for the monks of Glastonbury in the 1120s or 1130s. In it, he speaks of a feud between Arthur, king of all Britain, who could brook no opposition, and Gildas's brother, Huail, in which Huail is killed, though Gildas and Arthur are eventually reconciled. Gwenhwyfar (Guinevere) is violated and carried off by Melwas, king of the Summer Country (Somerset), to Glastonbury – 'an impenetrable place, defended by reeds, rivers and a marsh', virtually an island. Arthur comes up with all the armies of Devon and Cornwall, and a terrible battle is threatened, until the abbot and Gildas go out to mediate; they persuade Melwas to restore Gwenhwyfar and both kings reward the abbey with many lands.

This appears to be the first entry of Glastonbury, with its ancient history, into the Arthurian world and it is also the first abduction of Guinevere – whose kidnapping by sundry men and her responses were to become her major characteristic. The story deeply influenced the first French romance to star Lancelot and it had the makings of a long and potent tradition culminating in the destruction of the Round Table – though the 'Life of St Gildas' has nothing of that.

More interesting is the Welsh name given to Glastonbury: the City or Island of Glass. Derived from the Latin, this seems to be a misreading of the English name, the City or Island of the Glastings – just as the Welsh read summer into Somerset. More interesting still is the possibility that this City of Glass was a city of the Otherworld.

The Arthurian cycle, growing ever stronger in Welsh minds, begins to assume that mysterious, semi-pagan character which was to make it so attractive to minds reared in a totally different tradition. Something very like a City of Glass turns up in a poem, 'The Spoils of Annwfn', attributed to the sixth-century poet Taliesin. In a period singled out by the *History of the Britons* as witnessing the birth of Welsh poetry, Taliesin moved from the North, apparently to Powys, and enjoyed a successful career as a poet. But he was also raised by the Welsh into a prophet, a legendary figure with a miraculous birth, a shape-shifter who experienced many reincarnations, and in command of a dazzling array of esoteric learning. Called the Father of Inspiration, he plays a virtually deathless role, rather in the manner of William Blake's Bard many centuries later, and his image has dominated Welsh poetry to such an extent that a modern history of Wales can call itself *The Taliesin Tradition*.

• *Overleaf* The remains of the Abbey at Glastonbury, the 'City of Glass' first mentioned in connection with Arthur in the early twelfth century: 'an impenetrable place, defended by reeds, rivers and a marsh'.

Taliesin said that he accompanied Arthur on a mission into Annwfn, the Otherworld, where they encountered a fortress of glass. (There are plenty of parallels in Irish writing.) Arthur ran into the supernatural: 'Beyond Caer Wydr, the Fortress of Glass, they did not see the valour of Arthur. Three score hundred men stood upon the wall, it was difficult to talk with their watchman' – because all six thousand of them were dead! The expedition was a disaster:

> *Three freights of Prydwen went we into it,*
> *Save seven, none came back from Caer Siddi.*

Caer Siddi was a Faery City, where there was no sickness or old age and fountains tasted sweeter than white wine. The object was to seize a magic cauldron – the Cauldron of Rebirth of the Irish, which appears elsewhere in Welsh writing. There also seems to have been a 'flashing, deadly sword' – so *Caledfwlch* itself, the original of Excalibur, may have been one of the spoils. Geoffrey of Monmouth said that Arthur's sword had been 'forged in Avalon'.

Other early poems are full of Otherworld themes, as is *The Mabinogion*. The cauldron of inspiration and plenty was common to the Celtic world and Taliesin's first inspired saying was spoken from it – 'by the breath of nine maidens it was kindled'. These nine maidens crop up in any number of themes: the nine witches of Gloucester, the nine sorceress-queens of the classical description of an island off the coast of Brittany; the nine sorceress-queens, headed by Morgan le Fay, of the Welsh Island of Apples – the Island of Avalon.

The identification of Glastonbury as a City of Glass therefore *echoes*, and it echoes still louder because it was Taliesin who gave us the first description in literature of the Island of Avalon, where the mortally wounded Arthur was carried after the fatal battle of Camlan. And he did so in a conversation with Myrddin, who, as Merlin, was to loom as large in the imagination of Europe as Arthur himself.

There seem to have been two Merlins. An early, somewhat obscure Myrddin (Merlin) was a prophet who came to be associated with the town of Carmarthen in south-west Wales (Dyfed). The name of the town was derived from its Roman settlement, Moridunum – a sea-fort – but people trying to find an explanation of its Welsh name, Caer Fyrddin, probably identified it with a Myrddin who was linked to the town as early as the sixth century. *Armes Prydein*, an early tenth-century polemic, refers to an already well-known prophecy of Myrddin's which told of a restoration of the British race under the future leadership of Cadwaladr of Britain and Cynan of Brittany.

This same prophecy also appears in a clutch of early poems from a totally different environment. In them, Myrddin is fleeing from a battle of Arfderydd in the North, a battle dated 573 by annals and located by scholars at Arthuret near Longtown in Cumberland, a few miles north of Carlisle. It was a clan battle between Britons, under Rhydderch Hael, a much eulogized king in Dumbarton, and the defeated Gwenddoleu, a descendant of Coel Hen (Old King Cole). Rhydderch was renowned as a great friend of the Church, which has led to suggestions that Myrddin, who was a protégé, perhaps the court poet, of Gwenddoleu, was a pagan – a Druid. There might be something in this – the old religion had died hard – but the earliest poem about Myrddin was in fact extremely pious.

This poem, 'The Apple-Trees', has ten stanzas, each beginning with an address to the 'sweet apple-tree' growing in the forest of Celyddon (Caledon) in what is today southern Scotland. After the fall of Gwenddoleu, Myrddin hid in the forest for fifty years, having lost his reason in the battle. He was terrified of Rhydderch, felt painful regret that he had caused the death of the son of his sister Gwendydd, and uttered the prayer of the penitent that he be received into bliss by the Lord of Hosts. This may represent a 'conversion' of the Druid Myrddin, but one can hardly be sure.

The poem 'The Greetings' greets the little pig which is Myrddin's companion in the forest and advises him on how to escape Rhydderch's hunting dogs, though he is 'a rude bed-fellow . . . with sharp claws'. Other poems are full of prophecies by this Wild Man of the Woods who once drank wine with lords. In particular, the 'Conversation of Myrddin and his sister Gwendydd', which is composed mainly in *englyn* metre and cannot be earlier than the ninth century, teems with prophecies on British and Welsh history stretching from the late sixth century over six or seven hundred years. In it, Gwendydd admits to an estrangement between herself and Myrddin, but is concerned over his welfare. At one point, she addresses him as 'my Llallogan Fyrddin, sage, prophet'.

Llallogan is the Welsh form of Lailoken, who appears in another northern cycle which became Scottish. The source is the 'Lives of St Kentigern', where Lailoken is now a Fool at the court of Rhydderch, now a naked, hairy madman whom Kentigern met in a lonely wood and who had been the cause of all the slaughter. The heavens opened and a voice said, 'Lailoken, Lailoken, you alone will bear punishment', and there was a vision of 'numberless martial battalions in the heavens like flashing lightning'. He prophesied his own triple death through cudgelling, piercing and drowning – at the confluence of the Tweed with another river – at a tomb where 'the marshal of the British race will defeat the foreign race'. He was buried at the place of his choice, 'some thirty miles from the city of Glasgow'.

It seems clear that Myrddin and Lailoken are virtually identical. Several triads deal with the battle of Arfderydd and there was probably a rich saga about it. The Welsh Myrddin, however, developed entirely independently of it. Scholars assert that the great inflow of northern material into Welsh occurred at least in oral form from the ninth century and there were evidently two stories of Lailoken and Myrddin in existence simultaneously in what had become Wales and Scotland. Once relocated in Wales, it would have been hard to resist the pull of Carmarthen. One of the cycle of Myrddin poems, 'Dialogue of Myrddin and Taliesin', suggests it. The second part is full of northern material, which says among other things that 140 men of rank went mad at Arfderydd. But this is a sequel to the first part, which makes Myrddin the spokesman for the men of Dyfed in south-west Wales who fight off an invasion from north Wales in the first half of the sixth century.

But what on earth has all this to do with Arthur? To make a necessary anticipation, the link was the work of Geoffrey of Monmouth, who wrote in Latin and published a set of Prophecies before 1135 – in advance of his major *History of the Kings of Britain* – in response to request, for they were being much talked of – an interesting point in itself. In them, he launched the Merlin who was to capture the imagination of Europe. He took the marvellous youth Ambrosius from Glamorgan, of the earlier *History of the Britons*, made him Myrddin (which he Latinized as Merlinus), the son of a princess of Dyfed in Carmarthen, and erected a great structure of prophecies and miraculous achievements upon him, ranging the whole of Welsh tradition as he knew it. This was the Merlin which swept Europe – though Merlin actually fades out before the birth of the Arthur whose glory he had foretold.

Some twenty years later, Geoffrey of Monmouth had evidently discovered Merlin the Wild Man of the Woods and in a remarkable *Life of Merlin* in verse, replete with new knowledge and Latin philosophical and astronomical learning, he tried to fuse the two. This Merlin, a renowned prophet, is a king of Dyfed who, with the king of the north Welsh and Rhydderch Hael (!), king of the Cumbrians, fights with a king of Scotland. Three of his brothers are killed and he loses his reason. With a wolf for companion, he lives on grass and fruits, and is sustained by nineteen apple trees in the forest of Caledon. There is much to-ing and fro-ing between Caledon and the court. Kept in chains to prevent his return to the forest, Merlin reveals the adultery of his sister, the queen Ganieda, but is foiled by her. He is allowed back to the forest and promises his

• Merlin reads a prophecy to King Uther while Ygraine (Ygerna), wife of the duke of Cornwall, looks on from the battlements; Arthur, according to legend, was begotten of Uther and the innocent Ygraine by trickery.

wife Gwendoline her freedom, but on her wedding day a year later he turns up riding a stag, wrenches its horns from its head and hurls them at his rival, killing him instantly. In the end, he is permitted to return to Caledon, with a house provided for him and a hall with seventy doors, seventy windows and seventy secretaries to record his prophecies! When Rhydderch dies, his widow joins her brother Merlin in the wood, and so does the great poet-prophet Taliesin, who delivers a long discourse about Creation, the World and various natural phenomena. Merlin finds a spring which restores his reason and does the same for a man made mad by eating poisoned apples designed for Merlin by a former mistress, a svelte young thing (an anticipation of the later fey Viviane?). Finally, all four decide to spend the rest of their lives together in the forest.

This astonishing poem managed to fuse the two Merlins by blandly assuming that the Merlin of the mid-fifth century had lived into the late sixth. This proved too much even for the Middle Ages. By the late twelfth century it was generally believed that there had been two Merlins, Merlinus Ambrosius, the miraculous boy, and Merlinus Silvester or Caledonius of the Woods.

The link with Arthur in Geoffrey of Monmouth's work comes with Taliesin, who asks Merlin whether it is not now time to 'recall Arthur'. Merlin says no, the restoration of British liberties would come after many years, through an alliance of Welsh, Cornishmen, Bretons and Scots under Cadwaladr of Wales and Cynan of Brittany. Just before this, Taliesin had provided the first recorded description of Avalon, which was surely based on a Welsh tradition that probably existed much earlier than 1100.

Taliesin tells how Arthur was conveyed to Avalon, after Camlan, to be tended by Morgen and her eight sisters:

> The Island of Apples which men call the Fortunate Isle, is so named because it produced all things of itself. The fields there have no need of farmers to plough them, and Nature alone provides all cultivation. Grain and grapes are produced without tending, and apple trees grow in the woods from close-cropped grass. The earth of its own accord brings forth not merely grass but all things in superabundance. . . Thither after the battle of Camlan we took the wounded Arthur. . . With the Prince we arrived there, and Morgen received us with becoming honour. In her own chamber she placed the King on a golden bed, with her own noble hand uncovered the wound and gazed at it long. At last she said that health could return to him if he were to stay with her for a long time and wished to make use of her healing art. Rejoicing therefore, we committed the King to her, and returning, gave our sails to the favouring winds.

The Arthur who emerges from these fragments of a once abundant oral tradition is a vivid and often charming character. A disjointed picture begins to take shape – of a man who saved the Britons from the Saxons for half a century, a man of great power and nobility, but also of arrogance and tyranny, in whose fifty-year span there are hints of wider conquests. His legend grew to encompass many others, notably those of the Old British North, to create the Three Realms of a four-hundred-year tradition. Itself fairly light-hearted, the Arthurian story becomes enmeshed in the mists of the Celtic Otherworld, to end in a tragic civil war at Camlan and in Arthur's departure to the Island of Avalon, there to await his recall – an end which was not an end. His epic tale could never end.

The story would, however, remain fragmentary were it not for *Culhwch ac Olwen*, the Welsh tale which assumed written form, presumably after a long oral history, round 1080–1100, and was the first Arthurian 'romance', perhaps the first Arthurian masterpiece. It stands a little apart from *The Mabinogion* tales, with which it was later grouped. It had access, presumably pirated, to the triads, although it satirizes the guild of bards with their praise-poetry in court and is heir to a long, mocking tradition. Arthur and some of his men are nevertheless made real heroes and the tale seems to be directed at a different audience than that of the court poets. The author is at pains to produce a written story out of several oral tales and although it cannot be said that he succeeded, it remains a work of genius. Its humour, often biting, sometimes genial, strikes the reader first, along with its zest, imagination, sense of rhythm and often tumultuous progression. Welsh writing would be the poorer without it.

It begins, like all Celtic stories, by explaining the hero. His mother, as her time approaches, gives birth to him in a pig-run – hence his name, Burrow of Swine (Culhwch). Much later, his offended step-mother puts him under a 'destiny': 'thy side shall never strike against woman' until he wins Olwen, daughter to the monster Ysbaddaden, Chief Giant. The boy feels love in his every limb, 'although he had never seen her', and his father advises him to go to Arthur, his first cousin, to have his hair trimmed (an old ritual of recognition) and to ask his help.

Off goes the boy, cantering on his magnificent horse and equipped from head to toe with accoutrements which, in what became traditional style, are lovingly described according to their market value – each golden apple on his mantle is worth a hundred kine, the gold of his gear three hundred kine. And so he comes to Arthur's court, presumably at Celli Wig in Cornwall.

His first encounter is with the gate-keeper (in the style of *Pa gur?*). 'Is there a porter? There is, and thou, may thy head not be thine, that thou dost ask!' Glewlwyd

Mighty-Grasp says he is porter to Arthur on every New Year's Day, but names four deputies, one of whom is Penpingion, 'who goes upon his head to spare his feet . . . like a rolling stone on a court floor'. He refuses to open the gate: 'Knife has gone into meat and drink into horn, and a thronging in Arthur's hall. Save the son of a king of rightful dominion, or a craftsman who brings his craft, none may enter.' He offers him the hospice, 'with meat for thy dogs and corn for thy horse and hot peppered chops for thyself, and wine brimming over, and delectable songs before thee . . . and a woman to sleep with thee'.

Culhwch will have none of it and threatens to raise three tremendous shouts, which would be heard in the far depths of Cornwall, the North and Ireland. . . 'And every woman with child that is in this court shall miscarry.' The porter goes to speak to Arthur – 'Two thirds of my life are past and two-thirds of thine own' – and gives a long list of Arthur's battles and conquests, much of which would have made sense to a contemporary audience, if not to us. The places include 'India the Great and India the Lesser, Europe and Africa, the islands of Corsica and Greece', so Arthur was already a world-straddling colossus. The porter adds, of Culhwch, 'but never saw I a man so comely as this'.

'If thou didst enter walking,' says Arthur, 'go thou out running', for it was shameful to leave such a man in the wind and rain. Cei objects: the laws of the court should not be broken. 'Not so, fair Cei,' replies Arthur. 'We are noble men so long as we are resorted to. The greater the bounty we show, all the greater will be our nobility and our fame and our glory' – a neat exposition of the whole Arthurian ethos in Wales.'

Contrary to all custom, Culhwch comes clattering in on horseback. But Arthur treats him with honour, seating him among the warriors, with songs to entertain him and serving him drink from golden horns and hot peppered chops (which seem to have been the ultimate delicacy in medieval Wales). Culhwch says he has come to claim a boon. You shall have it, says Arthur, ritually trimming the young man's hair, 'as far as wind dries, as far as rain wets, as far as sun runs, as far as sea stretches, as far as earth extends, save only my ship and my mantle, and Caledfwlch my sword and Rhongomyniad my spear, and Wynebgwrthucher my shield and Carnwennan my dagger and Gwenhwyfar my wife' (apparently in that order!). Culhwch asks him to obtain Olwen for him and asks it in the name of all Arthur's warriors.

There follows a huge list of 227 warriors, which stretches over seven closely printed pages in the modern text. Familiar figures appear like Taliesin chief of bards, but the humour already evident at the gate takes over. Anyone reciting this list would have caused uproar in the hall. What is one to make of Drem mab Dremidydd (Sight son of Seer), who could see a fly rise in the morning in Scotland from Celli Wig in

Cornwall, or of Clust mab Clustfeinad (Ear son of Hearer), who, buried seven fathoms in the earth, could hear an ant fifty miles off when it stirred from its couch of a morning, or of Sugyn mab Sugnedydd (Suck son of Sucker), who could suck the sea up under three hundred ships? Or for that matter, of Sol, who could stand all day on one foot, and Gwefyl mab Gwastad – on sad days he would let down one of his lips to his navel, while the other would be like a cowl on his head – not to mention Gilla Stag-Shank, who could clear three hundred acres in a single leap, the chief leaper of Ireland?

A Wales inured to its royal courts endlessly wandering around, eating up district after district, would respond to Long Erwm and Long Atrwm, who would seize three cantrefs – local government units – for their feast; feasting till noon and drinking all night, when they went to sleep they would devour the heads of insects! And a Wales perhaps somewhat weary of poets chanting in complicated metres in court in endless triples might perhaps appreciate the three sons of Cleddyf Cyfwlch, with three gleaming glitterers their three shields, three pointed piercers their three spears, three keen carvers their three swords, their three dogs, three horses, three wives with names which meant Late-bearer, Ill-bearer and Full-bearer, their three grandchildren, Och, Scream and Shriek, their three daughters Plague, Want and Penury, and their three servants, Bad, Worse and Worst of All!

To encounter all this is to experience an abrupt and intense relief. From the high-minded and the half-understood, we are suddenly plunged into the world of Dylan Thomas, Gwyn Thomas and a familiar Welsh satirical streak. This is a 'Spitting Image' of Arthur's court. And among men with names like Fat-kine, Cat-claw, the Hewer, Bow-back (from the uplands of Hell these men were sprung), Cors Hundred-Claws, Canhastyr Hundred-hands, Llwch Windy-hand, Anwas the Winged and Sgilti Lightfoot the messenger (who always ran along the tops of trees and reeds and never a reed bent beneath his foot let alone broke), there are others perhaps more significant.

There was Morfan mab Tegid – 'no man placed his weapon in him at Camlan, so exceeding ugly was he: all thought he was the devil helping. There was hair on him like the hair of a stag'; Sandde Angel-face – 'no-one placed his spear in him at Camlan, so exceeding fair was he: all thought he was an angel helping'; and Cynwyl the Saint, one of the three men who escaped from Camlan and the last to part from Arthur on Hengroen his horse. Such descriptions give a sudden glimpse into the dense network of lost stories which must have enshrouded Arthur's last, tragic battle.

So, with some hints at the surly character of Cei and Arthur's feud with Gildas's brother, and a portrait of Osla Big-Knife (normally an enemy) whose sheathed knife, if laid across a torrent, would be bridge enough for the hosts of the Three Realms of Britain and its Three Adjacent Islands to cross with all their spoil (an anticipation of the famous Sword-Bridge of Lancelot many years later?), the interminable list of warriors draws to its close with mention of Bidwini the bishop, who blessed meat and drink (and did little else as far as one can tell), and all the gentle, gold-torqued maidens of the island, headed by Gwenhwyfar and including Essyllt Whiteneck and Essyllt Slenderneck, who conjure up Tristan and his Iseult.

Confronted with Culhwch's list, Arthur naturally complies, but messengers sent out come back empty-handed, so he summons his best men to accompany Culhwch. The first is Cei, who can go nine days and nights without sleep, and spend nine days and nights under water; no physician can heal a wound from him; he can be as tall as the tallest tree and when it rains, he remains dry a handsbreadth before and behind, 'by reason of the greatness of his heat'. And the second is Bedwyr, who never shrinks from any enterprise on which Cei is bound. None is as handsome in the island save Arthur and though he is one-handed, no three warriors draw blood faster. And then there is Gwalchmai, Arthur's nephew, his sister's son; the best of walkers and the best of riders, he never comes back without fulfilling his quest. With them go a guide and Menw, who can cast spells over a heathen land, and Gwrhyr, Interpreter of Tongues, who knows all languages. So, in what became the standard form, the group leaves the court with its ordered rituals and enters a world where anything might happen.

With great difficulty, they reach the castle of Ysbaddaden, Chief Giant, and meet a gigantic shepherd with a mastiff as big as a stallion. Menw casts a spell on him and the shepherd takes them to his wife, who is of equal stature. When she hears Culhwch, her nephew, is there, she rushes out to embrace them. Cei thrusts a log between her outstretched hands and she squeezes it so hard it becomes twisted. 'Woman, had it been I thou didst squeeze in this wise,' said Cei, 'there were no need for another to love me ever. An ill love, that!'

She tells them that it is death to approach Ysbaddaden; she has lost twenty-three sons by him and keeps the last in a coffer. But she tells them that Olwen comes every Saturday to wash her head and leave her rings; she promises to send for her.

And she came, with a robe of flame-red silk about her, and around the maiden's neck a torque of red gold, and precious pearls thereon and rubies. Yellower was her head than the flower of the broom, whiter was her flesh than the foam of the wave; whiter were her palms and her fingers than the shoots of the marsh trefoil from amidst the fine gravel of a welling spring. Neither the eye of the mewed hawk, nor the eye of the thrice-mewed falcon, not an eye was there fairer than hers. Whiter were her breasts than the breast of the white swan, redder were her cheeks than the reddest foxgloves. Whoso

beheld her would be filled with love for her. Four white trefoils sprang up
behind her wherever she went and for that reason was she called Olwen.

Here was the model for all future Arthurian heroines.

Filled with love, Culhwch leads them to the castle where they meet a violent
reception: three conversations end with Ysbaddaden hurling a stone spear at them,
which they throw back, to his damage, until he agrees to talk. 'Where are those rascal
servants of mine?' he says. 'Raise up the forks under my two eye-lids that I may see my
future son-in-law.' (Ysbaddaden with his eye-lids propped open turns up in our own
day in an episode of *Star Wars*.) He sets them some forty tasks to fulfil to obtain Olwen,
including the winning of magic vessels for the wedding feast and magic implements to
shave him. A dozen of the tasks are described in detail, among them the winning of a
giant's sword and beard, the freeing of a famous prisoner and the hunting of a giant boar.

On the way back, they see a great fort and are warned off by a 'black man bigger
than three men of this world', who turns up in other Welsh stories. But after an
encounter with the porter, which is a parody of the one with Arthur's, Cei by trickery
and ruthlessness wins the sword of Wrnach the Giant. Back in Celli Wig, Arthur decides
to lead them out on a hunt for the prisoner Mabon mab Modron. This was Son son of
Mother, who, as mentioned previously, had been a god in Roman Britain and probably
earlier, under the name of Apollo-Maponos, and whose mother Modron was a goddess
who, as Matrona, gave her name to the River Marne in France; as an earth-mother with
her son, she was almost certainly pre-Celtic.

Mabon must have been imprisoned since the beginning of time, for the adven-
turers decided, in a memorable passage, to consult the Oldest Animals in the World.
Through Gwrhyr the interpreter, they ask the Ouzel of Cilgwri whether he knows
anything of Mabon, 'taken when three nights old from between his mother and the
wall'. The Ouzel says that an anvil he uses to sharpen his beak on is not so much as a
nut now and he knows nothing, but he will take them to an animal even older than he.
So they go on, to the Stag of Rhedynfre, the Owl of Cwm Cawlwyd, the Eagle of
Gwernabwy and, finally, to the Salmon of Llyn Llyw near the Severn. He tells them
that he thinks Mabon is imprisoned in Caer Loyw, which is Gloucester. Arthur leads
his army into a siege of Gloucester, while Cei and Bedwyr ride the shoulders of the
Salmon up the Severn to rescue Mabon.

So it goes on. Arthur sails in *Prydwen* to Aber Deu Gleddyf (the Milford Haven
estuary) to get two whelps that God changes back into their human semblance for him.
An ant-hill is saved from a fire and the ants get them nine hestors of flax which
Ysbaddaden had demanded. One flax seed was wanting . . . 'and the lame ant brought

that in before night'. Cei and Bedwyr spot Dillus the Bearded, from Pumlumon behind Aberystwyth, 'in the highest wind in the world' and get his beard for a leash. Arthur sings a mocking *englyn* in praise of Cei and provokes a fearful quarrel between them. From that time on, Cei has nothing to do with Arthur, not even in his moment of need.

The tale comes to a climax in the hunt for Twrch Trwyth, a giant boar who had once been a king before God punished him (and who figures in Welsh legend very early). On a raid, Arthur's men seize the cauldron of Diwrnach the Irishman and learn that the Boar with his seven young pigs is laying waste a third of Ireland. So Arthur gathers together what warriors there are in the Three Realms of Britain and its Three Adjacent Islands, in France and Brittany and Normandy and the Summer Country (which suggests an overlordship, later 'documented' by Geoffrey of Monmouth) and crosses the sea. The Irish bring him tribute and blessings but Twrch Trwyth crosses to Arthur's country to do him damage, with Arthur and the Hosts of the World in pursuit.

Landing at Porth Cleis in Dyfed (south-west Wales), there follows a breathless, bloody hunt across the whole of south Wales, on a track which can be traced on a map to this day, through the Preseli, Nevern, the Tawe, the Tywi, the Amman into Gwent and the Severn. As they zigzag over Wales, Twrch Trwyth and his pigs turn on them repeatedly and inflict terrible losses on the Host, including a king of France. Finally, by main strength they drive Twrch Trwyth into the Severn and Arthur with all the champions of Britain plunge into the river, grab him and souse him. They take the shears and razor from between his ears, though two of Arthur's men nearly drown. But the Boar finds land with his feet and from that moment, there is no stopping him. They catch up with him again in Cornwall and whatever mischief was come by before is play to what happens then. In the end, they manage to snatch a comb from between his ears and Twrch Trwyth is forced into the sea and God knows where! Arthur withdraws to Celli Wig to bathe and rest.

Are there any more marvels left?, he asks. The answer is yes: 'the blood of the Black Witch, daughter of the White Witch, from the head of the Valley of Grief in the Uplands of Hell'. Off they go to her cave in the north. Two men go in and come out squalling and squealing. 'It is not seemly or pleasant to see thee scuffling with a hag,' they say to Arthur, and two more go in, to fare even worse. All four are shunted out on Arthur's mare, Llamrei. Angered, Arthur seizes the cave entrance and taking aim with his dagger Carnwennan, he strikes the Witch 'across the middle until she was as two tubs'. A twin-tub witch!

• Culhwch, hero of the first Arthurian romance,
Culhwch ac Olwen, depicted in Arthur Joseph Gaskin's
Kilhwych, the King's Son, 1901.

Then it is all over. Everyone who wishes ill of Ysbaddaden comes with Culhwch to his castle.

> And Cadw of Prydein came to shave his beard, flesh and skin to the bone and his two ears outright! 'Hast had thy shave, man?' asked Culhwch. 'I have.' 'And is thy daughter mine now?' 'Thine,' said the Giant, 'And thou needst not thank me for that, but thank Arthur.' Then they cut his head off and that night Culhwch slept with Olwen and she was his only wife as long as he lived. And the hosts of Arthur dispersed, every one to his country.

Culhwch ac Olwen makes a fitting climax to the Arthur of the Welsh, Cornish and Bretons. There was nothing of chivalry or feudalism in him, and much that was barbaric. But he was an Arthur of the Heroic Age, noble, gallant, but all too human, with a lot of humour about him and an audience wider than the courts of princes, an audience which could gather whenever anyone told a story around a fire.

The stories were being written down as the Normans came crashing in after 1066. They ripped the realm of England out of the Scandinavian world and drew it remorselessly into Latin Europe. They totally recast the Church. They tried to perform the same service for Wales. Marcher lordships sprang up along the border, replacing the local Welsh kings. In 1093, when the last legitimate king of south Wales was killed outside Brecon, 'kings ceased to bear rule in Wales'. For a brief time, the Normans swarmed all over Wales. But the Welsh fought back, beat them out of the west and established a frontier which was to last for nearly two hundred years.

The Marcher lords took over the loyalties of the old kings and were soon hopelessly enmeshed in a close network of intermarriage and cultural contacts with the Welsh. The translator became an honoured and responsible figure. The Marchers included Bretons, whose language (if they remembered it) was close kin to the Welsh; they listened to the songs and stories of the Welsh they inherited – and evidently found them fascinating. In little more than a generation Arthur and his people went cantering off, light as air, like Culhwch's horse, into the four corners of that Christendom which spoke French.

CHAPTER FOUR
THE·FRENCH CONNECTION

The most startling evidence of the swift British penetration of Europe comes from the Po valley in Italy. The nobles of Padua and Modena were christening their sons by the names of Arthur and his nephew Gawain (Gwalchmai) around the year 1100 and the earliest appearance of Arthur and his knights in art is on an archivolt over the north door, the Porta della Pescheria, of Modena cathedral. Dates suggested for the sculpture range from 1120 to 1140 – the building itself is recorded as being in place by 1106 – which makes the sculpture earlier than any surviving written works about Arthur other than those in Welsh.

The sculpture depicts an episode from the story of Yder (fiz Nudd), who is derived from Edern mab Nudd of the mythological world of the Welsh. Although names are altered, as one would expect, they are easy to recognize. Arthur appears as Artus de Bretania, with his supporters, Galvagin – Gawain/Gwalchmai – and Che – Kay/Cei; Carrado is Caradoc Freichfras. The source was probably French, possibly passed on by Bretons during the First Crusade.

What is notable about this sculpture which marks the first crossing of the Channel – and indeed the Alps – of the Arthurian story is that in the surviving Welsh manuscripts Edern mab Nudd plays a very minor role, yet his tale is singled out in Modena. Moreover, a hundred years later, as Yder, he was given his own French romance (which was distinctly hostile to both Kay and Arthur himself). This suggests that very much more was known about Yder/Edern in early years and that more Welsh material than we now have knowledge of was being transmitted in some form – which in turn suggests that the transmission was very early. So general is this predicament that scholars now turn to the early French Arthurian texts, which borrowed directly from Britain, for information on Welsh figures who had long since dwindled at home. For it was the French-speaking world, a world that embraced much of Europe and increasingly the Crusader states in the Middle East, which swiftly responded to the stories.

There was a striking early divergence between the two forms of French used in France. North of the Loire was the realm of the *langue d'oil*, identified by the way it pronounced 'yes'; south of it, but ever receding under pressure from the expansive north, was the similarly identified *langue d'oc*. It was the latter which most readily absorbed the British stories. It held sway over that great sweep of territory in southern France and across the Pyrenees in Catalonia: the realm of Provençal and Catalan, with its highly cultivated courts in Aquitaine, Auvergne, Provence, Toulouse, Montpellier, Narbonne and Catalonia. One of their historians, Rita Lejeune, says that when Geoffrey of Monmouth was writing his epic history in Oxford, Arthur was already well known in Poitou and that twenty years later the 'Matter of Britain' had long conquered Catalonia.

A book of instruction for poets compiled by a Catalan nobleman about the time – 1160s – that the northern Frenchman, Chrétien de Troyes, was composing the first of the French Arthurian romances, listed Artus, Tristan and Iseult, and Gawain among the familiar names which a *jongleur* (minstrel) should know. And some time around 1160 a nobleman from the Landes in Gascony was proposing as models to youth: Tristan, 'who knew how to love', Yvain (Owain), 'the first to wear furs', and King Arthur – 'He did not die and he never committed a fault . . . always he lived for love.'

Poets of the *langue d'oc* make much more frequent reference to Arthurian figures than do their counterparts in the northern *langue d'oil*, which became the dominant form of French. For Arthur, the proportions were 24 to 5, for Tristan 37 to 21, Iseult 22 to 7, Gawain 15 to 2. Nevertheless, time and time again, historians have to come back to the courts of Poitou in western, central France, then one of the major centres of civilization in Europe, to William, its duke, the son of a duke who was himself a troubadour, and the father of the beautiful and learned Eleanor of Aquitaine. She was a major patron of the Arthurian romances and her marriage to Henry II of England was, at least in its earlier years, the seeming embodiment of courtly love. It also made her queen of the great Angevin Empire over which Henry II presided. The northern poets were drawn to the successive courts of Poitou, where, the evidence suggests, *conteurs* and other entertainers, as one affronted court poet put it, spouted without end on Arthurian themes. Chrétien de Troyes himself wrote: 'As the popular saying goes, there are certain things we despise whose worth is far greater than we think . . . from a tale of adventure one fashions a very elegant composition.' He talks of tales 'which the professional story-tellers habitually fragment and corrupt in the presence of kings and counts'. One of those professional story-tellers, and the only one cited by name, was a Welshman, who was quoted as an authority without peer by several established French writers.

• Perceval witnesses the Grail procession at the castle of the Fisher
King; from a manuscript from northern France of 1274.

This flies in the face of the assumption, common until quite recently, that the agents of the Arthurian transfer from Britain must have been Bretons. The latter were certainly significant in the reception and diffusion of Arthurian material and may have been central as intermediaries. Bretons had been in close contact with the French since the eighth century and many were bilingual, particularly after the incorporation of French-speaking Rennes, Nantes and Vannes into Brittany. They were prominent among the Norman invaders of Britain after 1066 and they were great travellers. It has been plausibly suggested that the Arthurian traces in northern Italy and, later, in Sicily and near Bari in the south, stemmed from tales brought by Breton contingents in the armies of the Crusades.

But this identification, close to a fixation some thirty years ago, rests on an arbitrary interpretation of the meaning of the word *Britones* and its derivatives. In fact, the words are singularly ambiguous; they could mean Briton or Breton. The twelfth-century *Book of Llandaff* states baldly that the men of Wales and Brittany are 'of one race and language'. In the ninth, tenth and eleventh centuries many legends linked ultimately to Arthur were absorbed from the Old North and Cornwall, plus some from Ireland, into a Welsh pattern and from there delivered to Brittany. The lives of Breton saints focus on traditional progenitors in Wales, Cornwall and the North, rather than on Brittany, and Arthur was much more popular there than his alleged Breton ancestors, though there is no trace of any Breton text about Arthur. There is only one case of reverse transfer, of a Breton character being adopted into Welsh – the Enide of Chrétien de Troyes's *Erec et Enide*. The characteristic Breton *lai*, a short poem, was quite unlike the romances and although Breton lays are cited in some texts, notably those by Marie de France, who may have spent some time in England, they are only marginally Arthurian.

The rather disconcerting obsession with the Bretons seems irrelevant. Stories about Arthur and his men were commonplace in Wales, Cornwall and Brittany; and although the hope of his return was specifically described as the 'Breton hope', it was hardly so geographically constricted. Moreover, one salient historical fact demolishes the idea that only Bretons could act as a bridge into the French-speaking world: if Bretons had been in close contact with the French since the eighth century, why is it that French Arthurian stories did not appear until the twelfth? It is only after the Norman penetration of Wales and, in particular, of south Wales, that there is definite evidence of Arthurian stories in a language other than Welsh.

The pivotal role of south Wales may predate the Norman conquest itself; there were Normans installed in Herefordshire a generation before 1066. The first written versions of many Welsh stories emerge in south Wales and within a generation or two the southern March was, at least officially, bilingual. At that time in south Wales, there were four or even five languages in use: Latin, French, Welsh, English (though this was of minor importance then) and possibly Breton. Latimers – translators – emerged as a significant factor, men of substance who generally committed themselves to the Norman cause without losing their Welsh identity, as many others did. The area was to produce the three later Welsh Arthurian romances in *The Mabinogion* which were decidedly French in style. Latimers moved in a bilingual, even multilingual, environment; even the Arthur of *Culhwch* counted among his intimates Gwrhyr, Interpreter of Tongues, who of course knew every language on earth as well as several beyond it.

It was just such a man, and he may have been one of several, who was praised by French authors. Bleheris, born and bred in Wales, according to an anonymous author who tried to continue in the tradition of Chrétien de Troyes, is said to have told a well-received tale about Gawain and a dwarf knight to a count of Poitiers, assumed to be William VII, grandfather of Eleanor of Aquitaine, which would give him a date before 1127. Other anonymous continuators of Chrétien and writers on Merlin called him Blihis and an authority on the Grail; in the disguise of Blaise, he was hailed as an omniscient source for the early history of Merlin and Arthur, indeed he was Merlin's secretary. Thomas, the Norman author of a version of the Tristan story, described him as one who told the tale of Tristan best; he knew 'the history of all the counts and all the kings of Britain'.

Indeed, given the pertinent question posed by Rita Lejeune, a historian of the lands of *langue d'oc* – would such a developed culture there have absorbed stories which had not yet been fixed in form? – could Bleheris's stories, or some of them, have been written down? Significant here is the suggestion by Rachel Bromwich, distinguished scholar of the *Welsh Triads*, about two Welsh names included among the many in Chrétien de Troyes's first romance, *Erec et Enide*. He names, in passing, Caradoc Freichfras. In Welsh, *braich* means 'arm' and *bras* then implied 'strong' – hence, with the customary mutations, Freichfras carried the meaning of Strong-arm. But in Chrétien's French, the name was written Briebras, which neatly reversed the equation: *brie* reads as 'short' and *bras* was the French for 'arm', so the character in French became Caradoc Short-Arm. Suitable explanations were offered for the nickname! In the same romance, Owein mab Urien appears as Yvains le fiz Uriien, a rare case of the patronymic surviving the transfer to French intact (and Owein was later given a romance – Chrétien's best – to himself). This, Dr Bromwich strongly suggests, meant that the French versions were derived from a written text or texts in Old Welsh. Indeed, another scholar suggested, though without any evidence, that Bleheris might have been the author or compiler of books or manuscripts on Arthurian themes.

With or without such books, Bleheris has been quite plausibly identified with a Welshman of the early twelfth century (although the identification has been hotly disputed). Gerald the Welshman, writing later in that century, spoke of 'the well-known story-teller' Bleddri, who made a sly joke about coracle fishermen, telling his hearers that when Welshmen went hunting, they carried the horse on their shoulders to the field and carried it back when the hunt was over. This story-teller seems to have been Bleddri latimer ap Kadifor, specifically described as a translator, from the Carmarthen area, who made a gift to the priory there about 1130 and kept a nearby castle for Henry I. He would have been committed to the new order in Wales and one of a class of highly trained and cultivated professionals who served Normans and Welsh as liaison officers at every level.

The facts about the early transfer of Arthurian material into French, therefore, are established. More important is precisely what was transferred. What was it that made stories about an alleged hero of an offshore island and his many companions, all long dead, so attractive to French minds bred in a totally different school, and to many others ever since?

Here it helps to look ahead to the years after 1160 and to Chrétien de Troyes, author of the first Arthurian romances and a well-trained and highly skilled writer. Three of his romances are significant in this respect – *Erec et Enide*; *Yvain: The Knight with the Lion*; and *Perceval: the Story of the Grail* – particularly since they were echoed some years later by three Welsh romances collected in *The Mabinogion – Gereint mab Erbin*; *The Lady of the Fountain*; and *Peredur mab Efrawg*, which are now believed to be derived not from Chrétien but from a French or Welsh source or sources common to both.

All of the tales feature British heroes long since relocated in Wales and all of them teem with Welsh names. This is particularly true of the French *Erec*, which has long lists of the notables at Arthur's court, many of whose names have become incomprehensible in the processes of transition from Welsh to written French, but others of which are recognizable. They include Girflet fiz Do, who is Gilfaethwy mab Don, one of a dynasty of gods in *The Mabinogion*, and Carados Briebras, familiar as Caradoc Freichfras from the triads and elsewhere. Also present are Yder (Edern) of Modena cathedral, Melwas, lord of the Island of Glass (the ruler of Glastonbury), and Mabonagrain, who is a version of Mabon mab Modron, the mythical prisoner in *Culhwch*. Many were originally pre-Christian, Celtic or even pre-Celtic deities.

Underlying all three stories is a theme of Sovereignty, which is most fully developed in Irish sources of a very early date. A ruler was believed to be mated to a tutelary goddess of his realm. As the reign wore on, she turned from a beautiful young maiden into a hideous hag, who could be restored to her beauty (and the realm to its fertility) by sexual intercourse or a kiss. Gwenhwyfar herself (Guinevere) was on occasion described as *Prydein priawt* (Britain's spouse). By this time, the concept of the goddess had become divorced from its natural partner – the new man who would deliver the Transformed Hag and who usually won this right by single combat. This embodied the related idea that the fertility of the realm depended on the potency of its lord, which opened up the mystery world of the Maimed King, wounded in the genitals, with his country a Waste Land where everything could be restored by asking the right question or by some other magical act. The Welsh *Mabinogion* tales, no less than the Irish sources, are full of all this, usually in texts not technically considered 'Arthurian' at all, and often expressed in a manner which makes their meaning and interconnection tantalizingly obscure.

Sovereignty was often symbolized by the hunting of a white animal, usually a stag. The French *Erec* opens with just such a hunt, from Arthur's court in Cardigan, south-

---

• The later part of the story of Yvain illustrated in an early fourteenth-century manuscript: Lunete, the clever maiden who has helped Yvain, in prison; Yvain killing a giant; and Yvain, with his faithful lion, saving Lunete from death at the stake.

t met lescu deuant se saide	uil saide secours ᴢ aye
ue la flame mal ne li saide	la teste gentil ᴢ franche
ne il gerott par mi la gole	lespee sourbie ᴢ blanche
uil plus estott lee dun ole	a le felou serpent requerre
ly li lions apres lassaut	i le trenche iusques en terre
e la bataille ne li faut	les · ij · moittez retrondhne
ais quoi qlen auiengue apres	ierr ᴢ refiert ᴢ tant len dône
idier li naurra il ades	ue tout lamepuse ᴢ depieche
ue pites len semont ᴢ prie	ais de le keue vne pieche

west Wales. The killer of the stag had the right to bestow a kiss on his chosen lady, which, as Gawain warned at the time, could cause trouble in a court with five hundred beautiful, high-born damsels each with a bold knight convinced his lady was the fairest – a dilemma from which Arthur was rescued by the arrival of Erec with his unnaturally obedient Enide. This, to me, is a slightly ironic 'modernization' of what had, in the material available, become an established tradition.

Elsewhere in the same story, Erec comes to an enclosed garden, shut in by 'a wall of air' (a mist in the Welsh version), with a row of stakes topped by severed heads – a very Celtic notion! – and a horn. Having defeated a Crimson Knight who was actually Mabon mab Modron (originally a god), he blows the horn and lifts an enchantment from the place – the enchantment found in *The Mabinogion*, notably over Dyfed (south-west Wales) after the dalliance of its prince, Pwyll, with the Otherworld.

In *Yvain (Owain)*, there is a memorable opening sequence where the hero, riding through the Broceliande forest in Brittany, encounters a bad-tempered giant who is Lord of the Animals (in the Welsh version he is the giant black man met, in different guise, in *Culhwch*). Yvain/Owain is directed in detail to a magic spring (at Barenton) under a tree with a great slab beside it. Pouring water from the spring on to the slab conjures up a frightful storm, after which the tree is covered with sweetly singing birds. His joy, however, is short-lived, because, with a terrific clatter, a knight (a Black Knight in the Welsh) who is the defender of the spring arrives to confront him. The knight disposed of, Yvain/Owain duly takes possession of his lands, his mission and his lady – at least for a while, because he in turn will face the challenge at the fountain.

This is one of the oldest folk stories in Europe (and elsewhere) and one can derive some amusement from the efforts of French and Welsh writers to make the lady's prompt transfer of allegiance more psychologically acceptable!

But if such a tale is baffling but highly attractive it pales before that of Perceval the Welshman who arrives at the castle of the Fisher King to encounter a strange procession marching through to an inner chamber for a splendid dinner: a youth bearing a lance which drips blood is followed by two others with golden candelabras, and two damsels, one with a *graal* dish of pure, refined gold studded with gems, the other with a silver serving dish. Having been silent before the sequence of processions, Perceval wakes in the morning to find the castle deserted and to meet a maiden nursing the corpse of a headless knight, who tells him that because he failed to ask the right question, the maimed Fisher King goes unhealed, the land has become desolate and endless troubles await.

Chrétien left this story as it was, with only a pious reference to the Grail, that potent Arthurian symbol which first appears here. But his continuators made desperate efforts to make sense of and to thoroughly Christianize the Grail, dredging up yet more Welsh sources in the process, and the subject became one of the most riveting in the history of the Arthurian cycle in the days of the Cistercians, the Crusades and the Templars. For all this early British material is an echo of pre-Christian, Celtic and pre-Celtic religion. Not that the writers or redactors of the stories understood them as such – if they had, the tales would never have survived in the militantly Christian atmosphere of the time. The myths were so old and deeply submerged that their real meaning had been lost. In an infinite number of retellings, the stories had become fables.

And that surely was one reason for their attractiveness. Their readers or hearers were introduced to a sense of wonder, of fey adventure, of apparent inconsequence and the inexplicable, all increasingly embraced in the world of the great Arthur, whose court embodied all that was noblest and best. Outside that court, however, anything could happen. To quote Rachel Bromwich: 'It is not too much to say that the persistence of such obliterated themes of Celtic mythology has contributed largely to defining the special character of Arthurian romance. The evocation of ancient concepts which were no longer fully comprehended has constituted its most powerful attraction.' There was nothing else quite like it.

Whoever or whatever transmitted it into the French-speaking world – Welsh, Bretons, soldiers, Crusaders, pilgrims, the network of intermarriages, merchants, more formal Latimers like Bleddri, the clerics (perhaps the most important) – by the early years of the twelfth century Western Europe must have bubbled with story-tellers spinning yarns out of this hypnotic material. They were probably regarded as not quite respectable, perhaps like those science fiction journals of the 1930s which were then despised but are today considered classics. For as yet, the romances lacked any credible sense of a history behind them. Those who might have known something of British history before the Saxons, as Bleddri may have done, were rare. It was Chrétien de Troyes who sensed that a great literature could be made out of the material – 'there are certain things we despise whose worth is far greater than we think'.

By the time he came to write, the scene had been transformed. Around 1138 Geoffrey of Monmouth produced his *History of the Kings of Britain* and centuries of British history which had been blank were suddenly filled in, through a breathtaking and detailed narrative which swept through the ages to climax in a King Arthur who towered over the Europe of his day. It was this work which enabled Chrétien de Troyes to launch what was to become the most potent cycle of legends in Christendom.

ditur ee iste qm inuictus martir albanus dm̄
theret ad martirium. sicut ppi de ira arida ꝓ
clum montis ꝓduxit. De coronatōe Arthuri.

Defuncto aut̄ rege conueniunt pontifices
cum clero regni ⁊ ꝑfo iꝑmꝰ qꝫ infra clo
ram gigantium more regio himali̇uunt. Et
sed. dubꝛicius urbis legionum archiepꝝ socia
nt̄ q̄ epꝭ ⁊ magnatibꝫ: Arthurum filium el̄ iu
uenē·rv. annoꝝ in rege magnifice erigunt. Cunt
ent̄ mauditē iniuriis atꝗ: largitatis. in̄ tantam

CHAPTER FIVE

EMPEROR OF·THE·WEST

Geoffrey of Monmouth's Latin *History of the Kings of Britain* (*Historia Regum Britanniae*) was a sensation. Appearing about 1138, it swept Europe; over two hundred manuscript copies survive as testimony to its popularity. Largely fictional, it was nevertheless accepted by most writers, more or less, as historical truth for five hundred years. Some fifty chroniclers writing in Latin relied on it and there were myriad translations and adaptations. The English version, *Brut of England*, was so popular that there are 160 copies extant. A thirteenth-century bishop of Cracow took it as a model for his history of the Poles and by the fourteenth century there was even a rendering into Old Norse.

In Wales they were quick to adapt it. The triads were changed to take account of it and, alongside the Laws of Hywel Dda, the *bruts* or *brutiae* (chronicles – named after the mythical founder of the British race, Brutus of Troy) were the most frequently copied texts in Welsh literature, the *Brut y Brenhinedd* (*Chronicle of the Kings*) being one surviving example. Indeed, the Welsh conception of their own nation rested on the twin pillars of the Laws of Hywel Dda and the *History* of Geoffrey of Monmouth.

To this day, his brilliantly written work can grip a reader – and shake the common sense out of him! Above all, he created the Merlin and Arthur who have stirred our imaginations ever since. Thanks to him, Merlin became a figure of authority in France, Italy, Castile, Holland, even Iceland – 'There was scarcely a cranny of Christendom outside the Eastern Church which did not recognize Merlin as a great seer.' And Arthur, with his strange birth, his miraculous sword, his towering stature as virtual emperor of the West with a court of knights without peer, his tragic fall and mysterious departure to Avalon, was established as an unforgettable figure in 'history', one who inspired

---

• The coronation of Arthur, depicted in a manuscript of
c. 1230–50 by the great medieval artist Matthew Paris.

countless poets and story-tellers to make the 'Matter of Britain' the very stuff of the imaginative life of medieval Europe.

What kind of a man wrote such a book? We know a few facts. He called himself Geoffrey of Monmouth, though he was sometimes called Geoffrey Arturus, and it is assumed that he was born and spent much of his life in Monmouth – which would certainly have been familiar with the art of the *cyfarwydd*, the Welsh story-teller. Between 1129 and 1151 he was a witness to charters of the College of St George, Oxford, whose provost was Walter, archdeacon of Oxford, a friend and one of his major sources; he presumably worked in Oxford in a centre of learning and he may have spent some time in London. He was ordained a priest at Westminster and consecrated Bishop of St Asaph in 1152, but he never entered this Welsh see, then in the power of Owain Gwynedd, the leader of a successful Welsh campaign. He certainly displayed familiarity with the south-eastern March and particularly Caerleon, a Roman site whose ruins could excite the imagination. He died in 1155.

There is, once more, a persistent belief that he was a Breton – Monmouth itself had been founded by a Breton – but I think this belief stems from a misreading of his book. Geoffrey upbraids the Britons and their descendants, the Welsh, for lapsing into dissension and civil war, and holds up the Bretons as models of patriotic conduct. Ever since Little Britain had been founded, in legend, by the British Emperor Maximus, it had been a refuge of the true British spirit; the ancestry of Geoffrey's Arthur was Breton and so were his best soldiers and allies. It is assumed by his interpreters that the Bretons would be acceptable in Norman England in a way the rebellious Welsh were not.

There is, however, no evidence that Geoffrey knew any Breton. His own language was, of course, Norman-French, though he not only wrote in Latin, the language of the educated, but also displayed a mastery of classical models. But he was certainly familiar enough with the Welsh language to translate many documents; the vast bulk of his sources were Welsh. Denunciation of one's contemporaries for moral decay and the evocation of a golden age in the past or in some ideal community 'over the water' were commonplace. Gildas himself did no other. Geoffrey called himself 'an abashed Briton' and no medieval Welshman ever made the mistake of thinking Geoffrey anti-Welsh. His death is recorded only in the Welsh chronicles. I count myself one of the handful of historians who consider Geoffrey a Welshman even if a thoroughly Normanized one.

His purpose in writing was intensely patriotic: it was to provide the Britons and their descendants with a worthy and noble history comparable with that of the French and Charlemagne. Nor did he make it all up. In the Penguin edition of the translation of his work (1966), Lewis Thorpe lists 871 proper names in his index, many of which are the names of historical people and of places actually on the map. It was on inherited material that Geoffrey let his imagination play. He cited as a major source 'a very ancient book in the British language' which set out in order the acts of all the kings of Britain in an unbroken line from the founder Brutus to the last British king of Britain, Cadwaladr. It was written, Geoffrey said, 'in a style of great beauty', which he had translated, and had been given him by Walter, the archdeacon of Oxford, who was also a fount of orally transmitted wisdom on the subject. No trace of this book has been found and it is generally assumed to have been a fiction. On the other hand, there is nothing inherently unlikely about a book with historical material on Wales, South-west Britain and Brittany brought by Walter *ex Britanniae* – probably from Wales or Cornwall. Genealogies, king lists and annals were common to all those countries and Geoffrey certainly used them and many other Welsh sources, notably Gildas and the *History of the Britons*. Could this 'ancient book in the British language' be a compilation of the famous story-teller Bleddri, who was well known in both Poitou and Carmarthen, or something similar?

Of course, Geoffrey transformed, embellished and modernized his sources. The court of his Arthur resembles the Norman courts of his day, in which the idea of chivalry was being nurtured – in fact his court is a classic and a model for the future. He wrenches the court from Cornwall and locates it in Caerleon; he changes the names of Arthur's magical weapons. He has the customary cavalier attitude of his time to numbers; he invents speeches and conversations, and dwells in detail on campaigns that never happened. But he eschewed the wilder fringes of fantasy – there is no hunting of giant boars who were once kings, hags and the rest of the magical paraphernalia.

This is, in a sense, true even of his Merlin. He had reached the climax of his book, with Merlin's prophecies and the appearance of a brilliant star in the heavens heralding the birth of Arthur, when Alexander, bishop of Lincoln and a former member of the College of St George, begged him to publish *The Prophecies of Merlin* separately since they were being much talked of. Geoffrey published his *Prophetiae* or *Libellus Merlini* before 1135 and they were certainly sensational. Based on the marvellous boy in the *History of the Britons*, and recounting many prophecies which had been known since the ninth century, the work is full of boars and dragons and worms. The earlier prophecies clearly foresee the triumphs of Arthur; they forecast the coming of the Normans, 'men dressed in wood and in iron corselets', and the enslavement of the Saxon 'seed of the White Dragon'; and Geoffrey has his fifth-century prophet foresee the sinking of the White Ship and the death of Henry I's son in 1120.

• *Overleaf* King Arthur being crowned; from the *St Alban's Chronicle*, illustrated *c.* 1470 by Flemish artists.

Thereafter, except for the startling prophecy of the restoration of the Britons by Cadwaladr of Wales and Cynan of Brittany in alliance with Scotland, they become virtually incomprehensible, swathed in mystical beasts and ending in apocalypse – an apparently irresistible combination which engaged many of the best minds of Europe for centuries in the style of Nostradamus. Geoffrey in his *History* made Merlin the son of a princess of Dyfed in south-west Wales, but later, about 1150, he published *Vita Merlini*, a life of Merlin in a poem. Here, he had evidently discovered the other, probably earlier Merlin, the Wild Man of the Woods, and blandly combined the two by asserting that the prophet had enjoyed an inordinately long life! The prophecies did not alter much, but they included Taliesin's description of Avalon – which enormously strengthened the hope of a Return of Arthur.

It is intriguing to observe just what kind of a magician Merlin was. The magic is expressed in his gift of prophecy, central to the Welsh, but to many other peoples as well. And in some of the more miraculous achievements, such as the shifting of Stonehenge, he is presented rather as a superbly skilled construction engineer. He is credited with using drugs which were 'quite new and until now unheard-of in your day' – and is, as it were, a man ahead of his time. And while Geoffrey's Arthur has some mythical touches, they are kept to the minimum, for he was trying to produce a great and credible history which was also superbly readable. He certainly succeeded.

The chronicler, Henry of Huntingdon, was astonished when he came across the *History* at the abbey of Bec in Normandy in 1139, since he had been trying and failing to find works on pre-Saxon Britain. Geoffrey said much the same himself. He certainly filled the gap. He begins with the mythical founder of Britain, Brutus of Troy, who in his migrations founded the city of Tours. Hence both the French and Welsh subjects of the king (the Saxons are ignored) were descended from Trojans – a useful thought when England became part of the Angevin empire. Geoffrey makes the Welsh language, Cymraeg, a form of 'crooked Greek' – cam Roeg. Brutus lands in Totnes (which seems to have been uncommonly popular in these years), clears the land of giants and establishes the monarchy.

And on goes Geoffrey through the years, peopling his pages with mythical figures like Belinus and Brennius (gods originally), who sacked Rome, and authentic individuals like Julius Caesar and the pretenders to the Roman Empire who originated in Roman Britain, like Maximus, who is Maximianus in the *History*. Rome was to be the ultimate enemy of Arthur, but is assimilated, and the British kings roll on. All sorts of figures appear from the British pre-history of the Welsh, Cornishmen and Bretons – King Lear and his three daughters; Lud, who built London as Caerludd; Cymbeline; Constantine; Old King Cole (Coel Hen) – following on to the prophecies of the boy Merlin, which, as book seven, are right at the centre of the work and open the reign of Arthur, greatest king of the Britons, which fills a good fifth of the volume. Geoffrey draws to a close with the anti-climax of the British collapse into civil war and the assumption of the Crown of Britain by Athelstan, king of all Loegria (*Lloegr*: England). For his book is Providential history at its most unforgiving: the working out of God's will. It opens:

> Britain, the best of islands, is situated in the Western Ocean, between France and Ireland. . . a rich country, once graced by twenty-eight cities. . . Britain is inhabited by five races of people, the Norman-French, the Britons, the Saxons, the Picts and Scots. Of these, the Britons once occupied the land from sea to sea, before the others came. Then the vengeance of God overtook them because of their arrogance and they submitted to the Picts and the Saxons.

He then resumes the theme, present in the earlier Welsh tradition of the Island of the Mighty, of the Sovereignty of Britain and its loss to the Saxon pagans. It is the story of a favoured people, expressed in their single monarchy (though allowing for many sub-kings), who meet disaster because of their addiction to civil war, strife and dissensions.

This is not without historical warrant. To quote Merlin: 'Then the Red Dragon will revert to its true habits and struggle to tear itself to pieces.' At moments when a great leader emerges, the people could display unexampled courage, as they did at the climax of Arthur's reign, only to fall victim to treachery and betrayal, like Arthur. No true British leader is defeated in any other way, until the last British king, preparing to regain his kingdom from Brittany, is stopped by an Angelic Voice speaking to him in a peal of thunder – 'God did not wish the Britons to rule in Britain any more, until the moment should come which Merlin had prophesied to Arthur' (actually to Vortigern).

This stress on the debilitating horrors of civil war would have struck a chord among the Normans, who, when Geoffrey's work appeared, were locked into just such a war, between King Stephen and Queen Matilda. The Norman rulers knew that the Saxons before them had been incomers and originally pagans, and that there was a long, unknown British history behind them. There was nothing in Geoffrey's *History* to offend them; indeed, it offered them a much more distinguished *British* inheritance. Moreover, many of them would have been familiar with the romances spoken or sung in the Marcher courts. For Geoffrey wrote to please the Normans – what else could he have done? – and his search for preferment can be seen in the multiple and somewhat tortured dedications of his book! But it appeared at what must have seemed a tricky moment.

In what has been referred to as the twelfth-century Renaissance, Europe at this time had begun to cultivate new ideas of civilization, of kingship and chivalry; with the Crusades and ever-expanding colonization, pastoral peoples on the fringes were dismissed as barbarians. The Welsh had hitherto been treated neutrally or even favourably by English chroniclers – indeed, as late as 1130 the Worcester chronicler saw them as fellow-sufferers under the Norman Yoke – but a change had become visible from the 1120s or so. The scholar and contemporary of Geoffrey of Monmouth, William of Malmesbury, described them as barbarians, a term previously applied to pagans. William's ideal was French; it was not enough to be Christian, one had also to be cultivated, in all senses of the term. The English were only now entering this blissful state and the Welsh were nowhere. From this time onward, the tendency to look on the Welsh as barbarians grew steadily.

Geoffrey's book presented the Britons and, by extension, their Welsh heirs, as anything but barbarous. They had great kings, noble cities and a rich culture. There was without doubt an element of satire in his writing. It must have been with glee that he teased William of Malmesbury and others by making Caerleon, in a somewhat obscure corner of Gwent, the prime ecclesiastical centre of Britain, with a papal legate as its archbishop, and by having Bath, widely believed to have been founded by Julius Caesar, created by the British king, Bladud. But it made his whole-hearted reception among the mighty a little difficult.

The Normans, however, were facing more pressing problems. In their first impact, they had swamped Wales; Welsh kings disappeared, to be replaced by lords. To one Welsh chronicler, it seemed that the Normans were aiming 'to exterminate all the Britons completely, so that the Britannic name should never more be remembered'. As early as 1116, young men were led into revolt against Henry I by Gruffydd ap Rhys, a Welsh prince, inspired by 'an urge to restore and renew the Britannic kingdom'. After 1135, with the death of Henry I and the outbreak of civil war in England, the revolt became a tidal wave. Rebellions broke out all over Wales and inflicted severe defeats on the Normans. During the civil war, Stephen virtually abandoned Wales and, with interruptions, the revolt continued after the accession of Henry II, whose abortive Welsh campaigns in the 1160s settled a Marcher frontier which left much of the west in Welsh hands. This extraordinary development stemmed in the first instance from an unprecedented unity among leaders of the Welsh, north, centre and south; it was to be the age of Owain Gwynedd in the north and later of the Lord Rhys in the south.

• Arthur and his knights approach a fortified city from the
Romance of Guiron de Courtois.

Comment le roy artus mist ledit
le seneschal a raison / Et des cho
ses quil lui dist .

En ceste partie

More immediately there was an insurrection led by the brothers Morgan and Iorwerth ap Owain which killed the great magnate, Richard de Clare, and seized the castles of Usk and Caerleon, holding them until 1158. Morgan, based at Caerleon, actually styled himself a king and, moreover, was an ally of Robert of Gloucester, bastard son of Henry I, in the war against Stephen. And Robert of Gloucester, with his Welsh wife, was the very man to whom Geoffrey of Monmouth originally dedicated his book, which appeared at the crest of a wave of entirely unexpected Welsh success.

It has been suggested that these remarkable events influenced Geoffrey as he was finishing his history. When William of Newburgh made his celebrated attack on the book at the end of the century – that Geoffrey had 'disguised under the honourable name of History, thanks to his Latinity, the fables about Arthur which he took from the ancient fictions of the Britons and increased out of his own head . . . he made the little finger of Arthur thicker than the loins of Alexander the Great' – he might have been responding not only as an affronted historian but also against a current trend.

Geoffrey had been coy about Avalon and the Return of Arthur in his *History*, but was much more positive about this in his later *Life of Merlin*. Because it was precisely this which was at stake. It was probably in the 1140s that an Anglo-Norman wrote a *Description of England* in which he said of the Welsh revolt: 'Well have the Welsh revenged themselves. Many of our French have they slain. Some of our castles they have taken. Fiercely they threaten us. Openly they go about saying, that in the end they will have it all, by means of Arthur, they will have it back. . . They will call it Britain again.' Such feelings about the Welsh, and their belief in Arthur's return, may well have sharpened Geoffrey's writing about Arthur, but they made the assimilation of the story difficult and may explain his reticence about Arthur's end in the *History*. Not until the 'discovery' of Arthur's maimed body at Glastonbury in 1191 brought the intense relief of knowing that he would never come back could the kings of England whole-heartedly take him over as their own.

For there is no doubt that Geoffrey's section on Arthur with his preliminary Merlin is the climax of the whole book. Everything else led to this momentous period and in view of its transcendental significance, it is worth giving a full account of it.

The relevant section begins with the collapse of British resistance to the Picts, Scots and other barbarians after the withdrawal of the Romans – 'Thus it is when a kingdom is handed over to the safe-keeping of its peasantry.' An appeal to Brittany brought Constantine, the brother of its king, who defeated the barbarians but was stabbed to death by a Pict. The scheming Vortigern, who was rising to power in Britain, usurped the throne from Constantine's monkish son Constans, and Constans's two brothers, Aurelius Ambrosius (the Ambrosius Aurelianus or Emrys Wledig of history) and Uther fled to Brittany, where their looming presence remained a mortal threat.

At this point, Hengist and Horsa landed in Kent with a pagan army of Saxons. Ignoring their paganism, Vortigern enrolled them as allies against the Picts and Aurelius, and lavished lands on them. He was besotted with Hengist's daughter Renwein (Rowena), married her and permitted the Saxons to settle 'near the Wall between Deira and Scotland'. Revulsed, the Christian Britons took to the offensive under Vortigern's son, Vortimer, who drove the Saxons back to Germany. Renwein promptly poisoned him.

Vortigern resumed power and asked Hengist to return with a few men. He came with three hundred thousand! Renwein intervened once more and engineered a peace conference, in the Cloister of Ambrius (probably Amesbury). The Saxons came with knives hidden in their boots and, at a given signal, they 'cut the throats of about four hundred and sixty counts and earls who were thinking of something quite different'. With Britain's lords thus wiped out, the Saxons swarmed over the whole country, ravaging without mercy. The massacre became entrenched in Welsh tradition as *Brad y Cyllyll Hirion* (Treason of the Long Knives). Up to this point in his narrative, Geoffrey had been rehearsing, though with considerable embellishment, what had become the standard British–Welsh perception of recent history; he peopled his text with what are believed to have been historical figures. But after this, he starts to shift into the epic.

A disgraced and demoralized Vortigern fled to Wales and, on the advice of his 'magicians', started to build a strong tower into which he could retreat. But no sooner were the foundations laid than they sank into the earth without trace. It is not clear who the 'magicians' were. At this time St Germanus of Auxerre was on his missions to Britain against the Pelagian heresy and Vortigern, as opposed to the Catholic Aurelius, may have been a Pelagian. On the other hand, the magicians sound like a bunch of bloodthirsty Druids, for they advised him to find a fatherless boy, kill him and sprinkle his blood on the stones. A great search was launched.

At Carmarthen the weary seekers overheard two boys quarrelling at play. One said to another, 'Why do you try to compete with me, fathead? How can we two be equal? I am of royal blood on both sides of my family. As for you, nobody knows who you are for you never had a father.' The fatherless boy, Merlin, and his mother, daughter of a king of Demetia (Dyfed, south-west Wales), were promptly haled before Vortigern, when the mother confessed to having been seduced by a spirit who from time to time assumed human form. One of the magicians solemnly assured the king that this could be so, citing Apuleius in his *De Deo Socratis* on incubus demons. Stupefaction over such a history is, however, as nothing compared to what follows, when the *wunderkind* from Carmarthen totally overthrew the magicians.

Vortigern's men were told to dig beneath the foundations of the tower, where they found a pool which they drained to reveal two hollow stones. Inside them were two sleeping dragons. Wakened, they emerged and fought each other. And Merlin at this point launched into his remarkable series of prophecies, the first of which was that the Red Dragon of the Britons and the White Dragon of the Saxons would fight to the death for dominion over the Island of Britain. This has been taken as the start of the Welsh tradition of prophecy. The boy went on to forecast a fiery death for Vortigern, and all the vicissitudes that would follow for the Saxons until the moment when 'The Boar of Cornwall will eat them up'.

Even as he spoke, Aurelius was landing at Totnes. He burned Vortigern to death, destroying his castle on the River Wye, and drove the Saxons beyond the Humber. After a fearful battle in the north, Hengist was captured and 'packed off to Hell by cutting off his head'. Aurelius, moderate in all things and a prototype Arthur, buried him in a barrow after the pagan fashion and allowed the Saxons to hold land near Scotland as his subjects. He then restored the laws, churches and rightful heirs to the many estates now vacant.

When he came to 'Kaercardduc now called Salisbury', he was reminded of the men who fell at the Treason of the Long Knives and, seeking a fitting memorial for them, sent for Merlin. There followed the moving of the Giant's Ring from Ireland, the mighty gathering from all Britain, the Whitsun crown-wearing and the consecration of Dubricius (Dyfrig) as archbishop of the City of the Legions (Caerleon). Merlin then erected the stones at Stonehenge around the burial place of the 460 martyrs.

But the Saxons, 'striving by every means in their power to take complete control of the realm', came again from Germany, under Vortigern's son. Defeated in Britain, they allied with the Irish and landed at Menevia (St David's). The king sent his brother Uther to Wales, but a Saxon spy poisoned Aurelius on his sick-bed in Winchester. At this point, there appeared a star of great brilliance, sending out a single beam at the end of which was a ball of fire in the shape of a dragon. Two rays of light from his mouth beamed out on Ireland and Gaul. Everyone was paralysed with fear, including Uther, who sent for Merlin. He burst into tears, as he often did. He said that Aurelius was dead but urged Uther to fight on, saying that the dragon signified Uther himself and the rays of light a promise of great power for his son.

• Arthur prepares to do battle with the Saxons; from a
fifteenth-century Flemish copy of the *Chronicles of Hainault*.

luy soit faite de tous ses pechies
penitance z absolution mais que
par celle maniere icelle ne refuse
et en disant que chascun sarmast
il leur donna sa benediction. Et
tantost le roy artus vestus dun
haubert noble z digne tel que a
luy appertenoit mist ou chief le
healme dozet du quel estoit le
hachement le simulacre dun dza
thon z puis yetta sus ses espaules
son estu quil appelloit prinwem

la ou estoit paint limatge de le glo
rieuse vierge marie la quelle glo
rieuse vierge souuent en ses affai
res il reclamoit z appelloit. Conse
quanment il chaindit sa bonne z
noble espee quil appelloit calibur
ne qui moult estoit de grant es
pecialte z dist on qlle auoit este
forgie en lisle dauaalon. z puis
prist sa lance a la droite main q
il appelloit ron la quelle estoit
longue et grosse. Et tantost quil

Uther, accordingly, killed the king of the Irish and Vortigern's son, buried Aurelius within the Giant's Ring and, as king, ordered two dragons to be finished in gold with the most marvellous craftsmanship. One was given to the cathedral of Winchester, the other he carried with him on his wars. 'From that moment onwards he was called Uther Pendragon which in the British tongue means a Dragon's head,' adds Geoffrey, always anxious to tie up loose threads, even if he was mistaken in this case.

Back came the Saxons under a son of Hengist, but after a fierce struggle they were defeated at Mount Damen and Uther wore his crown at a great festival in London at Easter. There, he conceived an insatiable passion for Ygerna, wife of the redoubtable Gorlois, duke of Cornwall. Her enraged husband left the court, shut his wife up in Tintagel castle and went to face an equally inflamed Uther with a huge army at his back. In his torment, the king sent for Merlin. 'If you are to have your wish,' said the seer, 'you must make use of methods which are quite new and until now unheard-of.' The unheard-of methods were drugs which gave Uther the precise appearance of Gorlois. Off then at twilight to Tintagel to have his way with the innocent Ygerna, while at that very moment Gorlois was killed in a sortie, thus conferring a kind of posthumous legitimacy on the heir so begotten – Arthur.

The battle with the Saxons raged on. There was stupid arrogance on both sides, the Britons in particular refusing to obey their leaders. Loth, a lord of the North, stood in for Uther, who was ill, but who gave him his daughter Anna as wife. By her, Loth fathered both Gawain and Mordred. Uther, sick as he was, was in the end victorious, but was viciously cut down by the customary poison, to be duly buried within the Giant's Ring. By this time the Saxons, who had already overrun the whole stretch of land from the Humber to Caithness, sent for more men from Germany, made Colgrin their commander and 'began to exterminate the Britons'. It was under this mortal threat that Dyfrig, archbishop of Caerleon, called together the British leaders at Silchester. They decided to bestow the crown on Uther's son, Arthur.

'Arthur was a young man only fifteen years old, but he was of outstanding courage and generosity and his inborn goodness gave him such grace that he was loved by almost all the people.' On his installation, he gave gifts freely to everyone, until he ran out; he made up his mind to harry the Saxons so that with their wealth he might reward his retainers – *realpolitik* never deserted Geoffrey's Arthur! With his young men, he marched north, defeated an army of Saxons, Scots and Picts at the River Douglas and besieged Colgrin in York. Baldulf, rushing from the coast to help his brother, was ambushed and, alone, wandered through the British camp disguised as a minstrel with a harp before slipping over the wall to his brother's side. At that moment Cheldric came from Germany to Albany (Scotland) with three hundred ships. Arthur prudently withdrew to London and, as became his style, consulted the leading men. They sent for his cousin Hoel, king of Brittany.

Hoel was to prove his staunchest ally. Together they marched north, on the first of Arthur's great campaigns. He inflicted unheard of slaughter on the Saxons at Kaerluideoit – 'it is also called by another name, Lincoln' – and trapped the enemy within a ring of trees in Caledon Wood. Threatened with starvation, the Saxons handed over all their gold and silver, gave hostages and promised to pay tribute from Germany if they were spared. On their way home, however, they changed their mind, sailed to Totnes (again!) and depopulated the country as far as the Severn Sea, laying siege to the city of Bath.

Arthur 'was greatly astonished at their extraordinary duplicity' and hanged their hostages without more ado (a continuator of Geoffrey says that the hostages were twenty-four children); leaving Hoel ill in the town of Alclud (Dumbarton), he marched to Bath. Geoffrey evidently intended this to be a critical moment and though he does not name it, the ensuing battle is clearly that of Mount Badon and is treated as a crusade. 'You who are marked with the cross of the Christian faith,' declaimed Dubricius of Caerleon, 'fight for your fatherland and if you are killed suffer death willingly for your country.' Arthur assumes what were to become his familiar trappings, even if he changed the names:

> Arthur himself put on a leather jerkin worthy of so great a king. On his head he placed a golden helmet, with the crest carved in the shape of a dragon; and across his shoulders a circular shield called Pridwen, on which there was painted a likeness of the Blessed Mary, Mother of God, which forced him to be thinking perpetually of her. He girded on his peerless sword called Caliburn, which was forged in the Isle of Avalon. A spear called Ron graced his right hand; long, broad in the blade and thirsty for slaughter.

In a ferocious two-day battle around a hill, Arthur grew impatient. 'He drew his sword Caliburn, called upon the name of the Blessed Virgin and rushed forward at full speed into the thickest ranks of the enemy. Every man whom he struck, calling upon God as he did so, he killed at a single blow. He did not slacken his onslaught until he had dispatched 470 men with his sword Caliburn' (ten more than the Long Knives). Colgrin and his brother fell, Cheldric fled but was cut off from his ships by Cador of Cornwall and there was slaughter without mercy until they surrendered on the Isle of Thanet (another of Geoffrey's continuators suggested the more plausible Teignmouth).

Without a pause, Arthur swept north, relieved Hoel in Dumbarton, drove into Moray and, after three victories, penned up the Scots and Picts around Loch Lomond, which he besieged with a fleet of ships. As Scots died in their thousands he turned to deal with the king of Ireland, who had come with a huge horde of pagans. He cut them to pieces and returned to wipe out the Scots, treating them with unparalleled severity until 'all the bishops of this pitiful country with all the clergy under their command, their feet bare and in their hands the relics of their saints and the treasures of their churches assembled to beg pity. . . Their patriotism moved him to tears' and he allowed them to live.

Needless to say, Arthur was never very popular in Scotland. Indeed, the Arthur depicted here is very much the Arthur the Terrible of Welsh tradition. There followed a curious interval when Hoel commented on the wonders of Loch Lomond and its miraculous pool – its sixty islands, sixty streams, sixty crags with sixty eagles which gathered once a year to scream a shrill warning of portentous events. Arthur spoke of the equally miraculous Llyn Lligwy near the Severn, probably the home of the salmon, the Oldest Animal of *Culhwch ac Olwen*.

He celebrated Christmas at York, where he restored the churches, returned lands to nobles dispossessed by the Saxons and married Guinevere – 'she was descended from a noble Roman family and had been brought up in the household of Duke Cador of Cornwall. She was the most beautiful woman in the entire island.'

But as soon as next summer came, Arthur was off to assert his authority. He took Ireland by storm. The Irish army, 'which was naked and unarmed, was miserably cut to pieces' and their king captured. Thunderstruck, the remaining princes surrendered. Then, without a pause, he went on to Iceland, which he promptly subdued. Rumour spread through all the other islands that no country could resist Arthur and their rulers surrendered of their own free will. So the kings of Orkney and Gothland (a mythical island which haunted medieval maps, probably Greenland) submitted. These countries presumably replaced the Three Adjacent Islands of tradition – Wight, Man and Orkney (though Geoffrey sometimes treats Norway and Denmark as islands, too).

Arthur established a lasting peace and remained in Britain for twelve prosperous years. Geoffrey then introduces a note which had already appeared in the legends and which he now verified in abundance:

• Arthur and the Roman tribune Frollo in single combat outside the besieged walls of Paris after Arthur's invasion of Gaul; from the *Chronicles of Hainault*.

Tantost quilz furent entrez ou
camp sans plente dattente ilz
auallerent ses lances lun contre
laultre z ferrent cheuaulx des
esperons qui ses emporterent de
telle radeur quil sambloit que
ce fuist fourdze tellement fai
soient ilz sa terre resonner. si fe
rirent en ce venir lun sault ens
es pis si durement qil conuint
le dit flolon verser a terre tout
plat estendu z le roy passa oult

qui prestement retourna z auoit
ia sacquiet son espee pour ferir
le dit flolon le quel flolon es
toit ia releuez come tous confus
z honteur. et en trestirant desir
de venger sa honte auoit ahers
sa lance qui ly estoit volee par
et sen vint de grant ire embrasez
deuers le roy et assist sa lance
ens es ars du cheual artus tel
lement que il le tua mort par
terre z quey se cheual z le roy

Arthur then began to increase his personal entourage by inviting men from far-distant kingdoms to join it. In this way he developed such a code of courtliness in his household that he inspired peoples living far away to imitate him. . . even the man of noblest birth thought nothing of himself unless he wore arms and dressed in the same way as Arthur's knights.

Fear of Arthur spread and kings built fortresses for a refuge in case he should come. 'The fact that he was dreaded by all encouraged him to conceive the idea of conquering the whole of Europe.' No sooner said than done. Norway and Denmark were burned and blasted into submission and his army landed in Gaul. With all the young men of the islands in addition, he seemed irresistible – particularly since he had taken the precaution of buying up most of the opposing Gauls as well. Frollo, the Roman tribune who held Gaul for the emperor, was besieged within Paris, which was soon reduced to such a piteous state that Frollo challenged Arthur to single combat. Being a man of immense stature, courage and strength, Frollo presumably fancied his chances. Great crowds of armies along with the people of Paris watched the dramatic scene outside the city. Arthur unhorsed Frollo, but Frollo stabbed Arthur's horse and he fell. The Britons nearly broke the truce in their agony, but the two men stood face to face, trading blow for blow. Frollo found an opening:

> When Arthur saw his leather cuirass and his round shield grow red, he was roused to even fiercer anger. He raised Caliburn in the air with all his strength and brought it down through Frollo's helmet and so on to his head, which he cut into two halves. At the blow, Frollo fell to the ground, drummed the earth with his heels and breathed his soul into the winds.

Geoffrey is full of vivid detail of this riveting kind and the head-splitting stroke became something of an Arthurian tradition. The king split his army too and spent the next nine years subduing all Gaul, including specifically Poitou, Aquitania and Gascony. He held a great assembly in Paris and settled the government 'peacefully and legally', according to Geoffrey's somewhat elastic perception of those terms. It was then 'that he gave Neustria, now called Normandy, to his Cup-bearer Bedevere and the province of Anjou to his Seneschal Kay'. Which might have surprised their originals, Bedwyr and Cei. At long last Arthur decided to return home, to the Great Plenary Court at the City of the Legions in honour of the Hero who was now virtually emperor of the West – the climax of Geoffrey's account and indeed of the entire *History*.

Caerleon, says Geoffrey, 'was a match for Rome'. Lying by the River Usk, it had royal palaces adorned with gold-painted gables and two famous churches – one in honour of the British martyr Julius, which was graced by a choir of lovely virgins, and the other named after another British martyr, Aaron, which was served by a monastery of canons and was counted as the third metropolitan see of Britain. There was also a college of two hundred learned men who were skilled in astronomy and other arts and made careful computations for Arthur.

A sonorous roll-call follows of those invited to the Plenary Court. The kings and rulers of the Island came first – of Scotland, Moray, the Venedoti (north Wales), Demetae (south Wales) and Cornwall – followed by the archbishops of the three metropolitan sees, with Dubricius of Caerleon the primate of Britain and papal legate, then leading men from provincial cities – Gloucester, Worcester, Salisbury, 'Guerensis now called Warwick', Leicester, Caistor, Durobernia, Bath, Dorchester, and 'Boso of Rydychen, that is Oxford'. There were other famous men 'too tedious to tell', but all of them sported Welsh names and some were familiar, such as Peredur, better known as Perceval, and Kymbelin – Cymbeline. They were followed by the subject kings and lords – of Ireland, Iceland, the Orkneys, Gothland, Norway and Denmark; from across the Channel came Bedevere and Kay, twelve peers from the regions of Gaul, led by Gerin of Chartres and Hoel, king of the Armorican Britons. 'Once they are listed, there remained no prince of any distinction this side of Spain.'

They and their great trains of followers moved through the city. The king, enrobed, was conducted in due pomp to the metropolitan church, archbishops to left and right, and the four kings of Scotland, Cornwall, Demetia and Venedotia bearing golden swords in front. Clerics went before, chanting in exquisite harmony. From another direction the queen came with her own regalia to the church of the dedicated virgins, four kings with white doves before her and all the married women after her. So much organ music of such quality was played in the two churches, and so many choirs sang so sweetly, that 'the knights scarcely knew which of the churches to enter first'.

After High Mass, the king and queen put on lighter regalia and the king went off with the men to feast in his own palace, while the queen with the married women went to hers – 'for the Britons still observed the ancient custom of Troy' (which was in fact prevalent in Byzantine ceremony at Constantinople). Kay the seneschal, with a thousand noblemen in ermine, and Bedevere, with a thousand noblemen in miniver, served food and drink. Says Geoffrey:

> If I were to describe everything, I should make this story far too long. Indeed, by this time, Britain had reached such a standard of sophistication that it excelled all other kingdoms in its general affluence, the richness of its decorations and the courteous behaviour of its inhabitants. Every knight in

the country who was in any way famed for his bravery wore livery and arms showing his own distinctive colour; and women of fashion often displayed the same colours. They scorned to give their love to any man who had not proved himself three times in battle. In this way, the womenfolk became chaste and the more virtuous and for their love the knights were ever more daring.

Invigorated by food and drink, Geoffrey comments, they went out into the meadows outside the city. The knights planned an imitation battle on horseback 'while their womenfolk watched from the top of the city walls and aroused them to passionate excitement by their flirtatious behaviour'. So they passed three days, jousting, shooting with bows and arrows, hurling the lance, tossing stones, playing dice and a variety of other games, 'without the slightest show of ill-feeling'. Whoever won was awarded an immense prize by Arthur. On the fourth day, he rewarded all who had done him service with personal grants of cities, castles, archbishoprics and the like.

This is the classic picture of the Arthurian court, heart of chivalry, gallantry and noble worth under a peerless king. It was to haunt medieval Europe and still exerts its magical spell over a sceptical twentieth century. And it is located in Caerleon, capital of the Island of the Mighty, Britain, with its Three Realms and its Three Adjacent Islands.

Into this joyful spectacle came twelve emissaries from Lucius Hiberius, procurator of the Republic of Rome (who somehow managed also to serve the Emperor Leo). The message was an insult. Outraged by Arthur's insolent behaviour, it demanded restoration of the lands snatched from the empire and a resumption of the tribute paid by Britain since the days of Julius Caesar. Arthur was given until August to present himself in Rome. This was a challenge from what Geoffrey clearly saw as the Ultimate Enemy. It was to be a clash of Titans.

It opened Arthur's last campaign, which Geoffrey relates in such loving detail that the reader has to keep hold of his wits to remember that none of it ever happened! The leaders withdrew to a gigantic tower outside the city, where Cador of Cornwall, a merry man, burst out laughing. He had been afraid that their life of ease, 'playing at dice,

---

• Arthur depicted as the Christian sovereign of the thirty kingdoms of the earth; his shield is emblazoned with the Virgin Mary and infant Jesus, and his crowns range from France, Rome and Denmark to Egypt and Babylon; from the early fourteenth-century *Chronicle of Peter Langtoft*.

burning up their strength with women', had weakened the Britons; he welcomed the challenge. Arthur made a long speech, proclaiming Geoffrey's own theme-song: 'When these men landed with their armed band and conquered our fatherland by force and violence at a time when it was weakened by civil dissension, they had been encouraged to come by the disunity of our ancestors. . . Nothing that is acquired by force and violence can ever be held legally by anyone.' Worthy sentiments, if a trifle rich in the circumstances! Hoel of Brittany complimented Arthur on his 'Ciceronian eloquence' and the king of Scotland waxed fierce over the treachery of Germans and Romans. They all pledged their support and an enormous army. Arthur sent a harsh reply to Rome, where the Senate promptly summoned all the kings of the Orient and an army of about four hundred thousand men. Arthur handed over the defence of Britain to his nephew Mordred and Queen Guinevere, and set off with his army from Southampton.

After a mid-Channel dream of a conflict between a bear and a dragon, which his men said presaged a battle with a giant but which Arthur interpreted as an omen of Roman Empire, they landed at Barfleur, where they were distracted. A hideous giant had carried off Helena, daughter of Hoel of Brittany, to Mont St Michel. Bedevere, sent on in advance, climbed one of the two peaks to encounter an old, weeping woman, Helena's nurse, who said that the girl had died rather than submit to the monster's embrace so that she herself had been raped instead. Arthur dismissed Bedevere and Kay and went on alone. 'The inhuman monster was standing by his fire. His face was smeared with clotted blood of a number of pigs at which he had been gnawing.' They grappled. A blow from his club deafened Arthur, who struck the giant till he was blinded by his own blood. He grabbed Arthur, but the king wrestled free and at last drove his sword the whole length of the blade into the giant's skull. The creature gave a great shriek and collapsed. Bedevere cut off his head and carried it to camp, while Hoel raised a chapel on the peak. To his day, according to Geoffrey, it was called Helena's tomb.

After this diversion, they encountered the Romans on the River Aube. Arthur sent a delegation to order Lucius to withdraw; it included Gawain, Arthur's most loyal knight but an impetuous man. When Lucius rejected the order, 'his nephew Gaius Quintillanus was heard to mutter that the Britons were better at boasting and making threats than they were at proving their courage and prowess on the battle-field'. Incensed, Gawain rushed at him and cut off his head. The Britons ran for their horses as the affronted Romans pursued them. Marcellus Mutius, keen to avenge a friend, caught up with Gawain, who 'swung round and with the sword which he brandished clove him through helm and head to his chest, bidding him, when he got to hell, to tell Quintillanus . . . that this was why the Britons were so good at boasting'.

96

A running fight followed, with much marching and counter-marching, until the armies got to grips at Saussy, south-west of Langres. After set speeches on both sides, it became a frightful slaughter, 'with a bedlam of shouting and with men tumbling head foremost or feet first to the ground all over the place and vomiting forth their life with their heart's blood'. In the battle Arthur lost his closest companions; Bedevere was killed and Kay mortally wounded. 'No better knights than Hoel and Gawain have ever been born down the ages,' said Geoffrey, as they saved the day. 'What the devil are you doing, men? Are you letting these effeminate creatures slip away unhurt?', shouted Arthur, waving his wonderful sword Caliburn. 'Think of your own right hands . . . which have subjected thirty kingdoms to my sovereignty!' In the end he prevailed, avenging centuries of oppression. But the cost was dreadful. Bedevere was buried in his city of Bayeux (founded by his grandfather Bedevere I, says Geoffrey, in a touch that no doubt intrigued his Norman readers!) and Kay in a wood near Chinon belonging to a convent of hermits, 'as was fitting for a Duke of the Angevins'. The body of Lucius was sent to Rome as the only tribute it would receive from Britain. The army wintered in France and in the summer set out for Rome. They were moving into the Alps when appalling news came from home. Mordred, Arthur's nephew, had treacherously placed the crown on his own head and was living adulterously with Guinevere, who had broken her marriage vows. It was the end of a disastrous expedition. Arthur's magnificent empire dissolved in domestic and public tragedy.

'About this particular matter, most noble Duke, Geoffrey of Monmouth prefers to say nothing'; he would, he said, simply tell the story which he found in his British treatise and which he had heard from Walter of Oxford. In this unaccustomed reticence, his conclusion was brief. Only the island troops and their kings fought with Arthur in the ensuing civil war, though Mordred brought back the Saxons. There was a fierce, contested landing at Richborough, where Gawain was killed along with the king of Scotland. They marched on Winchester. When Guinevere heard the news, she gave way to despair, left York for Caerleon and became a nun in the church of Julius the Martyr. There was another slaughter as Britons desperately fought each other at Winchester. Mordred fled into Cornwall and Arthur fought his last great battle there at the River Camblam, which was presumably the dread Camlan. The accursed traitor Mordred was killed and thousands of his men with him.

Arthur himself, our renowned King, was mortally wounded and was carried off to the Isle of Avalon, so that his wounds might be attended to. He handed the crown of Britain over to his cousin Constantine, the son of Cador Duke of Cornwall: this in the year 542 after our Lord's Incarnation.

eschiffleroit branques. et quant le
roy artus entendi ceste chose la
nuit subsequente venue enuiron
le mienuit il print kayus le senes
cal z beduer le boutillier z se par
ti secretement des tentes si print
le chemin que pour aler vers le
mont z euantdit come celi q riens
ne sauoit de la force du monstre
euantdit qui seul estoit assez

fors que pour vaincre z destruire
vng tyrant ost. et come ilz fuissent
approchies z venus prez du mont
ilz virent vng feu ardant sur le
haultesce du mont et puis virent
encore vng aultre feu vng peu
mendre le quel nestoit point trop
loins de laultre feu. Si doubterent
a sauoir au quel des deux feux le
euantdit nayant se pooit tenir

• *Above* Arthur fights the Roman general Lucius; painted
c. 1415 to illustrate a historical narrative probably composed
for Prigent de Coetivy, later admiral of France.

• *Left* Arthur's fight with the giant of Mont St Michel, an
illustration by Guillaume Vrelant in 1468 from the Arthurian
part of the *Chronicles of Hainault*, one of the Flemish manuscripts created for Duke Philip the Good of Burgundy.

And that was it. The epic of Arthur came to an abrupt and almost incomprehensible end. The rest of the *History* was a sorry tale of disharmony and defeat until the Angelic Voice told the Britons that they were no longer fit to rule in their Britain.

The Voice, however, added that 'as a reward for its faithfulness, the British people would occupy the island again at some time in the future, once the appointed moment had come' – that moment captured by Merlin when he declaimed: 'The mountains of Armorica shall erupt and Armorica itself shall be crowned with Brutus' diadem. Kambria shall be filled with joy and the Cornish oaks shall flourish. The island shall be called by the name of Brutus and the title given to it by the foreigners shall be done away with.'

Geoffrey of Monmouth, that ambiguous Welshman, created the Arthur of 'history' and stimulated creative energy in the European mind for centuries. But in the end it is still Arthur, hero of the Britons, whom he celebrates and through him we hear the voice of a small people with big memories and even bigger hopes, who against all the odds cherished the belief that the hero would return, 'that in the end they will have it all. By means of Arthur, they will have it back. . . . They will call it Britain again.'

CHAPTER SIX
CHIVALRY AND·CHAUVINISM

Geoffrey's *History* came into a feudal French world of chivalry which was beginning to respond to the strange mix of British stories with their mysterious overtones. His direct impact was on history and the Latin culture of scholars. This gave warrant to the romancers, but to have an effect on the imaginative literature of the day, Geoffrey's work needed to be translated and adapted to the cultures of the vernacular in Europe.

The process began with a freewheeling translator, Maitre Wace, a Jersey-man born about 1100, who, after a youth in Caen and the Ile de France, spent some time in southern England, probably in Sherborne, which was linked to Caen. He was able to correct Geoffrey on some details and gave his translation of the *History* to Queen Eleanor around 1155; he was commissioned to write a history of the dukes of Normandy, his *Roman de Rou*. He died in 1174, the possessor of a canonry at Bayeux.

He translated Geoffrey's book into French verse, which was presumably more popular in court circles, but despite this urge to romanticize, he was a rational, sceptical man. He omits Merlin's prophecies as incomprehensible, places great store on eyewitnesses and says that in the long period of peace which Arthur enforced, so many adventures and wonders happened that they had been turned into fables, 'not all lies or all true'. He went to the great forest of Broceliande in Brittany, which was starting to figure in many stories, 'to seek marvels; I saw the forest, I saw the land; I looked for marvels but I did not find them. A fool I went, a fool I returned!' (an experience which, having repeated it, I heartily endorse!).

He made two additions to the canon which have proved enduring. Arthur's magical sword had been *Caledfwlch* in Welsh, implying lightning and the old lightning gods; Geoffrey called it *Caliburnus*, forged in Avalon. Wace transformed it into *Excalibur*, a name which displaced all others. And it was Wace who was the first in literature to refer to the *Round Table*.

• The Round Table and the Holy Grail; detail of an
illustration from the third volume of the *Roman de Tristan*
manuscript *c.* 1479–80.

Because of quarrels over precedence among his 'barons', Arthur established the Round Table where all sat equal. Some forty years later, the first account of Arthur in English, by Layamon, spoke of a quarrel over precedence at a Christmas feast where several were killed. Arthur had the knight who started it beheaded with all his kinsmen, while their women had their noses cut off! A carpenter in Cornwall then made for him in four weeks a round table which could be carried everywhere and at which 1600 men could sit in perfect equality!

There was a story that a round table, said to have been that of the Last Supper, had been seen in the Holy Land, but this by-product of the Crusades seems a later version. Both Wace (who spoke of Bretons, probably accurately in his case) and Layamon hinted at native origins and there seems to have been some version of a Round Table already extant in Welsh and Breton stories. Celtic warriors who gathered around the fire of their local king used to sit in a circle so that none should have precedence and this could easily translate into a round table. Arthur and his friends did not at first sit there; they were on a dais at a higher level. In time, he was to join the circle, whose number was limited, in some cases to as few as thirteen, and the whole concept of a Round Table with its Siege Perilous (Perilous Seat) and elaborate rituals was to grow into a mystical idea and the model for both the Grail and the great knightly orders of late medieval Europe.

Wace's influence was short-lived but intense: more copies of his translation survive than any other French work of the Middle Ages save one. In particular, he, together with the potential offered by popular tales, seems to have inspired Chrétien de Troyes, who was the first serious writer to naturalize the British stories in the French of cultivated court circles and in the process to have established the framework for the whole Arthurian cycle.

Chrétien, born before 1130, was associated not only with Troyes, with its international fairs, but with the court of Marie de Champagne, the highly cultivated daughter of Queen Eleanor who was imbued with the courtly love of the troubadours. Trained in the classics, Chrétien's first love was Ovid, and his *Art of Love* and his poems were meant to be read not declaimed. Writing octosyllabic verse in rhymed couplets, he nevertheless achieved a remarkable flexibility in tone. He was given to long mini-sermons on Love, Kingship and Morality, but he was full of humour, of the lightly burlesque – and of a rather heavy-handed psychology. There are times when he seems long-winded, padding things out to achieve his target length, but he was without doubt the creator of the style and manner of Arthurian literature in Europe.

He was, of course, imbued with the feudalism which had reached its highest point in France and was spreading throughout an insecure Europe and the Crusader states.

Kings and lords presided over a complicated network of dependence, knit together by the act of homage and the knight's fee. The knight was the key figure. Holding land and dependants by military service, he provided his own horses and equipment at high cost. The much valued war-horse, the *destrier*, cost two hundred times as much as a workhorse and the knight needed in addition a palfrey to get across country, plus spare mounts. (To leap straight into the saddle scorning stirrups, the 'Welsh leap', was a mark of distinction.) His armour – the hauberk of chain or ring mail (plated armour came in later) with its leggings, hood, padded jerkin and helmet – plus his weapons (thrusting lance and heavy sword) also did not come cheap. He commanded a small retinue, including his trainee squire and an archer, known as a *lance*; mercenaries were known as *free lances*. The tournament or tourney, where fortunes could be made and lost, was the natural habitat of such men, who fought in single combat with blunted weapons under strict rules; all was swathed in elaborate ritual and morality, and in the growing practice of heraldry with its colourful insignia – which the Church denounced as 'detestable'.

Chrétien is steeped in this macho, warlike culture – which gave him a wider audience among the oligarchical 'democracy' of the lord's hall and mixed retinue. But Chrétien's women were not all ciphers. His Guinevere is a haughty, imperious, unpredictable woman, his maidservant Lunete a girl of resource and character. But in his writing it is taken for granted that, while a woman travelling alone was safe, if she was escorted by a knight, his defeat would leave her fair game! The women tend to become an undifferentiated mass, fixing a tournament to decide whom they would marry, swooning *en bloc* over Lancelot. So do the 'lower orders' of any kind, the 'townsfolk', who are a veritable Chorus, now lavish in praise, now unanimous in warning, now despicable and vile. For it was also an aristocratic culture – though open to outsiders and of course to 'evil knights', without whom there would be no story!

In such a culture, and given Chrétien's own high estimate of kingship, Arthur proved irresistible. He was the great Christian hero fighting pagans and he and his men were wreathed in the atmosphere of a lost golden age and all the mysterious, forgotten pagan rites that came with it. Chrétien, who has been called 'the Ovid of a disintegrating Celtic mythology', was at first close to his Welsh or British sources, but he rapidly drew away from them. His remarkable listings of Arthur's knights include familiar figures, but also plenty of dubious characters and, in what became standard Arthurian style, such type-figures as the Handsome Coward and the Ugly Brave, not to mention Bilis, King of the Antipodes and Lord of the Dwarfs (many of whom were Good Dwarfs, a perhaps understandable feature of Welsh mythology!).

Though his first romance was apparently a version of the Tristan and Iseult story (now lost), Chrétien disliked the theme of adultery. What he cherished was a high ideal of kingship and a commitment to married love. His feeling that marriage and the chivalry of young men were incompatible is caught perfectly in two of his stories, *Erec et Enide* (*c*.1176) and *Yvain: the Knight with the Lion* (*c*.1177–81), where the same problem is approached from opposite directions.

Erec, hitherto unknown but second among the knights of the Round Table, joins Guinevere in the train of Arthur's stag-hunt from Cardigan, south-west Wales, but the Queen has been insulted by Yder fiz Nudd (Edern mab Nudd) and his evil dwarf, so he pursues them seven leagues to a city, where he is sheltered and armed by a poverty-stricken vavasour and his shabby but lovely daughter, Enide. He decides to marry her and, to the admiring gasps of the Chorus, leads her out in a battle to win a symbolic sparrow-hawk. Victorious, he despatches Yder to Arthur's court where he is received courteously, and follows with Enide, to a rapturous reception.

They are married with much splendour – a hundred men take a ritual bath before being knighted, and all Arthur's vassals are present – and they then attend a great tournament between York and Edinburgh, where Erec defeats many knights (and, in good tourney style, makes a lot of money!), before going off to Erec's father's castle. Theirs is the love of equals – 'The hunted hart, panting for thirst, does not so long for the spring, or the hungry sparrow-hawk come so readily to the call, that these two were not still more eager to come naked into each other's arms. That night they indeed made good all the time they had lost.' Each part of the body had its due and in the morning, Enide was a new lady! So much so that Erec gives up tournaments and all knightly arts and spends his time playing the lover to his wife. There is much muttering that he has been corrupted by love. Enide hears the rumours, weeps in the night and, under pressure from an enraged Erec, confesses the truth – a big mistake, which opens an epic of testing and self-testing, in which she outdoes even the Patient Griselda.

Erec orders her to wear her best dress, ride always in front of him and never to speak under any circumstances, and he gallops off, amid long soliloquies from Chrétien and incredulous laments from all. There follows a string of astounding adventures: encounters with robber knights where Enide is punished for warning him; a meeting with Count Galoain, who lusts after her and threatens to kill Erec, but whom she tricks into delaying the deed until morning, when they escape, pursued by the Count and a small army. Erec, in a terrific fight, foils them and on they go to the next adventure –

• *Overleaf* Two knights fighting in the lists; an illustration from *Froissart's Chronicle*, a fifteenth-century manuscript.

a mistaken battle with the Good Dwarf Guivret, when Enide goes out of her mind until they are reconciled. Incognito, they meet Arthur's court. Kay tries to force them to come to Arthur – 'You'll both go, just as the priest goes to the synod, willy-nilly!' – but is upended; Gawain in the end seduces them into it, but Erec, though wounded in every limb, will not stay but goes on to rescue a knight carried off naked by two giants. He sends him back to Arthur, after splitting one giant down the middle, but collapses into a coma from his wounds.

Enide wails uncontrollably and eloquently. Up come the knights of the Count of Limors – is she Erec's wife or his mistress? 'Both the one and the other,' she replies. With the 'corpse' of Erec present, the Count marries her against her will. She refuses to eat at the wedding feast and the enraged Count strikes her; his lords intervene and they wake up Erec, who attacks the Count with his sword, 'beating out his brains and knocking in his forehead without a word.' The lords, terrified, rush from the room crying, 'Flee! Flee! here comes the dead man!' Erec lifts Enide on his horse and at last forgives her! Which is big of him!

Another clash with Guivret follows and, 'more than thirty Welsh leagues away', the famous adventure at the great Brandigant castle of King Evrain. Here, all are terrified at the dangerous passage through an inner garden, but Erec, leaving Enide in great distress, penetrates it to meet the wall of air, the awesome row of stakes with helmeted heads, a maiden on a silver bed and a horn. He fights, with a green sword of Vienne steel, the Crimson Knight Mabonagrain (Mabon mab Modron), who, defeated, says that his lady asked him a favour without naming it and, as a result, he has been imprisoned ever since (together, one presumes, with all those who lost their heads in the challenge). Erec blows the horn and, amid general ecstasy, proclaims the Joy of the Court, in which the knight's imperious lady finally joins when she learns Enide is her cousin!

The story ends with a great coronation ceremony at Nantes in Brittany, ordered by Arthur, to which Erec is called from Tintagel after his father's death – 'grief is not becoming in a king'. At the sumptuous ceremony four hundred knights are dubbed and there are two ivory thrones for Arthur and Erec (Enide presumably knew her place), plus a robe from the Roman philosopher Macrobius, inscribed by four fairies with the four Liberal Arts of the Quadrivium – Geometry, Arithmetic, Music and Astronomy. Guinevere 'was so above herself for joy that you might have used her for hawking'!

Erec's twin and opposite, *Yvain*, in both the French and Welsh versions, opens with a prologue, set in Carlisle and Caerleon respectively, in which Arthur retires to sleep and Kay is his usual sarcastic self as Guinevere, Yvain/Owein and others listen to a story told against himself by Cynon in the Welsh and Calogrenant in the French. The Welsh opening is the more vivid.

Cynon, travelling 'the bounds of the world and its wilderness' in search of challenge, comes across a castle by the sea run by a curly, yellow-headed man with sons to match and twenty-four delightful maidens. Here he is directed through the forest to a giant black man with one eye in the middle of his forehead, one foot and a giant club. He is the Lord of the Animals – 'I will show thee, little man' – and he gives a stag a terrific clout with his club and his mighty belling brings countless animals, all of which – serpents, lions, vipers – crowd to do him homage. Ugly in visage but not disposition, he directs Cynon on to a fountain under a great tree, with a marble slab beside it. Cynon takes a silver bowl on a silver chain and pours water over the slab. With a great peal of thunder, torrents of rain and hail rip away every leaf and threaten Cynon's very life. Then, abruptly, the storm ceases and the tree is covered with uncountable flocks of birds in full song, until, with a great panting and groaning up the valley, a fully armed black knight comes; he denounces Cynon for the storm he has caused and attacks him so ferociously that he is unhorsed and sent stumbling back in disgrace. The French version says much the same except that it is set in Broceliande forest seven years earlier, the giant is not black but a 'churl' ignorant of chivalry, and the fountain, whose water boils, and the slab are much richer.

'After dinner, there are more words in a potful of wine than a barrel of beer,' mocks Kay, while Guinevere sharply reprimands him – if his tongue were hers, she would charge it with treason. Arthur wakes up to hear the story repeated and he swears to get to the fountain in a fortnight, on the eve of St John the Baptist. Yvain, knowing that Kay and Gawain will otherwise have the first crack at the knight, leaves court against the rules and rides into the forest, going through the ritual at the fountain, but, forewarned, he mortally wounds the knight and chases him, holding on to his back saddle-bow, up to a great castle. The bridge is lowered and the gate opens as the pair career madly in, but the far gate closes and the portcullis crashes down, slicing Yvain's horse in two and cutting off his spurs level with his heels. ('Caught between gate and portcullis' became a favourite cry of love-lorn Welsh poets in later centuries.)

There follows a remarkable section in which Lunete/Luned, the archetypal soubrette, pretty, pert, brunette and intelligent, who knows Yvain, gives him a ring to make him invisible to crowds ranging the streets to kill him, urged on by a strikingly beautiful but distraught Laudine, mortified by the death of her husband, the Knight of the Fountain. Lunete works on Laudine, her lady, stressing that as the loved one is dead she needs a champion to defend the fountain, recommending the renowned Yvain fiz Urien. With the city elders in support, she offers to send for him, while he swoons secretly from love. Only half-deceived, Laudine agrees and she and Yvain are married with great pomp – just as Arthur and his crew come clattering up to the fountain.

In his new role as keeper of the fountain, Yvain sends Kay somersaulting over his saddle, to everyone's joy, and reveals himself. There is much rejoicing all round, while Gawain flirts outrageously with Lunete, before he raises the key issue. 'It's amazing how people set store by a life of perpetual comfort,' he says, urging Yvain to return to the tourneys and the combats – 'What? Will you now be one of those who lose in merit because of their wives?' Yvain begs leave from Laudine, who grants him a year but says her love will turn to hate if he overstays. A triumphant year in British tourneys ensues, till Gawain and Yvain set up their tents outside Chester and Arthur's court comes to them! As an appalled Yvain suddenly realizes that he has overstayed his leave, up comes a damsel on a black palfrey, rips Laudine's ring from his finger and denounces him as a disloyal traitor. Yvain promptly goes mad and undertakes a journey of redemption similar to Erec's.

The madman flees naked to the woods, killing animals and eating them raw, and finds some sanctuary with a hermit. Rescued by two ladies (originally water-fays) who treat him with an ointment from Morgan le Fay, he saves them in turn from Count Alier and his men, to the acclaim of the Chorus. Rejecting all pleas to stay, he goes on to rescue a lion from a serpent; in an amusing scene reminiscent of Androcles, the lion pledges himself to Yvain for the rest of his life – and indeed is to prove vital. By accident, Yvain reaches the dread fountain and, in agony, swoons and wounds himself. He hears Lunete moaning in a chapel: undone by his betrayal and beset by three villains, she is to be burned at the stake in the morning. Yvain promises to help but has to find sanctuary. He does so at a castle where there is great grief because Harpin of the Mountain, an evil giant, has killed the lord's sons and threatens to give his daughter to the 'vilest, foulest, serving-lads'. In a tense passage worthy of the *Perils of Pauline*, Yvain stays in the morning as long as he can; then, with the aid of the lion he sees off the giant but, scorning the pleas of the Chorus and the offer of the lord's daughter, he rides like mad to the fountain to rescue Lunete. Her three accusers are burned instead but, with Laudine looking on in bewilderment, he then rides off again, carrying the lion.

By this time, the fame of the Knight with the Lion as a defender of ladies has spread, but Chrétien, to buttress his plot, introduces a new theme. 'The Lord of Noire Espine had a dispute with death' which he lost. His elder daughter, trying to exclude the younger from her inheritance, rushes to Arthur's court, where Gawain, rashly and anonymously, agrees to be her champion. The younger daughter, desperate, searches for the Knight with the Lion through the scenes of his past triumphs. When she finds him, however, there is another adventure to face – in the town of *Pesme Avanture*.

• Yvain finds sanctuary with the lord of the castle near the
spring; from an early fourteenth-century manuscript.

Here they find that the lord, his beautiful daughter and everyone else have been prisoners since two devil's sons, born of a woman and a goblin, had captured the king of the Island of Maidens (an old Celtic conceit) and forced from him an annual tribute of thirty maidens. Over three hundred of them are housed in a yard, enclosed by pointed stakes, sewing furiously with gold thread and silk, and getting a mere one-sixtieth of their proper earnings! (This unexpected scene, possibly a protest against the exploitation of female labour in Champagne, seems to make Yvain a prematurely Red Knight – or at least his lion?) For the lion, by cheating, helps Yvain finish off the devils, to tumultuous jubilation. And Yvain, declining yet another offer of a daughter, goes with his companion to Arthur's court.

There follows a battle, much enjoyed by Chrétien, with long sermons on love and hate as twins, between anonymous Gawain and Yvain. It lasts for hours, till in one break Gawain confesses his identity. Yvain casts away his sword and broken shield; they embrace and both acknowledge the victory of the other, until Arthur in the end blackmails the elder sister into giving her sister her share. Yvain then goes back to the fountain, where he raises such a storm that Laudine fears for her city. Lunete, 'well versed in courtly manners', again tricks her, this time into a sworn promise to do her best for the Knight with the Lion. Whereupon, in veritably Shakespearean manner, all is revealed.

Yvain, like Erec, is packed off at last to lead a respectable married life as a good lord, leaving knighthood and tourneys, no doubt, to young stags in the mating season. The lion presumably enjoys a well-earned retirement. It remains unclear whether the dread cycle of the knight at the fountain is broken.

There were other versions of these two stories in circulation. The Welsh one, several decades later, replaced Erec with the Welsh Gereint mab Erbin, omits the coronation at Nantes and locates the sparrow-hawk battle in Cardiff. Hartmann von Aue's *Erec* of 1190 also omits Nantes. Hartmann, a south German, stresses the knightly virtues, but, while accepting his rude nature, keeps Kay as a great hero, as do several later French works. The Welsh version of *Yvain*, *The Lady of the Fountain*, is less complicated and subtle, but has a supremely vivid opening, while Hartmann's *Iwein* (c.1202) is far simpler, idealizing Frau Minne, the goddess of love, sniffing somewhat at Lunete and declaring it boorish to conduct a sword fight from the saddle!

These variations, however, pale before a third story by Chrétien, *Lancelot*. Lancelot was to become the greatest of all knights and his love for Guinevere a key element in the disintegration of the Round Table, though this does not figure yet. Chrétien evidently knew of the stories about Lancelot which were then in circulation, but he refers to them only in passing, assuming knowledge among his audience – rather like a *Guardian* editorial on tabloid stories which have never sullied its news pages. What those stories may have been like can be seen from a third-rate German version of an Anglo-Norman tale, written around 1194–96, which was given to Ulrich von Zatzikhoven, a Swiss German, by one of Richard the Lionheart's hostages. In this version Lanzelet was carried off when less than two by a water-fay and brought up ignorant among women until he was fifteen, when he left the Island of Maidens, was trained as a knight and set off on adventures. After the usual encounters, he apparently married a lady called Iblis and was called to Arthur's court, where he became the defender of the queen, Ginover. One Valerin abducted the queen, who was only rescued with the aid of the wizard Malduc, and Lanzelet returned with Iblis to his own kingdom to live happily ever after.

These names would be incomprehensible to anyone versed in the Welsh–British tradition and it seems significant that there is no Welsh version of Chrétien in this case. The whole question of Lancelot is mysterious. There is a belief that Lancelot was a French-Breton name localized in Cornwall, but in effect there is no Lancelot in the surviving British–Breton tradition. Yet even in von Zatzikhoven's lame story there was clearly some distinctly Celtic character. Lancelot's nurture by a Lady of the Lake was to become a permanent feature of his story, but it was Chrétien de Troyes who launched the later familiar Lancelot, though his version, too, moves dramatically into the geography of illusion.

Lancelot (the Knight of the Cart) is based, very loosely, on the kidnapping of Guinevere by Melwas of Glastonbury, City of Glass, in the *Life of Gildas*. It opens with Arthur, one Ascension Day, leaving Caerleon and holding a magnificent court at *Camelot*. Whilst it may have figured in lost tales, this is the first mention of Camelot in literature. Its context fixes its first appearance. Whereas *Erec* and *Yvain* have some anchorage in real life, *Lancelot* is set in fairy-tale country, a never-never land. It seems to me that, whatever Camelot developed into, here Chrétien chooses it as a splendid, dream city of desire, a never-never capital.

Moreover, it is the seat of an utterly unprecedented humiliation of both Arthur and Guinevere. In comes a bold knight who turns out to be Meleagant, wicked son of the noble Bademagu, King of Gorre, the Land of Glass, from which no stranger (particularly from Arthur's realm Logres/Lloegr – England), ever returns. Meleagant

• *Overleaf* Scenes of Lancelot's adventures from a manuscript dated 1344: Lancelot crossing the perilous Sword Bridge, fighting lions and jousting with Meleagant, Guinevere's abductor.

says that he holds many of Arthur's people prisoner and demands to take the Queen. Arthur, in shameful cowardice, agrees. Kay blows up, declaring that he is leaving this degenerate court for ever, but is dissuaded by Guinevere, who prostrates herself before him, muttering in misery for a pusillanimous Arthur and longing for an (unmentioned) Lancelot. They go off, an inadequate Kay as her saviour.

Astounded, Gawain addresses Arthur – 'Sire, you've done an extremely silly thing!' and thunders out after them. He comes across Kay's bloodstained horse and a knight walking an exhausted animal. Though it is not revealed until much later, this is Lancelot of the Lake, a knight without peer but absolutely besotted by Guinevere. He promptly commandeers one of Gawain's horses, leaping straight from the ground to the saddle (to scorn stirrups is the mark of a 'real man'), and gallops wildly away. Gawain follows in hot pursuit, to find Lancelot walking behind a cart driven by a dwarf, the horse having died from hard riding.

Chrétien, in an incomprehensible passage, described the cart as the Ultimate Shame, used for criminals – and, significantly, for those defeated in judicial combat. At that time, he claims in defiance of obvious truth, there was only one such cart in every town, whereas 'today, there are three thousand'! In fact, the reference is to a suppressed 'memory' of annual kings; the king defeated in single combat at a fountain or some other magical place would be dragged through the town at the foot of a cart, to be pelted in mud and filth by the inhabitants.

Lancelot hesitates for two steps (which damages his reputation with Guinevere, who, miraculously, knows all about it), but then gets into the cart (which, at once known to all and sundry, damages his reputation with them too!). Gawain, bemused but loyal, follows on. They come to a castle where they are offered shelter by three maidens but denied a sumptuous bed, which is to be slept in only by those who merit it – not the likes of Lancelot of the Cart. He insists on it. This is the Perilous Bed which became famous. At midnight, like a thunderbolt, a lance with a flaming pennon comes down, narrowly missing Lancelot and setting fire to the bed. He throws it into the middle of the hall and goes back to sleep. In the morning they see a procession go by, Meleagant leading a sad Guinevere and a crippled Kay on a litter. Gawain, character-istically chatting up a maiden, sees Lancelot about to throw himself from a window. He restrains him, but the maiden says Lancelot is right – his life, after the cart, is now shameful. On they go, till they meet another maiden, who demands that they serve her in return for information. Gawain gladly agrees, but Lancelot reserves his love. She tells them of the kingdom of Gorre and offers them a choice of two routes there – by the Water Bridge or the even more perilous Sword Bridge. Lancelot, of course, chooses the latter.

The usual string of adventures follows. Lost in reverie of Guinevere (the duty of a lover), Lancelot does not notice a ford until the knight guarding it hits him into a stream. He nearly pulls the knight's leg off until he grants him leave to collect his weapons, whereupon he makes mincemeat of him, granting him life at the begging of a maiden. It emerges that the custom of Logres is that a maiden travelling alone is sacrosanct, but if a knight defeats her champion, he can do what he likes with her! This is nothing to the challenge he meets next, when a girl offers him hospitality if he will sleep with her. After much dawdling over the meal, he hears a cry – the maiden, stripped to the navel, is being raped across a bed by a knight protected by two swordsmen and four men with axes. With incredible agility and without arms, Lancelot is defeating them when the maiden calls them off. They spend the night in bed together, Lancelot sweating with apprehension, until the girl gives up. No-one she has met, she declares, is worth 'the third of an Angevin penny compared to this one'.

She goes on with him, to find a comb of gilded ivory with a handful of hairs left by Guinevere. He swoons over these – 'he would not exchange them for a cartload of emeralds or carbuncles. He is confident he will never suffer from boils!' His companion laughs. Chrétien's mockery is a reminder that there is a lot of Don Quixote in Lancelot. They continue on, to run into a son who lusts after Lancelot's companion, but is dissuaded by his father, and into a company who give up games and dancing out of contempt for the Knight of the Cart, but think twice of it, till they reach a church where Lancelot prays and a monk shows him graves already inscribed with the names of Gawain and Yvain and a massive tomb with a slab that no-one can lift. Lancelot promptly does so, which marks him as the superhuman liberator of all the foreign prisoners of the land of Meleagant. The monk remarks that 'no knight to match this one was ever born'. Girl and lustful son give up at this point, but on goes Lancelot, through a Stony Passage where no-one harms him and a fortress where the ring given him by the Lady of the Lake protects him from enchantment, till they run into a revolt against Meleagant by the men of Logres. Bent on Guinevere, Lancelot presses on and comes to a house of a man from Logres – 'with the first course came a bonus in the form of a knight outside the gate, looking more arrogant than a bull' – where he triumphs yet again, in the end cutting off the knight's head after a second battle, in response to a plea from a damsel who turns out to be Meleagant's sister. So he comes to the Sword Bridge.

Displaying supreme courtesy to all, Lancelot strips off his hand and foot armour and crosses, bleeding from his wounds. There is a stark confrontation. The king, Bademagu, who has sheltered Guinevere from his son, offers help and the Three Marys' Ointment, but Meleagant is unrepentant – 'You be as moral as you like, but let me be cruel!' They fight. Lancelot is saved by the sight of Guinevere in a window (at one stage,

• Lancelot being driven in a cart – 'the ultimate shame'
according to Chrétien de Troyes; decorated initial from an
early fourteenth-century *Romance of Lancelot du Lac*.

staring besottedly at her, he fights his foe with his back to him). The father intervenes and a combat is arranged at Arthur's court in a year's time. All the captives are freed.

Guinevere, however, turns angry at Lancelot's hesitation before the cart. He goes to find Gawain; natives try to trap him and rumour reaches the court that he is dead. Guinevere is overcome with remorse – 'had I but held him once, with both of us naked for my greater pleasure'! She tries to kill herself. Lancelot hears she is dead and tries to hang himself from his horse. Both stories are proved false and after a long, long seduction, enlivened by sermons from Chrétien, Lancelot finally prises open the bars of Guinevere's window and they enjoy each other. But he leaves blood on the bed and the wounded Kay is blamed. Lancelot, as Kay's champion, fights another long, inconclusive fight with Meleagant, until his father again intervenes. Lancelot goes to seek Gawain, is betrayed by a dwarf and led off to imprisonment, while Gawain, freed half-drowned from the Water Bridge and believing Lancelot has gone to Arthur, releases everybody and they all go off to a great tournament at Nouaz.

This tournament is described in great detail. The ladies had arranged it, to decide whom to marry. Knights who had been unhorsed or taken the Cross interpret the shields and the coats of arms, but Lancelot turns up incognito, having wooed the wife of a seneschal of Meleagant to obtain his scarlet arms, and having promised to return to imprisonment. A herald recognizes him – 'Now the one who will take their measure has arrived,' he shouts (the first time this expression was used, says Chrétien) – and Lancelot indeed proves all-powerful, winning the hearts of all the ladies, until Guinevere, who suspects his identity, tells him to do his worst. An appalling performance ensues, but in the morning the Scarlet Knight is back and all-conquering. Further contradictory orders from Guinevere leave him supreme, with all the ladies yearning for him and Guinevere highly amused. But, true to his word, he returns to Meleagant's country.

At this point Chrétien hands over to another writer! Meleagant turns up at Arthur's court, having jailed Lancelot in a great tower on an island, and demands satisfaction. Gawain goes to seek Lancelot, promising to fight Meleagant himself, if necessary. There is a final confrontation between Meleagant and his father, where his sister, in debt to Lancelot, realizes that he is imprisoned, seeks him out, frees him and nurses him back to health. Then comes the final combat. Gawain is overjoyed to see Lancelot appear and the court adjourns to the fairest heath this side of Ireland, with a sycamore on a patch of green grass which has never withered, where a clear, fast-flowing spring with a bed of gold gushes. King Arthur, recovering his dignity, sits there with the people. Both men are unhorsed and fight on foot. Lancelot severs Meleagant's right arm, smashes his nose-guard, unlaces his helmet and cuts off his head, to general joy. And the story abruptly ends.

Chrétien, having blamed his patron, Marie de Champagne, for insisting on the fulfilment of Guinevere's adultery, nevertheless tells the story with great erotic gusto, right down to plans to conceal the adultery from Arthur. Such romances were to prove models and writer after writer in French developed them, peopling them with characters some of which came out of inherited lore but more of which came out of their own imaginations. In a triumph of the story-teller's art, the romances spread, in endless complexity, all over a Europe that was succumbing to the culture of chivalry and the tournament – to southern France, Italy, Spain, Germany and, a little later, to England, the Low Countries and Scandinavia.

In the stories, Arthur, a Christian king battling the pagans, is supreme, though his enemies, the Saxons, dwindle. And already in Chrétien one can detect significant shifts among the major characters, which were to become permanent. Arthur, of course, remains a great hero and, increasingly, the greatest king in Christendom; his end remains enigmatic. But in the day-to-day life of his court, what does he do? He merely presides. He becomes a *roi fainéant*, a king who does nothing, a 'hero without deeds'. In the end he is an object of pity and contempt, as he drags his tragic, broken self to the final conflict.

Kay, while still a hero in some hands, goes remorselessly downhill to end up a villain. Even Gawain, most generous of knights – who remains so in England – is betrayed by his fondness for women and threatens to follow Kay downhill. There remains Lancelot, the greatest knight of them all, but one whose love for Guinevere will in the end destroy the Round Table.

Was there anything behind these shifts other than fashion and the whims of writers? The whole Arthurian epic, in its rise through Europe, mirrors the rise and decline of the Crusading ideal. From the First Crusade which culminated in the liberation of Jerusalem in 1099 and the installation of Godfrey de Bouillon as its Christian king, through to the final loss of Jerusalem in 1244, the Crusade dominated European imaginations. A blend of zeal and greed, of colonialism and an aspiration to holiness which sent men tramping 2500 miles to the Holy Land and forming monkish knightly orders, the Crusades and their ideals seemed to fit the Arthurian model perfectly. It was only when Jerusalem fell that Camelot lost its glamour. It was militant Christianity, in its many contradictory forms, that gave the writers of romances the measuring rod they were seeking. Chrétien's last story, which he began around 1181 and, perhaps significantly, could not finish before his death around 1190, was *Perceval; the story of the graal*. The Holy Grail began to cast its long shadow over the Round Table.

CHAPTER SEVEN
HOLY·GRAIL
AND·UNHOLY·POWER

The story of Perceval the Welshman, who appeared briefly in an earlier romance, Chrétien says he found in a book and wrote up for Philippe of Alsace, count of Flanders, who died in 1191 in the Third Crusade. It is the story of a young man brought up in a great dark forest in Wales by his mother in complete ignorance of chivalry, of which she has a horror, having lost her husband and two sons because of it. He does not know what a 'knight' is or even a 'church'. His pilgrimage through knowledge to a state of grace is unequalled by any other of Arthur's knights and is linked to the first appearance of the Grail or *graal* in literature.

'The Welsh are by nature more stupid than grazing beasts,' declares one of five knights to his lord. Young Perceval has met them by chance, thinks they are angels and falls to his knees, saying the prayers his mother had taught him. His endless questions, however, are unconsciously offensive and he determines to get to Carlisle to see Arthur, who 'made knights'. His horrified mother faints, but in the end sees him off, dressing him in the Welsh manner and taking away two of his three javelins, with which he was expert, 'because he would have looked too much like a Welshman'. She gives him advice which he misinterprets and she swoons into despair.

He lurches on through misadventures, comic in his innocent arrogance. He kisses a girl in a tent and causes trouble with her lover, makes a farcical entrance at Arthur's court, is insulted by Kay, but impresses a far-sighted maiden, kills with his javelin a Red Knight who had insulted the court, is trained in arms by the kindly Gornemant de Gohort and saves the maiden Blancheflor from her enemies. She comes to his bed and they lie 'mouth to mouth' till dawn. But in his new glory, he sets out to find his mother.

There follows the celebrated encounter with the Fisher King. He comes to a deep, rushing river, sees two men fishing from a boat and asks the way to shelter. He is directed to a marvellous castle, which suddenly appears and where he is greeted warmly. He meets one of the fishers, clad very sumptuously and leaning on his elbow on a couch before a great fire. This man is unable to get up, but they eat a splendid meal together. In comes a youth bearing a magnificent sword specifically destined for Perceval. Then, at every course, a strange procession passes through to another room: a youth holding a white lance which drips blood on to his hand, two other youths bearing gold candelabras, a beautiful girl carrying a *graal* or grail of pure refined gold with many precious stones. Once she has entered, a great radiance floods the room; she is followed by a girl holding a silver carving dish.

Perceval is transfixed, but dare not speak: Gornemant had warned him against loquacity. It is an error, for when he awakes the castle is deserted, the gate closes mysteriously behind him and he meets a weeping girl nursing a headless knight. She tells him that she is his cousin, that his host had been the rich Fisher King who had been wounded 'through both thighs' (a euphemism for genitals) and is in deep distress. She denounces Perceval for not having asked the meaning of what he had seen. Many misfortunes now await him because of the wrong he has done his mother, who has died of grief. She warns him that his new sword will fly to pieces if he uses it and tells him to take it to no-one but Trebuchet the Smith.

A bemused Perceval goes on, redeeming the girl in the tent whom he had wronged, defeating her misguided lover, the Haughty Knight of the Heath, and sending him to Arthur, who holds court at Caerleon with three thousand knights. Here, Kay creates the usual brouhaha, until Gawain breaks into Perceval's deep reverie – the sight of three drops of goose's blood on white snow had set him thinking of Blancheflor – and he is honoured at Arthur's court as a full Knight of the Round Table. The celebrations are, however, interrupted by the entry of a maiden of astounding ugliness riding a mule – eyes like a rat, nose like a monkey, lips like a donkey, yellow teeth and her black face bearded – known in the parlance as the Loathly Damsel. She curses Perceval for his failure to ask the question which would have healed the Fisher King: now 'ladies will lose their husbands, lands will be laid waste, maidens left orphaned and helpless and many knights will perish'.

She also, however, offers the knights various challenges. Gawain elects, of course, to rescue the Maid of Montesclaire, but Perceval 'spoke quite differently'. He defies Fate. He swears never to stay two nights in one place, never to shun any adventure or single combat until he has learned who was served by the Grail and why the Lance dripped blood. At this point Gawain and his multiple adventures take over and by the time the story returns to Perceval five years have passed, during which he has sent sixty distinguished knights back to Arthur as prisoners but never remembered God on his Cross, never entered a church.

• The early adventures of Perceval carved on a fourteenth-century Parisian ivory box: Perceval in his holy fool's clothing meets the knights for the first time.

He meets three knights with ten ladies, wearing hoods and hair-shirts, and walking barefoot. They are doing penance for their sins on Good Friday, when, Perceval hears, Jesus Christ who gave us the New Law was slain and no-one should bear arms. Nonplussed, Perceval is given Christian instruction and directed to a nearby hermit, who turns out to be his uncle and the Fisher King's brother. He learns that it was his sin against his mother which stopped him from asking questions and that the Grail is to serve the Fisher King's father, who himself served from it and who for twelve years has never left his room, surviving on a single, consecrated Mass wafer, even though the *graal* is big enough to hold a salmon. The hermit tells a weeping Perceval how to atone and they fast together. 'That is how Perceval came to the recognition that on Friday God was put to death and crucified' and received communion. The story now returns to Gawain's endless adventures and then cuts off.

Presumably Chrétien would have continued the tale by having Perceval ask the crucial question to end the misery of the Fisher King and his Waste Land. Gawain was presumably intended as a worldly foil to the young Welshman; he forgot about his promised quest to discover why the Lance dripped blood. What was this Bleeding

Lance and the Grail carried by a woman in a castle? Who was the Fisher King? Chrétien preserves the mystery even if he wraps it in Christian morality. Small wonder that over the next thirty years there were no fewer than six attempts at prologues and continuations, a compilation which owed practically nothing to Chrétien – and an attempt to provide an integrated story – all of them centring on the mystery of the Grail.

An *Elucidation* of Chrétien, which is distinctly unlucid, cites Blihis (Bleddri) and tells of maidens who lived in wells, serving food and drink to travellers. They were raped, whereupon the land became desolate and the court of the Rich Fisher could not be found. This folk-tale figures in Glamorgan, south Wales. Another story serves as a reasonable introduction to Chrétien, but names Perceval's father as Bliocadran, a name unfamiliar generally.

Two continuations of Chrétien's tale were both probably written before 1200. The first is lively but almost wholly concerned with Gawain's countless adventures, with a chunk inserted about Caradoc Freichfras. The Grail castle is in stark contradiction to that described by Chrétien. It is now reached by a long causeway running out to sea. There is no procession. The Grail becomes an automatically moving food-producing vessel. There is a corpse on a bier and a sword broken in two which has to be joined by the quester. The lance no longer drips on the hand, but stands in a rack and drips blood into a vessel – and it is identified as Longinus's lance which pierced the side of the crucified Christ. Evidently there were several versions of the story.

The second continuation deals with Perceval's adventures and ends with a procession in Chrétien's style, including the Grail, the Lance and a broken sword. This version specifically states that the Grail holds Christ's blood. Perceval joins the sword pieces, but the seam still shows and the quest is only partially successful.

Other developments of Chrétien's story include the *Gerbert*, written some time after 1225, perhaps by a monk, and which is very didactic, and the *Manessier*, written before 1227. The latter finishes the story by having Perceval encounter Satan in various guises and the youth has to carry out a mission of vengeance to heal the Fisher King. The Grail magically provides food and is not a blood relic. Perceval is at last crowned as a successor to his uncle the Fisher King, but when he dies, Grail, Lance and Serving Dish are carried off to heaven.

The story of the Grail and the Lance is riddled with contradictions. If the Grail is a chalice, why is it big enough to hold a salmon? How is it carried by a maiden, since women had been banned from handling the Host since the sixth century? Where does the Bleeding Lance fit in? And what place does the Maimed King and the Waste Land occupy in Christian theology? It is clear that, in essence, the story is pagan.

A striking parallel is found in the Irish story, 'The Prophetic Ecstasy of the Phantom', composed before 1056. In this tale an Irish king is invited to the palace of the phantom Lug, whom he finds seated on the throne; his wife, seated on a crystal chair, represents the Sovereignty of Ireland. She serves ale in a cup, repeatedly asking, 'To whom should I give this cup?' Lug gives the names of all the princes who are to succeed to the throne of Tara. The queen/sovereignty plays the role of the Grail Bearer; she provides food in an Otherworld dwelling, but she also assumes a hideous appearance – a Loathly Damsel? And the spear of Lug drips blood and is held before a cauldron of blood.

Wales, however, was a more immediate source for the story than Ireland, from which the Welsh absorbed much material, including the Irish Cauldrons of Rebirth, which figure largely in Welsh mythology. Among the triads there is a list of the 'Thirteen Treasures of the Island of Britain', which include a *corn*, a horn of Brân mab Llyr – 'whatever drink might be wished for was found in it' – and a hamper (*mwys*) of Gwyddno Long-Shank – 'food for one man would be put in it and when it was opened, food for a hundred men'. Dishes moved of their own accord. In particular, there is a *dysgl*, a largish serving dish like the original *graal*, which had originally belonged to Brân mab Llyr, a god associated with the sea. Brân, like the Fisher King, was wounded by a spear in battle, an event followed by the Wasting of Britain. He had a brother whose stepson, Pryderi, was his nephew, just as Perceval was a nephew of the Fisher King. Pryderi brought on the desolation of Dyfed (south-west Wales) by sitting on a Perilous Mound before a banquet; Perceval, according to one version of the French story, brought on the calamitous enchantment of Britain by sitting on the Siege Perilous before a banquet. The evidence is compelling.

The first continuation of Chrétien's work, to take one example, offers excellent evidence. Gawain was partly successful in his Grail quest. At the castle, he saw clerics chanting a vigil for the dead about a body – a *cors* (*corps*) – when a tall king entered. A rich *graal* served them seven courses, though no hand held it, and he saw a bleeding lance held upright over a silver vessel. Gawain asked about the lance, but as the king was explaining, he fell asleep! He woke to find himself lying on a cliff above the sea and the land, hitherto Waste, was partly restored to fertility because he had asked 'the momentous question about the lance'.

Clearly the Welsh and Irish stories provided the first outline of a Christian Grail, as they did about so much else. But the major impetus came from the Crusades, which opened up the Holy Lands and brought a flow of holy relics back to the Benedictine monasteries of the West, hungry to satisfy the fashionable cult of the Holy Blood. And there was the influence of the Eastern Byzantine Church. Although it was despised in

the West – and indeed was to be a victim of the Fourth Crusade – Byzantine ceremonies had for centuries been far more elaborate than any practised at Rome, with the Holy Vessels elevated high and processions not unlike Chrétien's.

But particularly significant, I think, in the way the tale developed is the well-attested confusion between the Welsh *cors* (*corn*) meaning horn and the French *cors* (*corps*) meaning a body – as in the *cors* over which Gawain witnessed monks chanting a vigil. The horn of Brân could mutate into the body of Christ! Moreover, Joseph of Arimathea, whose home had been the Holy Land and who took custody of the sacred body of Christ and safeguarded it, first appears in French Arthurian writing about the

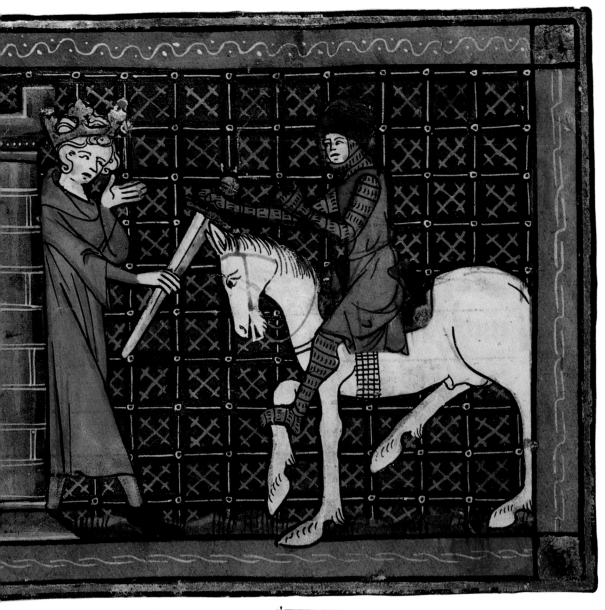

• Perceval at the Grail castle presented with the Sword of the Dolorous Stroke by the Fisher King. Inside, the Grail and the Bleeding Lance are carried to the banqueting table; from a fourteenth-century version of Chrétien de Troyes' *Perceval*.

same time as the continuations of Chrétien, which run into the first decade of the thirteenth century.

Robert de Boron, a knight who lived near Montbéliard in eastern Burgundy, seems to have started a large-scale attempt to fuse the by now numerous Arthurian stories into a whole. A bold and imaginative man, though not a very good writer, he composed a poem, *Joseph*, and seems to have written another on Merlin, of which there were also prose versions. There was, further, a prose *Didot Perceval*, so named after the owner of the original. Robert seems to have known nothing of Chrétien. His sources were the often harsh Apocryphal Gospels and other fictions about Jesus, Geoffrey of Monmouth and the wealth of originally Welsh stories and traditions then available. The *Didot Perceval*, on the other hand, shows familiarity with Chrétien and was presumably by another hand. The great aim of Robert was to provide a Christian 'prehistory' for the suspiciously pagan Grail. The *Didot* rounded things off.

The story begins in de Boron's poem *Joseph*. The sacred communion vessel of the Last Supper passes to Joseph of Arimathea, who caught Christ's last drops of blood. Imprisoned by the Jews, he is visited by the risen Christ who gives him the vessel, saying that only three men, including Joseph himself, will have it. Released after forty years during which he has miraculously lived without food and drink, Joseph with some companions moves to the west, where several succumb to adultery and all to starvation. Whereupon Joseph sets up the table and service of the Grail in memory of the Last Supper and on it places the vessel and a fish (Christian symbol) caught by his brother-in-law Bron – about whom, says Robert, many tales are told and who seems to be a confused memory of Brân mab Llyr, or the Blessed, of Welsh and Irish legend. Only those who believe in the Trinity and live cleanly may sit at the table, where they will have all that their hearts desire. A sinner who sits in the vacant seat reserved for Bron's unborn son is swallowed up by the earth and the Voice of God declares that it shall not be filled until Bron's grandson sits there.

Alain, Bron's son, is to go west, preaching Christ. One Petrus is also to move west, to the *vaus d'Avaron* – the vale of Avalon – and await the coming of Alain's son. Finally, Bron, known as the Rich Fisher, goes there too, taking the Grail which he will deliver to his grandson.

The prose version of Merlin resumes the story. A council of demons, infuriated by Christ's descent into hell and deliverance of the Righteous Jews, plots to ruin mankind through a prophet, half human, half devil. They corrupt Merlin's mother, but she confesses, so when Merlin is born, he has a hairy body, a mischievous streak and preternatural knowledge, but no will to evil. He saves his mother from death and before he is two years old, he dictates to Blaise (Blihis/Bleddri) the history of Joseph and the Grail! Having satisfactorily introduced Merlin, the story then roughly follows Geoffrey of Monmouth's account of Vortigern and the dragons and the shifting of Stonehenge. Merlin persuades Uther to set up the Round Table on the model of the Grail; he puts Arthur into fosterage with one Antor and secures his coronation.

Here Robert de Boron introduces another familiar theme, *The Sword in the Stone*. The barons are uncertain over Arthur's succession as king, but he passes the test of drawing the sword (which was not Excalibur) from the stone – or rather off the anvil placed on it – though he has to draw it several times before they are convinced. Another Celtic tradition is thus woven into the French story.

The sequence is rounded off with the *Didot Perceval*. Alain, in Britain, has a son, Perceval, who acquits himself brilliantly at Arthur's court, but rashly takes his seat on the stone Siege Perilous. This splits with a roar, great darkness comes out of the earth and a voice proclaims that, as a result, Bron will not be healed, nor the stone joined, nor the enchantment removed from Britain until a knight who surpasses all others asks the right question.

Perceval swears his familiar oath never to stay two nights in one place until he has found the home of Bron the Fisher King. A string of adventures follows, familiar from Chrétien or his continuators: Perceval triumphs over Orguelles de la Lande (The Proud One); enters the Castle of the Chessboard (a memory of the magic chessboard of Gwenddoleu in Welsh tradition?); hunts a White Stag; fights the Black Knight of the Tomb; meets the Loathly Damsel; and fights Urbain and his flock of black birds at a ford (Owain and his ravens?). Finally, he gets to the Grail castle and sees the procession – but this time it is a youth who holds the Grail. He fails to ask the question and wanders seven years without God, until he meets his uncle the hermit and does penance. A long account of a tournament intervenes before he finally reaches the Grail castle again and asks the disenchanting question.

The Fisher King is healed, instructs his grandson in the secrets of the Grail and dies. Merlin announces to Arthur the fulfilment of the Grail quest and dictates the account to Blaise. And on into the final 'Mort Artu', the end of Arthur as told by Geoffrey. Merlin takes leave of Perceval and Blaise, and has never been seen since.

At about the same time, before 1212, a romance appeared which is one of the most striking in the cycle, *Perlesvaus*. Its author writes in the style of north-eastern France and it draws heavily on Welsh precedent. It was to be popular, in translation, in Wales. Full of brooding menace – the truth is beset by enemies within and without – it is also intensely human. Its aim is to prise the whole Arthurian enterprise out of this world and charge it with religion. But what a religion! Fiercely opposed to evil Jews and Muslims and all heathen, it contrasts the New Law of Christ with the Old Law of the Jews – and heathen – and, like the Crusades in their first phase, it seeks to hammer hell out of the infidel and force him to Christ. Arthur and his men are to impose the New Law at sword-point. Perceval, presented as a kind of alter ego to Christ, takes hair-raising

• *Above* Merlin, as the wise old tutor of Arthur, from
Meliadus by Hélie de Borron, mid fourteenth century.

• *Right* Arthur passes the test of drawing the sword from the
stone and is proclaimed king; from a Flemish manuscript
written in French *c.* 1290.

revenge on his enemies. Heads are carried around like Celtic trophies. It is belligerent
and individualistic: Lancelot boasts of his love for Guinevere. Seemingly Benedictine
in inspiration, though hermits people its pages, it is unlike many of the secular stories
in restoring Arthur to his central position and it consciously judges the key figures –
Gawain, Lancelot and Perceval – by their approach to the ideal.

Although not as skilled as Chrétien, the author uses a tapestry technique to
memorable effect. His work begins with Perceval's failure to ask the key question.
Desolation results. Arthur loses his urge to win honour and practise largesse, and his

knights are leaving him. On Ascension Day at Carlisle, Guinevere prevails on him to visit St Austin's chapel in Wales, where he has great difficulty entering. A hermit who had known his father urges him to mend his ways and support the New Law. Arthur is cured. The rest of the story deals with the successive Grail quests of Gawain, Lancelot and Perceval.

Gawain earns most space. He meets the Damsels of the Cart, messengers of Fate, wins the sword that beheaded John the Baptist, without which he cannot enter Grail country, and finally reaches the Fisher King. He is obsessed with the three drops of blood that fall from the Lance and fails to ask the question. As he departs, a voice shouts to him that the King of Castle Mortal, having renounced the New Law, is attacking the Fisher King.

If Gawain is worldly charm personified, Lancelot is the perfect knight, except for his love for Guinevere. His adventure at the Waste City leaves his head in peril, since he swears to return in a year's time to receive the return blow – an echo of the ritual kings. He sits at the 'ivory table', but the Grail fails to appear.

The only hope is Perceval, who is with his uncle King Pelles. Pelles upbraids Lancelot about Guinevere, but Lancelot defiantly replies that he hopes he never loses the will to love. Perceval leaves his uncle, has various clashes with Red Knights and sees the body of Loholt (Llachau), Arthur's son, whom Kay has treacherously killed. He takes a frightful revenge on his mother's enemy, the Lord of the Fens. The Damsels of the Cart arrive and urge him to destroy the Old Law by delivering the Grail castle from the King of Castle Mortal. Perceval retakes the castle and the Grail reappears, with Lance and Sword. The King of Castle Mortal kills himself, but, the Fisher King having died, no procession takes place and no question is asked.

Arthur now enters the scene with his own quest. A maiden comes with his son's head and Arthur hears that Kay has joined Brian des Illes in a revolt against Lancelot and himself. Guinevere, overcome with grief over her son, dies. When Arthur finally beholds the Grail at Mass, it appears in five shapes, the last of which is the chalice, and for the first time in the literature Arthur is instructed in the use of the chalice and the bell. In the war against Brian and Kay, Lancelot is reconciled and the King and Gawain, followed by Lancelot, go to mourn at Guinevere's tomb; the place is described in terms that leave no doubt that it is Glastonbury.

The story ends with Perceval's journey to the island Castle of the Four Horns, which is drawn from the Otherworld of the Welsh *Annwfn*. There he is welcomed by thirty-three monks in white robes and led to a glass case in which stands an armed but silent knight. Perceval retires from the world. Pelles's son remains at the Grail castle till he dies, whereupon it falls into ruins. Those who visit it fail to return, except for two Welsh knights who lead saintly lives ever after.

The author of this romance knew Robert de Boron's work – he refers to Joseph of Arimathea and Alain le Gros, father of Perceval – but there is a special Welsh imprint to it. He names Arthur's son, drawn from a real historical character, and Pelles is almost certainly Pwyll, prince of Dyfed, who was also lord of the Low People, like Bilis, lord of the dwarfs, and Beli, a dwarf king. They may all have been the same person. The Welsh translation of *Perlesvaus* was influential and as late as the fifteenth century an abbot of Valle Crucis near Llangollen in Wales, who had a memorable encounter with the last, rebel Welsh Prince Owain Glyndŵr (Glendower), sent the poet Guto'r Glyn to Glamorgan to collect the copy of the work kept there – 'the goodly Greal, the book of blood, the book of heroes, where they fell in the court of Arthur; a book still in the Briton's hand – the race of Horsa could not read this'.

What all these first expositions of the Grail do is to wrench the whole epic of Joseph of Arimathea, the sacred Vessel, the holy circles of the Round Table, the Grail Table and the Last Supper, the grace abounding that rewards the peerless knight, into the west and locate them in the Britain of King Arthur. And did those feet in ancient time. . . ? Well, at one remove they certainly did. For everything comes to a focus on Glastonbury. *Perlesvaus* states specifically that its story 'was taken from the Isle of Avalon, from a holy religious house which stands at the edge of the Lands of Adventure; there lie King Arthur and his queen'.

Yet at that time Glastonbury – founded in A.D. 700, but with a longer history behind it – knew nothing of the Grail. Situated near the Bristol Channel, 'at the edge of the Lands of Adventure', the monastery received a constant stream of heroic and mythic tales out of Wales, Cornwall and Ireland, as well as participating in the French and Latin culture of Norman and Angevin England. It attracted scholars from the old Celtic world and was already celebrated as the City of Glass and the Isle of Avalon. As early as the year 1000, a biographer of St Dunstan had said that the first preachers of Christ in Britain found a church there which had been built by no skill of man and which was consecrated to the Virgin. William of Malmesbury in the early twelfth century suggested that the preachers were sent over from Gaul by St Philip and in a forged charter of St Patrick of 1220, this suggestion became a claim that twelve disciples, sent over by St Philip and St James, had built the old church at Glastonbury.

Glastonbury did respond to the French stories of the Grail, but slowly. In 1247 a reviser of William of Malmesbury said that the leader of Philip's mission had been Joseph of Arimathea himself! But it was not until 1367 that the abbey claimed to 'discover' the body of Joseph, by which time such discoveries may have become a clerical tradition: in 1191 the monks had announced that they had discovered the bodies of Arthur and Guinevere buried in the Isle of Avalon. The announcement must have had a dramatic effect, for by then the idea that Arthur would some time return had become quite widespread.

In sharp contrast with France, however, the development of Arthurian literature in England was slow, late and often mediocre. There were a couple of early versions of the Tristan story, but there is no Grail literature in Anglo-Norman and little in Middle English – and that is of French derivation. The great exception, the Arthurian writings of Layamon in full Anglo-Saxon style in the late twelfth century, was succeeded by a yawning gap until about 1350. English rhymed and prose romances on Arthurian themes begin between 1250 and 1300, Latin romances around 1280 at the earliest. There was to be a huge expansion in the later Middle Ages, producing masterpieces, but English celebrations of Arthur can generally be said to mount to a peak about the time that the massive French production, and everything else European, went into decline.

This, no doubt, stems from the peculiar circumstances of the island that had given birth to Arthur. The Welshness of much of the tradition must have been a bar. The idea of a Return of Arthur was a prime obstacle and not until that idea was buried and Wales itself conquered, could England wholeheartedly embrace the legends, in that characteristic blurring of Britain with England which has been the bane of lesser breeds who occupy the fringes of the island ever since!

It was the French-speaking monarchy, at first largely alien to things English, which was the prime mover. The Normans and after them the Angevins were active promoters. Henry II, in particular, and his wife Eleanor of Aquitaine, were very enthusiastic, pressing Arthur on the Scandinavians and anyone within reach. It was on one of his abortive campaigns in Wales that Henry heard a story that Arthur was buried in Glastonbury, though whether he was active in promoting the 'discovery' cannot be ascertained. A fire at the abbey in 1184 destroyed the old chapel and many of the relics on which the abbey depended for its prestige, and the king was lavish with funds to restore the damage: the Lady Chapel was built by 1186. It was in 1191, two years after Henry II's death, that the monks announced the discovery of Arthur and Guinevere's bodies.

The best report of this discovery is from a letter at the abbey of Margam, in south Wales. Digging to bury a fellow-monk between two 'pyramids' on which certain letters 'could not be read because they were cut in barbarous style and worn away', the monks found a coffin containing the remains of a woman's corpse, her hair still intact; below that was another coffin containing a man's bones and below that was a third, decorated with a lead cross turned inwards and inscribed in Latin: 'Here lies the famous King Arthur, buried in the Isle of Avalon.' The monks transferred the bones from the latter to a marble tomb in their church and claimed that the other remains were those of Mordred and Guinevere.

To identify one corpse out of the three buried together as Mordred, betrayer of the Island of Britain, was poetic but stupid. By the time Gerald the Welshman visited Glastonbury, Mordred had been dropped as one of the discoveries and the inscription on the cross had been modified to include Guinevere. This is highly suspect, as is the description of Arthur as a *rex* or king: no Welsh or British inscription of the sixth century

• The discovery of Prince Arthur's Tomb by
John Mortimer, *c.* 1767, a drawing inspired by the
Glastonbury monks' claim in 1191 to have found the
bodies of Arthur and Guinevere.

would have described him as such. The discovery seems to fall into place with
Glastonbury's many other claims – Joseph of Arimathea as its founder, his staff planted
to become the Glastonbury Thorn, the tip of the Holy Lance driven into Jesus's side,
making him the Maimed King. A pilgrimage to Glastonbury under its mysterious Tor
was shortly to reap greater promises of Indulgence than journeys to Canterbury, Rome
and Jerusalem put together.

In the end, despite Gerald's circumstantial evidence of a very large thigh bone, a notably high brow and ten wounds in the skull, and despite the purported existence of the cross – a copy of which, in suitably crude lettering, was made by the seventeenth-century antiquarian William Camden – historians are virtually unanimous in describing the discovery as a fraud, in the old monkish tradition. That ancient cross, however, still gives many pause.

Forgery or not, the effect was visible. Most chroniclers henceforth accepted the discovery willingly – it figured quite early in *Perlesvaus*. At last the pesky Welsh and Breton notion that Arthur would return could be ruled out. With him dead and buried, there was no longer a focus for future rebellion and the monarchy was quick to respond to the now safe Arthurian legend. Richard the Lionheart, glamorous hero of the Crusades, renowned for his personal duel against the noble Saladin of the Saracens, called his sword Excalibur and his circle stimulated Arthurian romance in Germany. After the loss of Normandy in 1204, the monarchy grew more self-consciously English, though the English language was not to attain respectability until the fourteenth century. Early in the previous century Richard, Duke of Cornwall, the brother of Henry III, seems to have rebuilt Tintagel castle simply because it figured so prominently in the tales and it was probably Henry III who ordered the making of the original Round Table at Winchester.

But it was Edward I who most clearly used the Arthurian legend. He snuffed out the last independent Welsh prince and tried to conquer Scotland in the name of his 'Britain', basing his claim to Scotland on Geoffrey of Monmouth. He proclaimed the Arthurian inheritance as his own on every possible occasion and went with his queen and the archbishop of Canterbury to Glastonbury where he had the famous bones removed from a casket and put on show. Later, he reinterred them before the High Altar of the abbey church, where they remained until the sixteenth-century Dissolution of the Monasteries, at which time they vanished.

Between 1279 and 1302 Edward I also took part in at least five *Round Table* ceremonies, held in imitation of the Arthurian tradition. At that of 1299, to mark the sixty-year-old king's wedding to Marie de Brabant, there was a tournament and three interludes celebrating Edward's triumphs over the Welsh, the Scots and the barons. The event began at sunrise with a mock battle in which the knights who had taken Arthurian names had the best of it, except for Kay, whose saddle-girths had been cut and who took a tumble, to roars of laughter. At the banquet, after the first course, a page disguised as a squire rode in, spattered with blood, and called for vengeance on the Welsh, which the 'knights of the Round Table' promised to wreak (a striking inversion). The second course was followed by a squire riding in on a sumpter, his hands and feet tied, to be freed by 'Lancelot' and to deliver a challenge from the king of Scotland; while the third course heralded the arrival of a 'Loathly Damsel' with a nose a foot long, a goitre on her neck and teeth a finger-length out from her mouth, who called on 'Perceval' and 'Gawain' to destroy Simon de Montfort (leader of the barons and ally of the Welsh) and reduce their stronghold of Kenilworth.

How did the Welsh, major promoters of Arthur after all, though now deprived of their deathless hero (at least in the official historiography), respond to this royal exultation? The Arthurian tradition remained strong in the three 'French' romances of their *Mabinogion*; there were to be later translations from the French; and belief in Arthur's return still persisted. But the thirteenth century saw the crushing of Wales. Although the House of Gwynedd in north-west Wales established a virtually independent Principality of Wales which was formally recognized in 1267, it was to last only ten years before being extinguished and all political independence with it, in two major campaigns which revolutionized English military society and reached their climax in 1282–4. In this sustained battle, crushed between the Crown, the Marchers and Gwynedd, the ancient kingdom of Powys – possibly the original home of Arthur in history – was pulverized. Out of Powys came the last effective Arthurian story in Welsh. And a sour thing it is.

The Dream of Rhonabwy (Breuddwyd Rhonabwy), composed between the late twelfth and mid-thirteenth century, is something completely new in Welsh – a written story composed by a single (unknown) author with complete mastery of his material. It is a satire on the whole Arthurian tradition – ambiguity and parody are its life-blood – and it is often brilliantly done. The tale is of Rhonabwy, a fictional character from Powys, who sets out to seek the brother of Madog, who ruled successfully over the kingdom from 1130 to 1160. While sleeping in extremely uncomfortable quarters on a yellow heifer-skin he is granted a vision in a dream.

He is transported back to the Arthurian world – with Iddawg the Embroiler of Britain as his guide! But what a world this is! Arthur and Owain mab Urien are supposed to be massing their forces to fight Osla Big-Knife in the crucial battle of Badon – the fatal battle of Camlan has apparently happened seven years earlier – but in this world turned upside down, they simply play *gwyddbwyll*, a Welsh form of chess. Arthur's men attack Owain's ravens; they retaliate. Both Arthur and Owain say they must do something, but never move. It's like waiting for Godot! In the end, they strike a truce

• *Overleaf* Tintagel Castle, Cornwall, rebuilt in the early
thirteenth century by Richard, Duke of Cornwall, in tribute
to its key role in the Arthurian stories.

and Arthur's followers are told to gather in Cornwall. The whole futile, if riveting exercise is summed up by one comment of this despised Arthur: 'I am not laughing; but rather how sad I feel that men as mean as these keep this Island, after men as fine as those that kept it of yore.'

There will be a resurrection, but in the thirteenth century the Arthurian world is dead for the Welsh. In Europe the great epic of Arthur rises to a glittering climax, but the Welsh give up on him. We wuz robbed!

CHAPTER EIGHT
VULGATE TO·VULGAR

Who, I say, does not speak of Arthur the Briton, since he is almost better known to the peoples of Asia than to the Britons, as our palmers returning from the East inform us? The Eastern peoples speak of him, as do the Western, though separated by the width of the whole earth . . . Rome, queen of cities, sings his deeds, nor are Arthur's wars unknown to her formal rival Carthage. Antioch, Armenia, Palestine celebrate his acts.

This assertion, confidently penned in the twelfth century and redolent of the Crusades, came true in the thirteenth and fourteenth centuries. Score upon score of romances poured out in French, English, German, Italian, Castilian, Catalan, Dutch and Scandinavian tongues. There was even a Hebrew Arthur, probably a translation in 1279 from the Italian. The Arthur of the *langue d'oc* had an even longer run. In our own day, the people of the Philippines enjoy a tale in the Tagalog language, set in the realm of Camalor under King Artos and Queen Ginebra – names which survive from the only Arthurian romance in Provençal, *Jauffré*. Jauffré himself is recognizable as Girflet fils Do, whose ancestor was originally Gilfaethwy mab Don, a god from the Welsh *Mabinogion*.

As the tales moved away from their British originals, an interlocking world of Arthurian literature was created. The technique of interlacing – starting one tale, breaking off to tell another, returning to the original – was used with differing degrees of sophistication. Stories fed on each other and there were almost endless first and second versions of a post-this and post-that. Names and characters were invented in bewildering profusion; new knights appeared like Sagremor or the Saracen Palamedes, who was noble enough to figure in pageants. There were intriguing oddities. *Diu Krone*, written in Austria around 1230 by Heinrich von dem Turlin, is a compendium of romances in which Gawain was the hero of the Grail quest, while a Dutch work,

Walewain, includes Gawain's adventures with a talking fox. The French *Chevalier du Papegau* is almost the only work since *Culhwch ac Olwen* to treat Arthur himself as a knight-errant hero and it offers the entertaining spectacle of the once and future king led on his way by a talking parrot in a gilded cage.

France, first in the field of the Arthurian romances, remained the focus. Of some 280 tales singled out by scholars, around 120 were French and of those about sixty were considered worthy of serious consideration. England, somewhat later, supplied some thirty tales. German, Dutch and Spanish romances were less in number but seem to have been marked by quality. The tremendous vogue in France in the thirteenth century spilled over into other countries and, besides the myriad Arthurian references which appeared in works on other subjects, the first productions of the tales in most countries were translations or adaptations of the French, addressed to courtly audiences. Then, as that audience grew to include the bourgeoisie, the tales were absorbed into vernacular literature and adapted to its taste; mysticism was minimized, action maximized and out of this, running into the hostile Renaissance, came original works which enjoyed an intense if brief vogue.

In this world, the 'lost golden age' theme of the originals dwindled. While the Crusade fever lasted Arthur was revered as a Christian king battling the Infidel, but as it subsided, the status of Arthur generally shrank. It was his knights, multiplying endlessly in equally endless adventures, and still carrying the semi-pagan inheritance, who were now the heroes. They became household names throughout Europe. Their adventures figured on Sicilian bed-spreads, backs of mirrors, tapestries and embroideries – on the walls of bourgeois no less than aristocratic homes. Striking late Romanesque frescoes at Schloss Rodeneck in the Tyrol celebrate Hartmann von Aue's *Iwein*, while Gothic frescoes depicting Tristan's story adorn nearby Schloss Runkelstein. Indeed, Arthurian frescoes (though now badly damaged) can be found from the Auvergne through Thuringia to the Baltic at Lübeck. Ivories were also particularly popular. A casket with scenes from *Tristan* in early thirteenth-century Cologne seems the first to survive, but the bulk of ivory pieces were turned out in Paris between 1300 and 1340; they memorialized Perceval, Gawain and Galahad, and Tristan and his Iseult – and found their first and best patrons in ladies of high birth. But the greatest works were without doubt the miniatures in illuminated manuscripts, which became a tradition from the mid-thirteenth century. One particularly captivating example is an illuminated *Lancelot* from northern France, dating to about 1316, which points ahead to the great imaginative works of the fifteenth century.

Then there were the largely royal and aristocratic Round Tables – ceremonies with jousts, feasting, dancing and pageants where the heroes were impersonated and their adventures re-enacted, sometimes with uncanny precision. The places where such Round Tables were held ranged from Acre in the East, in 1286, to Dublin in the West, in 1498, from Valencia in 1269 to Prague in 1319. The first was in Cyprus in 1223, when the lord of Beirut celebrated the knighting of his eldest sons; when Henry II of Cyprus was crowned king of Jerusalem in 1266, there was another, with impersonations of Lancelot, Tristan and Palamedes. In Britain there were eight between 1252 and 1345. They were, of course, especially popular in France and seem to have been peculiarly favoured by the kings of Aragon in the thirteenth century.

Appearing in every type of parade, pageant and display were also the Nine Worthies – the supreme warriors of pagan, Jewish and Christian history. Arthur invariably figures in the latter history, alongside Charlemagne and Godfrey de Bouillon, the first Christian king of Jerusalem.

The majority of the romances were adventure stories which everyone loved, although the long series of more and more incredible feats in the later stories now make for tedious reading. But among those stories which approached literature in the thirteenth and early fourteenth centuries, two great determinant themes can be distinguished: love, in all its manifestations, and religion, in its most austere and demanding form. These two themes came to dominate Arthurian literature in its own golden age.

Love is probably best exemplified by the Tristan story, which, in so far as one can tell, originated in the West, probably coming from Brittany. The tale relates that Tristan, orphaned son of Rivalen and Blancheflor, sister of Mark, king of Cornwall, comes incognito to Mark's court, where he distinguishes himself by knightly feats, in particular killing Morholt the Irish champion who came every seven years to demand a tribute of young men and women. Morholt's niece, Iseult, finds a piece of Tristan's sword in her uncle's body and swears to avenge him. When Tristan comes to Ireland to seek a bride for Mark, he kills a dragon to win Iseult, but succumbs to the dragon's poison. A seneschal claims the credit. Iseult, having noted Tristan's guilt from the gap in his sword blade, but afraid of the seneschal, refrains from killing him. He takes her back to Cornwall as his uncle's bride, but a magic love philtre, intended for the wedding night, is given to Tristan and Iseult instead. What ensues is an all-absorbing passion which can stand no restraint.

The pair resort to all kinds of tricks, which are related with loving care, to fool Mark – beginning with Brangain, Iseult's maid, taking her mistress's place in the wedding bed. Mark, suspicious, orders Iseult to undergo the ordeal of holding a red-hot iron. She arranges for Tristan to appear as a pilgrim, stumbles into his arms and swears she has never been touched by anyone in her life save the king and the pilgrim, so she survives. Later Mark banishes both of them, but comes across them in a forest sleeping side by side with a sword between them and is convinced of their innocence yet again. But in the end he banishes Tristan to Brittany.

There, Tristan marries Iseult of Brittany, sister of the prince Kaherdin. The marriage is never consummated, but to prove there was no insult, he takes Kaherdin in disguise to Cornwall to see Iseult of Ireland. Kaherdin falls for Brangain. They have to return to Brittany where, after many adventures, Tristan is wounded by a poisoned arrow. He sends for Iseult of Ireland to heal him and tells the messengers to hoist black sails if they fail to bring her, white sails if they are successful. Iseult of Brittany, out of jealousy, falsely tells him the sails are black. Tristan dies of grief, as does Iseult of Ireland because she arrives too late.

This story, shorn of added adventures, was immensely popular and figured in all kinds of later material. The startling glee with which the lovers deceive Mark was quite shocking, but hardly diminished the story's appeal, with its moving portrayal of the pair's perfect love. Early romances were written some time after 1150 by Thomas, a Norman at the court of the Plantagenets, who quoted Bleddri as his master, by Eilhart von Oberge, a German who used a different French version after 1170, and by Beroul, another Norman, writing about 1190. The tale was only marginally Arthurian: in Thomas's work, Arthur does not appear at all, since Mark is a king of England, and though Arthur and his court appear in Beroul and Eilhart's versions, they feature very little.

The sophisticated and strong story of Tristan, which also figures in the *lais* of Marie de France, changed relatively little in plot over the centuries; writers developed their skills in the details. In Eilhart and Beroul's versions, primitive cruelty abounds. Iseult is about to be burned at the stake for adultery when a company of lepers suggest a more fitting fate would be to make her their whore. The authors differ on the love potion, but agree in seeing Mark in a purely legalistic light. They make physical desire the mainspring; their lovers lack fire. It was Thomas who subordinated the story to a study of feeling, with the crux the truth of their love. He introduces the *Salle aux Images* (Hall of Statues), where Tristan retreats to worship an image of Iseult, but Thomas does not realize the full glorification of their love because he is too true to the original.

This glorification was supplied in abundance by Gottfried von Strassburg, who wrote his *Tristan und Isolde* in Strasbourg in the first two decades of the thirteenth century. His version is virtually a hymn to Minne, the goddess of love, and is beyond both courtly and merely physical love. Scorning even the most sacred act of knighthood – the initiation – he speaks only to 'noble hearts'. The power of an elevated passion is presented as a 'philosophy' in its own right:

A man, a woman; a woman, a man
Tristan, Isolde; Isolde, Tristan

In a masterpiece of erotic literature, he raises the lovers and their equal love above the ways of the world. Tristan has every skill, chess, harping, war; he knows Breton, Welsh, Latin, French, all languages – while Isolde is already perfect. If true love exists, as he is saying it does, it must be incompatible with society. When the pair retreat to the wilderness and take shelter in the Cave of Lovers, it is a perfect haven. 'Their high feast was Love who gilded all their joys; she brought them King Arthur's Round Table as homage and all its company a thousand times a day! What better food. . . ? Man was there with Woman, Woman with Man. What else should they be needing?'

Gottfried's book, in part based on Thomas, was wholly remarkable for its time, but while many cited him as a great author, few dared imitate him. He was left to modern times and to the dubious immortality conferred by Wagner's opera. Far different was the fate of a major French work, known as the *Prose Tristan*, which appeared in two forms, one around 1235 and the other, a much fuller version, later in the century. It fixed the Tristan story for posterity; it has its own grandeur and finally succeeded in integrating the tale into the Arthurian network.

The *Prose Tristan* departs from the original in many ways. Tristan is a knight-errant in the style of Lancelot; he is actually made a knight of the Round Table. Mark is a villain and a traitor, and is treated by Arthur and his men as such. A long account of Tristan's ancestors precedes his birth, when he is rescued by Merlin, whose brother Mark has killed. A near-fatal intrigue in Gaul brings him to the court of Mark, where the story resumes traditional form. The break comes with his decision to marry Iseult of Ireland and the shipwreck which follows.

He is washed up in Cornwall and people run after him at Tintagel as a madman, shouting '*Veez le fol, veez le fol!*', until he is rescued by his dog! Banished from Cornwall, he resolves not to join Camelot till he has proved himself and he launches into the usual series of jousts, tournaments and knight-errant adventures. But the basic theme remains and his death is characteristic: he is stabbed by Mark with a poisoned lance as he sits singing to his harp before Iseult, whose healing powers cannot save him. This kind of death is an old Welsh tradition – and so I believe is his friend Dinadan, happy and cheerful and yet determined to question this whole crazy world. His speeches would fill a volume; knight-errantry bemuses him – 'May God protect me from such a love!'; fighting battles to prove valour leaves him cold – 'My cowardice lets me live!'. Such a note had not been heard since *Culhwch*. Another innovation is Palamedes, who cherishes an unrequited love for Iseult but remains a fine and noble man.

• *Above* Wolfram von Eschenbach preaching religious
tolerance towards the Jews; from his romance *Willehalm*.

• *Left* Page from Wolfram von Eschenbach's *Parzival*
c. 1250: Parzival and Feirefiz arrive at Arthur's court where
(centre) the Grail messenger Kundrie asks for Parzival to be
forgiven and (below) leads him to the Grail castle.

The vast and rambling *Prose Tristan* achieved a popularity almost without peer; it blotted out the poems and became the only recognized form of the Tristan story. It greatly influenced Sir Thomas Malory's *Sir Tristrem* and its impact can still be felt in Tennyson and Swinburne in the nineteenth century. The magic and tragedy of Gottfried's work may have been lost to the *Prose Tristan* but at least it was spared Wagner!

Very different indeed were the tone and style of those writings which grappled with the Grail and the problem of charging the Round Table with the highest and most spiritually rewarding commitments of Christianity. The first advance on Chrétien, de Boron and the author of *Perlesvaus* came in the first decade of the thirteenth century, when Wolfram von Eschenbach wrote his *Parzival*. A Bavarian knight from a family of *ministeriales* – knights in imperial service who were technically serfs: 'at home the mice have rarely enough to eat!' – he married after a series of amorous adventures during wide travels and he cherished married life as well as the high ideal of chivalry, regarding it as natural to the Round Table. He disliked the court rowdiness at Eisenach, fief of the Landgrave Hermann von Thuringen, which was a literary centre he kept his wife away from. He liked to quote a colleague who said that the Landgrave, far more than Arthur, needed a seneschal as intimidating as Keie (Kay).

He was a humorous man. He boasted of his scorn for polished writing, to the rage of Gottfried von Strassburg, and whimsically made the Wildenberg near his home the model for the Grail castle, Munsalvaesch (Wild Mountain). But although his work is full of a light and teasing irony, his purpose was serious. In the age of the Teutonic Knights, he advocated religious toleration. Man in his state of doubt, half in heaven, half in hell, was as black and white as a magpie. He gave Parzival a half-brother, Feirefiz, pagan son of a pagan mother who was yet worthy enough to join the Round Table and be Parzival's chosen companion to claim the kingship of the Grail – even though his skin was striped black and white.

Broadly, Wolfram sticks to the outline of Chrétien's *Perceval*, but making his own inimitable innovations. Parzival marries Condwiramurs – Wolfram's version of Blancheflor – and does not sleep with her for three days; Feirefiz is converted and marries Repanse de Schoye, virgin keeper of the Grail; even Gawan (Gawain), whose adventures, as usual, fill most of the text, marries the proud Orgeleuse, who in the French tradition was a much more unsympathetic character. In general, Parzival follows the pattern of a 'holy fool' advancing in maturity, while his friend Gawan acts as a worldly foil. In some startling passages, Parzival in his unredeemed state defies God – 'the Welshman said "Alas, what is God? . . . If He hates me, that hatred I will bear." '

The hermit Trevrizent converts him, until he ends in grace with the healing of the Fisher King and his own installation as Keeper of the Grail.

Wolfram's text became the most popular German manuscript of the Middle Ages, but he differs radically from Chrétien and the rest in his description of the Grail. He claims he heard his story from a man called Kyot (Guiot) of Provence, who in turn picked it up from a half-Jew in Toledo in Muslim Spain, where it was written in the 'heathen' (Arab) tongue. Historians doubt this provenance, ascribing it to Wolfram's imagination, but to the German, the Grail was a small, intensely powerful Stone, with its own religious Order, the Knights of the Grail, which he greatly admired. These knights were real – the Knights Templar.

The fighting Knights Templar were one of the most important Orders in the history of the Crusades; they were the cutting edge of the enterprise. Their head-quarters were at the newly liberated Temple Rock in Jerusalem itself and they owned vast estates throughout Europe, secured by patronage and a prodigious accumulation of wealth. But they were also Cistercian monks, clad in white mantles and bound, in theory, by the oaths they took to individual poverty and chastity. Their 'little death' of knightly vigil and initiation into the Order mimics Christ's descent into hell and his resurrection, and they shared to the full the austere mysticism of the Cistercian movement.

The Order was founded in Cîteaux in 1098 in reaction against the worldliness of the Benedictine monks. The Cistercians withdrew to the wilderness, but in a precious irony they became extraordinarily wealthy, through the wool trade in particular, and were enmeshed with Italian bankers and the state finances of half Europe. It was they who paid most of the ransom for Richard the Lionheart after he had been taken prisoner on his return home from the Crusades. Their great preacher, St Bernard of Clairvaux, a man of compelling eloquence, provided much of the impetus behind the Crusades and generated the animus against the Albigensian sect in southern France. Joachim de Fiore, a Cistercian and mystic, called the Order a 'city of the sun'. Rome had become the Whore of Babylon, the true Church was the New Jerusalem of the spirit, a mystic vision with its earthly focus in the great Cistercian abbey of Clairvaux.

At a time when the Crusading spirit was fragmenting in wars against Christian Byzantium in 1204 and in crushing the Albigensian heresy in southern France, and as the Crusader states in the Middle East struggled vainly to withstand the Turks, the holy quest shifted towards the purely spiritual and it was the Cistercians, with their mysticism, who were the moving spirit behind the most comprehensive and popular Arthurian text to emerge from the Middle Ages.

Known as the *Vulgate Cycle*, and completed about 1230, this text represents the climax of the French and European celebration of the Arthurian legends. It was a response to the urge to unify all the stories which characterized the early thirteenth century. It is vast: the printed version runs to eight huge volumes. Other attempts at synthesis have left fragments – the *Suite de Merlin* (which influenced Malory), the *Livre d'Artus*, remnants of a *Roman du Graal* – but it is the *Vulgate Cycle* which holds the field.

It is five stories in one, of which the last three are the crux. They brilliantly integrate the doomed love of Lancelot and Guinevere into the tragedy of Arthur and weave it into the epic of the Grail and the Round Table. The first of the last three stories, the *Prose Lancelot*, is a huge compendium of adventures by innumerable knights – a knight may disappear for three hundred pages and the reader is expected to know just who he is when he re-emerges – and sometimes the central figure of the legend appears to be not Arthur but Lancelot. But if you cut through the jungle, the story which emerges is stark and riveting. There follows the *Queste del Saint Greal*, where the Cistercian influence is most clear in its uncompromising austerity. Finally comes the *Morte Artu* with its tragic end and the first time the story is told of Excalibur being hurled back into the lake. The general belief is that the integration of these stories was the work of an unknown 'architect' who left the component tales to others.

Preceding the three crucial stories in most versions of the *Vulgate Cycle* are two texts of inferior quality which were written later, under the compulsion to fill in the gaps, notably the early years of Arthur. The *Estoire del Saint Greal*, derived from de Boron, has Joseph of Arimathea with his virgin son Josephé sailing in an Ark to the city of Sarras to convert the natives. (This city's Sarrasens were frequently confused with the Saracens (Arabs) and Sarras was placed in the East, but there is good reason to believe that the 'holy city' of the pagans was in Britain and might have been Stonehenge.) They encounter Solomon's Ship, which figures in the later *Queste*, and, with their converts, end up in Britain, where the Grail works miracles. It is committed to Alain, first of the Fisher Kings, who moves to an unknown *Terre Foraine* (Strange Land) and builds for it the castle of Corbenic, where successive guardians of the Grail await the coming of the Perfect Knight. The story's most memorable feature is the consecration of Josephé as First Bishop of Christendom by Christ himself.

Then comes the *Vulgate Merlin*, which is de Boron's Merlin with a long and monotonous historical sequel. In two interminable epics, it deals with Arthur's battles

• Galahad is introduced to Arthur and the knights of the
Round Table at the feast of Pentecost (Whitsun); from a
North Italian manuscript, *c.* 1370–1400.

te saint qi portoit sor ses espaulcs. a par
te dunt estoit folee dunt biaus saint.

Vant il la uestu et appellue se li dit. ue
nez aps moi sir. chr. et il li fist et ulle
meine tot droit au siege pilleus. de les en
tance. se seoit. et leue le ma3 dont il estoit
couers. qe lanc. ui uoit fete mettre se troue
les lettres qi disoit c est la siege galahin.

I preudens regarde les lettres se de
troue escrites le noms se dont il huit qe
cel de leens loent. Sire. chr. asser uos cu
au est leu e uit. Et cil sa siet tot seure
ment. a dit apris tome. O uirer uos apo
e ale. qe bien aues fet ce qe len uos co
manda. saluer moi tos. ces a tos cellus
del saint ostel. a mon aie le roi pilleu

et mon lxsauel le roi pesqueor. et li dites
de pir moi qe le li uii ueou au plus tost
qe ge porc et qe ge en uuai loisir.

Tant se puit li putxes. de leens. a coma
de ateu nre seigneu. le roi a toute sa y
pignie. et qnt il uoustret de ma3re. qil
estoit. sine tint onques pler aanz. ainsi le
ur rssont tot pleniemant. qil ne lor uiu
ue roi pir au il le sauoier bien en cor tot a
cuns s'il losoiet demander. O uirer au me
stre bres ueu paler qi dont estoit si le o
uit. a uesant dinil lechiegni ulla cort a
troue. chra. aulsi grande qe tot la sou
roient. et ssoiet mi acoluls e u doi
e euo en tiel meniere qil ne sout pluer
te sor eluz a oile force.

with his barons running parallel to the combats between Christian Britons and pagan Saxons. Merlin is present throughout and finally achieves a reconciliation, clearing the way for the life and death struggle. The work draws heavily on existing material in the *Vulgate*: Arthur's habit not to eat on a feast day until some adventure occurs; Arthur's incest with his sister which produces Mordred; his marriage with the False Guinevere. But Merlin's enchantment by Viviane (who appears elsewhere under many names), which leads to his permanent imprisonment under a rock, is treated more sympathetically. Merlin is fully aware of his fate and, subject to a morbid passion, is resigned to it. The setting is shifted to the Broceliande forest in Brittany.

The *Vulgate Cycle* then enters into its major themes. Lancelot, greatest knight of them all, is a child of calamity. Snatched away by the Lady of the Lake, he spends his first eighteen years in her palace concealed in a magic lake which is an illusion. She then brings him to Arthur's court, delivers a long discourse on knighthood, designed to protect the weak and serve the Holy Church, and arms him herself. Arthur knights him, but forgets to gird him with his sword. Guinevere does this, establishing an obligation. Lancelot falls hopelessly in love with her, while she is intrigued. On then, into a maze of vows, combats, enchantments, which lead up to Lancelot's discovery, at the *Douloureuse Garde*, of a tomb with his name on it. After he has lifted the enchantment, he renames the place the *Joyeuse Garde*. There, his body will lie, alongside the man whom he clearly loves, Galahault.

This man, lord of the *Lointaine Isles* (Far-away Isles), invades Logres (England) but, smitten with Lancelot, submits to Arthur. They become the closest friends; indeed, one could argue they were more than that. Galahault arranges the first romantic rendezvous with Guinevere, but it is only after a long interval of separation that the lovers reunite, in Scotland – where they lie together on the very night that a faithless Arthur lies with the false enchantress Camille, in anticipation of his later infatuation with the False Guinevere created by Morgain la Fey and the persecution of the True. Galahault withers into jealousy; nightmares plague him. With only four years to live, he ends his days in a proud melancholy like 'a medieval Hamlet'. Only in death are the friends reunited.

After this memorable passage, the adventures continue, but Lancelot is beginning to suffer premonitions. He is losing his primacy as the best knight in the world. Some of his ardour and magnanimity is gone; he no longer shows mercy to defeated foes. His cousin Bors comes to the fore, indeed is marked as one of the Elect, though he, too, is marred by the loss of his virginity. At this point the preparations for the Quest begin.

Pelles, the Grail king, welcomes Gawain. His daughter carries in the Grail, but Gawain is inadequate: he receives no food from the Grail, is wounded in the Perilous

Bed by the flaming lance and, in an odd echo of Chrétien's Lancelot, is driven away on a Cart of Shame. Bors has similar experiences, but is not humiliated and remains one of the Elect. There are anticipations of the later *Mort Artu*, of the discovery of Lancelot's adultery, Mordred's treachery and the final catastrophe. Guinevere, too, has premonitions – 'It would have been better for me that I had never been born.' Love for her becomes a torment. She drives Lancelot away and he goes mad. Cured by the Grail, he lapses into what is a second seduction by the Grail king's daughter.

In the meantime he has achieved his fate. Under the influence of a potion administered with the connivance of King Pelles, he lies with Pelles's daughter under the impression that she is Guinevere and engenders his son Galahad – the perfect hero who will win the Grail. All of this, cutting through the endless maze of adventures, moves steadily away from a sympathy with the lovers and Galahault, towards the Church and particularly the Cistercian view that adultery is an absolute sin.

It leads us into the *Queste* proper. At Pentecost, AD 454, Galahad is knighted by his father in a nunnery. Bearing vermilion arms, he is brought to Arthur's court by an old man in a white robe. He passes the tests of the Siege Perilous and draws the Sword from the Stone; he is clearly the long-awaited Deliverer. With a clap of thunder and in intense light, the Grail floats in, covered by white samite. It circulates round the table, serving each whatever he wishes. The Vessel vanishes and the knights swear to go in search of it. They leave together but soon separate. Most of them, among them the most illustrious, fail, including Gawain. Warned by a hermit, Lancelot confesses his guilt, but although denied the supreme vision, he is able to visit the Grail castle and enjoy a brief ecstatic trance.

The Elect are Galahad and the less pure Perceval and Bors. One day they are joined by Perceval's sister on a great ship, built by King Solomon to carry a message two thousand years later to the virgin knight, who is of his lineage. The sword of King David lies there on a bed. This is the Word of God. Three spindles from the Tree of Knowledge, taken by Eve from Paradise, lie in the form of a cross on the bed-head. Perceval's sister replaces the hempen girdle of the Sword, representing the inferior doctrine of the Old Testament, with one of gold thread and her own hair, and hangs it on Galahad as the symbol of the New. Having given her blood to a leper woman, she dies and is carried off by ship.

At last the three are welcomed at Corbenic and are joined by nine other knights to make an apostolic Twelve. With great solemnity the Maimed King is borne in, Bishop Josephé descends from heaven and sits before the silver table which carries the Grail, while angels bring in the Bleeding Lance. Josephé performs the sacrament of Mass, the wafer takes the semblance of a child and from the Grail the crucified Christ emerges

• *Above* On his quest for the Grail Lancelot confesses to a
hermit living in a wicker hut in a tree; from a
French manuscript of *c.* 1300.

• *Right* King Arthur discovers paintings by Lancelot
which reveal his love for Guinevere; from the *Romance of
Lancelot du Lac*, 1470.

to administer the sacrament to the Twelve. Galahad anoints the Maimed King with the
Lance and cures him.

All three are wafted away to the land of Sarras, where they find the body of
Perceval's sister and bury it. Galahad enters into the Kingdom of Heaven, openly sees
the ultimate mystery within the Grail and dies in ecstasy. A hand removes Grail and
Lance to heaven and no-one has seen them since. Within a year in Sarras, Perceval also
dies. Bors alone returns to Camelot, which is a broken court.

In the last section, the *Mort Artu*, Lancelot lapses into his old sin. Wounded in a
tourney at Winchester, he is nursed by the Fair Maid of Escalot, who falls in love with

Comment le Roy artus trouua en la chambre
de mortgram lhistoire de lancelot dot Jese doubtr
fort de lamo de la Royne geneure et de lancelot

him. Rumours reach Guinevere, who is maddened by jealousy, but a barge comes down the river bearing the body of the girl with a note saying her death was due to Lancelot's rejection. Arthur is now deeply suspicious of him. A visit to Morgain's castle, where he sees Lancelot's paintings of his love, confirms his suspicions. Guinevere is charged with trying to poison a knight; only Lancelot's victory in judicial combat saves her. She and her lover are trapped, but Lancelot carries her off from the stake where she is to be burned to death, unwittingly killing Gawain's beloved brother.

As Gawain erupts in rage, war between Arthur and Lancelot breaks out, splitting the Round Table and paving the way for Mordred, here depicted as Arthur's son by incest. The dream collapses into tragedy. Arthur besieges *Joyeuse Garde*, the Pope persuades him to take Guinevere back; he persues Lancelot into his own kingdom of Gaune and only when Gawain receives a severe head wound does he withdraw to Meaux in France. There he learns of the invasion by the Romans. He defeats them and kills the emperor, when news comes that Mordred has usurped the throne. At the landing in Dover, Gawain is killed, but sends a message to Lancelot before he dies, begging forgiveness. Despite dire warnings, Arthur advances on Salisbury Plain, kills Mordred, but is himself mortally wounded.

In the first example of this marvellous scene in literature, he reaches the sea with the faithful Girflet. He tells him to throw Excalibur into a nearby lake, in Celtic style. A reluctant Girflet does so only on the third occasion, when a hand rises from the water, flourishes the sword and sinks back. Heralded by a shower of rain, the barge with Morgain and the ladies comes and bears the king away, but a few days later Girflet finds his tomb in the Black Chapel (*Noire Chapelle*). Guinevere dies repentant. Lancelot and his friends return to Britain and kill Mordred's sons. They pass the rest of their lives in penance as dedicated hermits. Lancelot's soul at his death is borne skywards by angels and his body is interred alongside his friend Galahault at *Joyeuse Garde*. And the *Vulgate Cycle* ends.

This breathtaking work, for all the maze of adventures it follows through, skilfully weaves everything together. The Round Table gets a mission. Arthur, even in his weaknesses, becomes a great tragic figure. His end is more dramatic than ever – even the shower of rain adds a touch of Celtic mystery – though the tomb in the Black Chapel probably represents a compromise with the widely accepted 'fact' of Glastonbury. Before the last battle Arthur foresees his own death in a vision of the Wheel of Fortune, delegated by Providence to control the vicissitudes of human life. When Mordred splits Yvain's skull, Arthur cries, 'Ah God! why do you suffer what I see? The worst traitor on earth has slain one of the worthiest men alive!' To which Sagremor replies, 'Sire, these are the sports of Fortune.'

The knights tend to represent types of humanity. Gawain, good friend and lover of ladies, is treated with respect but with irony. He is excluded. Of the Elect, Bors is the lowest because of his involuntary sin. He compensates by humility, the mortification of the flesh, a resistance to the myriad temptations of the devil and a warm devotion to kinsmen. Perceval, here made a virgin, retains much of his ingenuousness; he is so incapable of evil that he cannot perceive it in others. And in the end he hears a voice proclaim, 'Perceval, thou hast triumphed!' But the major achievement, without doubt, is the dual character of Lancelot, whose whole life has been Guinevere, who repents and lapses in turn. He is treated with sympathy and has his reward. In fact he dominates the text.

But these people are also made flesh and blood. Gawain is seized with vindictive rage, Guinevere is ravaged by jealousies, Arthur, tormented by suspicion, becomes pathetic. Lancelot, told of Gawain's bitter hatred, replies – 'He cannot ever hate me so much that I will not love him.' Even Galahad, who is a veritable 'monster of piety', his very name derived from Gilead in the Vulgate Bible and one of the mystic appellations of Christ, can be very appealing in his scenes with his father.

The whole work is of course governed by the doctrines of the Cistercian Order, which are seen at their clearest in the *Queste*. The first of the virtues is virginity, followed by humility, patience, justice and, last of all, charity! Unchastity is the root of all evil; wives and mistresses are not allowed to accompany the knights on their quest. The very first sentence of the *Queste* has the tables laid in Arthur's hall on the eve of Pentecost at the hour of nones after service – in exact accord with the rules of Cîteaux. Central is the problem of grace. The Grail at once signifies grace and is also the dish from which Christ ate the lamb at the Last Supper and the vessel containing the Host.

It is in the remarkable scene at Corbenic that the full significance of transubstantiation and the communication of grace through the Eucharist to the Elect is achieved in full Cistercian style. There are three themes: divine liturgy, unification of the Church and the heavenly host in the Mass – hence the presence of angels and the Josephé who died three hundred years earlier; apostolic communion – a re-enactment of the Last Supper where Christ himself appears to knights who have been brought to the apostolic number of twelve; and the miracle of transubstantiation, made visible by the descent of an infant from the heavens, his incorporation in the sacred bread and the emergence of the crucified Saviour from the holy vessel. This intensely mystical vision is conveyed in translucent, precise prose, which lacks colour in accordance with Cistercian austerity, but is nevertheless charged with animation and fire – the words of an orator rather than a poet, as its major interpreter Jean Frappier says, with justice.

For all the tedium of adventure following on adventure, for all the sense of running into an all-wise hermit on every other page, this is a magnificent and memorable work which makes a fitting climax to the whole Arthurian cycle.

The *Vulgate Cycle* also marks the beginning of the decay of the Arthurian legend. The Church, though it supplied some of the authors, had always been wary of it. The alien-sounding, 'Oriental' mysticism of the Cistercians deepened that suspicion. The terrible crusade against the Albigensians in southern France, which destroyed the whole civilization of the *langue d'oc*, had thrown up St Dominic and the Dominicans with their Inquisition – which soon became general. With the collapse of the Crusader states, the Templars' mission was gone; the Order withdrew to Europe, where its immense wealth attracted greedy kings, while its mysterious doctrines provided a motive for persecution.

The romances of the Holy Grail seemed highly suspect, full of visionary ideas which were at root a pagan heresy. In 1304, all over Europe, Templar leaders were arrested and tortured; many were burned at the stake. Years of trials, investigations and witch-hunts followed, until in 1312 the Templars were suppressed by papal decree. Their wealth went, but the alleged mysteries, the treasures of Solomon's temple, the shroud which wrapped Christ's body, the crown of the kingdom of Jerusalem, their esoteric knowledge, remained to haunt a new mythology.

The particular mysticism of the Cistercians suffered a cruel blow. And it was followed by the Great Schism in the Church, with a French pope at Avignon confronting one in Rome; by the conciliar movement around 1400 to reunite the Church, with its attendant new nationalism; and by the first stirrings of Protestantism. In these circumstances, the quest for the Grail lost all meaning and one vital ingredient of Arthurian romance was lost.

What was left? The world of Celtic yearning had long gone; the Grail had gone; all that was left were adventures with a semi-pagan and amorous theme. This was the point when the great changes in Europe, stemming from the plagues and the rise of new interests, began to tear apart the fabric of knightly society. Its trappings proved remarkably resilient, but as France moved out of the old-style landlordism and all over Europe merchant capitalism began to set the pace, the bourgeoisie and its many dependants grew in importance.

This was reflected in the audience for the Arthurian complex. Beginning in the old-established centres like mercantile northern Italy and industrial Flanders, the audiences spread until their adherence to the romances became noticeable. Of course, they had little direct knowledge of the world of chivalry, their interest was confined to the sheer adventure. In response, the stories became more and more long-winded, more and more fantastical. Something of the same kind is visible in our own day!

The bourgeois Round Tables, in imitation of the aristocratic ones, began quite seriously in Flanders, but they soon acquired a humorous note. In Magdeburg as early as 1261, for example, the burghers issued challenges to Goslar, Brunswick and other towns to compete in a tournament, with Dame Feie (Fay) as the reward. In the event, an old merchant won and he gave Dame Feie enough money for her to quit her immoral life and get safely married! Similarly in 1330, the bourgeoisie of Tournai formed a society of the Round Table, with a golden vulture as prize.

This frivolous attitude found its best examplar in the south German farces of the fifteenth century. At Shrovetide, apprentices went from house to house collecting money in the cause of three plays, all dealing with the chastity test common at Arthur's court and which made use of a drinking horn, a mantle and – something new – a crown which, worn by a cuckold, sprouted antlers on his head. The antics were calculated to provoke ribald guffaws at the idealistic chivalry of Arthur's court, a wholesale mocking assault on all its values, and it is difficult not to feel that most Arthurian writing of this period is marked by decadence.

The whole Arthurian cycle had in fact become irrelevant in the age of the great discoveries, the wrenching of Europe's centre of gravity to the Atlantic seaboard, the great religious divide between Catholics and Protestants (who regarded the romances with horror), the influx of Greek thought, rationalism, the humanism of Erasmus. The Renaissance regarded Arthurian romance with indifference, even detestation. Dante might be so moved by one passage of the *Vulgate* that it influenced his Paolo and Francesca's first tremulous kiss, but Rabelais in France was bitterly hostile – and it was in France, the old heartland, that the new Italian and Classical styles made most headway.

Not that the old order died quickly. It was in the fifteenth century that the royal library of France became a great centre for Arthurian manuscripts, that huge illuminated versions were made for Jacques d'Armagnac and many compilations for the court of Burgundy. The same century was a golden age for Arthurian miniatures. Some belonged to the great collector Jean de Berry, others were made in Flanders for the Burgundian court. A notable set adorn the *Chronicles of Hainault* by Guillaume Vrelant. One of the last commissions, with superb full-page miniatures from an obscure romance, was by a knight of the Golden Fleece about 1475. And good works were still written – *Amadis de Gaula* in Castilian, *Tirant lo Blanc* in Catalan.

But these seem the afterglow of a dying culture. The advent of printing led to a reprieve; many of the romances were printed as books and enjoyed a brief vogue –

though the sheer bulk of many works posed a problem. But the mainspring had been broken. From the fifteenth century the whole Arthurian cycle in its many forms – a yearning for a lost golden age, the quest for the Grail, the glorification of knighthood and chivalry – which had captivated some of the best minds of Europe for about three hundred years, stumbled, groped for a place in the new order and disappeared into the murky world of antiquarians, eccentrics and folklore. In effect, it died and stayed dead for four hundred years. Its harshest epitaph was penned by Cervantes, whose *Don Quixote* precisely satirized it: 'What is more, their style is hard, their adventures are incredible, their love-affairs lewd, their compliments absurd, their battles long-winded, their speeches stupid, their travels preposterous and lastly, they are devoid of all art and sense and therefore deserve to be banished from a Christian commonwealth, as a useless tribe.'

There was one great exception to the general decline, an exception which witnessed a literary renaissance, a seminal work and a wholly unexpected political transformation. That exception was England.

CHAPTER NINE

MALORY·AND·THE PECULIARITIES OF·THE·ENGLISH

Nowhere are the 'peculiarities of the English', to quote the late Edward Thompson, more visible than in their reception of the Arthurian cycle. Geoffrey of Monmouth's influence was of course paramount, particularly after the difficulty of a Return of Arthur had been resolved! Edward I, who was so keen to make sure the once and future king was safely buried at Glastonbury, included 'Arthur's crown' among his regalia and claimed Wales and Scotland for his 'Britain'. Edward III, who is recorded as owning one or two manuscripts on the subject of the Grail, followed suit, making a costly visit to Glastonbury with his queen in 1331 and authorizing a 'seer' to search for the body of Joseph of Arimathea. As the Hundred Years' War was breaking out, he staged a Round Table carnival and seriously contemplated the re-foundation of an Order of the Round Table with three hundred knights – an idea which in 1348 led to the formation of the Order of the Garter at Windsor.

Among the upper, educated classes, the French stories clearly circulated freely, but the development of a vernacular tradition was seriously hindered by what was for many years the depressed status of the English language. (I had vivid experience of this myself, years ago, while working on medieval London. I came across an early fourteenth-century case in the city courts which used French. An English clothes-dealer and his Welsh friend had been fined for causing a fracas in a brothel, whereupon they made a habit of standing at the roadside and neighing like horses whenever the aldermen rode by! Rebuked, they replied with ribald snorts of 'Trrphut! Trrphut!' (perhaps the first recorded raspberry?) – described as a rude 'English' expression!)

Yet it had begun in fine, Anglo-Saxon style with Layamon's continuation of Geoffrey of Monmouth's work in the 1190s. At that time, as in future centuries, most

¶Here begynneth the fyrſt boke of the mooſt noble and worthy prince kyng Arthur ſomtyme kyng of grete Brytayne/now called Englande whiche treateth of his noble actes and feates of armes & chyualrye/and of his noble knyghtes of the table roûde and this volume is deuyded in to .xxi. bokes.

¶How Utherpendragon ſente for the duke of Cornewayle and Igrayne his wyfe/and of theyr ſodayn departynge agayne.   Capſm.j.

IT befell in the days of ÿ noble Utherpendragon whã he was kynge of Englande and ſo regned/there was a myghty and a noble duke in Cornewayle that helde longe tyme wærre agaynſt hym. And ÿ duke was named the duke of Tyntagyll/& ſo by meanes kynge Uther ſente for this duke/chargynge hym to brynge his wyfe w hym for ſhe was called a ryght fayre lady/& a paſſynge wyſe/& Igrayne was her name. So whan the duke & his wyfe were comen to ÿ kynge/by the meanes of grete lordes they were bothe accordeð/& the kyng lyked & loued this lady well/and made her grete chere out of

a

writers needed the patronage of a nobleman or churchman of substance to be able to carry out their work and make headway. But Layamon, the parish priest of Areley Regis on the upper Severn in Worcestershire, wrote his *Brut* in an English language which precluded any patronage or reward; it was, presumably, a labour of love for a local or invisible audience.

A translation of Wace's version of Geoffrey's *History* with touches of his own, Layamon's work cuts out courtly love and chivalry, and is closer to the Welsh tradition; his are the oldest heroes of all: Kay, Bedevere, Gawain, Arthur himself. He has a way with simile – knights dead in the Avon are 'steel fishes lying in the stream' – and takes ferocious delight in defeats inflicted upon what one assumes to have been his own ancestors. His Arthur is frightening – 'Even if you desired to go to heaven, you shall go to Hell, ever to remain there, never to return,' he says over the corpse of the Saxon leader Colgrin – and he hangs twenty-four child hostages without compunction.

Layamon replaces the mid-Channel dream with a vivid one of Mordred and Guinevere tearing down Arthur's hall, with Arthur and Gawain clinging to the roof. In the end Arthur kills Mordred and his own wife, but while being carried by a golden lion to the sea-shore, he loses his grip on it and is finally rescued by a giant fish. This almost barbaric account closes when Arthur is carried off to Avalon by Queen Argante and her elves: 'The Britons still believe that he is alive, living in Avalon with the fairest of the spirit-folk, and they continue to expect Arthur to come back. . . A wise man whose name was Merlin: he said in these words – and his words were true – that an Arthur should yet come to help the English.' This astonishing idea of rescue of the 'English' by a 'British' hero, which seems as futile as *The Dream of Rhonabwy*, was nevertheless to become commonplace.

Layamon's work was a solitary jewel for over a century. Twenty-three English prose and rhymed romances survive from the years 1300 to 1500, which is late in European terms, and the great majority of them derive from the French: there are five straight translations. In these romances the Grail and Lancelot hardly figure at all; there are versions of Tristan and Chrétien's Yvain, and of Perceval's boyhood, and translations of parts of the *Vulgate Cycle*, with perhaps the most impressive a stanzaic *Morte Arthure*. But the quality is generally poor. Scholars identify the authors as translator-versifiers, often writing in the style of minstrels, virtually anonymous hacks without hope of patronage. Some of them rise a little higher – a London merchant, Henry Lovelich, with his *Merlin* and Thomas Chestre's *Sir Launfal*.

• The opening page of Wynkyn de Worde's 1529 edition of
Thomas Malory's *Le Morte d'Arthur*.

Yet, though mediocre as literature, these romances score by their directness and poignancy; they inhabit a much simpler world near to folklore. And some stories have adventures not found in French. The heroes are the old Welsh ones, Kay, Bedevere, Gawain and, above all, Arthur. In *The Avowing of King Arthur, Gawain, Kay and Bawdewin*, Arthur, based on Carlisle, hunts a great boar to his lair in Inglewood Forest near Hesketh, where all the hero knights make vows: Arthur to kill the boar, Gawain to keep watch all night at the haunted Tarn Wadling, Kay to ride through the forest and kill anyone who opposes him, Bawdewin never to be jealous of his wife, never to refuse food to a man, never to fear death. All vows are fulfilled except Kay's – and Gawain rescues him.

The same localities crop up in other stories and, while the native English tradition underwent profound change in the South and the Midlands, in the North Midlands, the North and even Lowland Scotland, it revived in strength in a local tradition focused on Gawain, even resurrecting the old Anglo-Saxon alliterative style. Above all, one work of native genius emerged during these years – *Sir Gawain and the Green Knight*.

It was written between 1360 and 1390 by an unknown author who was familiar with court life, with feasting and hunting, and who could read Latin and French; he might have been a clerk in minor orders, with John of Gaunt a possible patron. He shows a mastery of the alliterative style, in a poem that was meant to be recited rather than read. It opens in Camelot around Christmas and New Year. A gigantic Green Knight appears and challenges any of the knights to strike off his head with his own axe, provided he accepts a return blow in a year's time. Amid general paralysis, Gawain restrains King Arthur and strikes the blow himself. To everyone's astonishment, the Green Knight picks up his head, warns Gawain to meet him at the Green Chapel in a year's time and rides off with his head under his arm!

In a year's time, Gawain makes ready. He rides through Logres (England) to the wilderness of Wirral by way of Anglesey, Holyhead and the coast! At Christmas in a vast, dreary forest, he kneels to pray and a splendid castle appears. The lord of the castle invites him to stay until New Year and proposes a bargain: he will hunt every day while Gawain stays at the castle with his wife; in the evening they will share the spoils. Hunts take place with full ceremonial, while the lady tries to seduce Gawain, to be turned off by his courteous speeches. He gives one kiss for some deer on the first day, two kisses for a boar on the second. On the third day the lady gives him a magic green lace girdle, which Gawain keeps, thus breaking the pact. The next grim, grey morning, at the Green Chapel, he hears an axe being whetted and braces himself for the blow. Twice the axe is raised but let fall; the third time it lightly grazes his neck.

The Green Knight then reveals himself as Bercilak de Hautdesert, lord of the castle, whose wife had been carrying out his instructions. The graze was for the lace girdle Gawain had falsely kept. It was Morgan le Fay who had arranged the adventure to test the knights of the Round Table and frighten Guinevere. A shamed Gawain is forced to keep the girdle and Arthur decrees that all the knights shall henceforth wear a green baldric in memory of the adventure.

This ultimately good-humoured and vivid story, full of suspense, skilfully weaves together two themes: the Beheading Game, best exemplified in Irish romances which were transmitted through France; and the Temptation Tale, best shown in the Welsh story of Pwyll, prince of Dyfed, in his dealings with the Otherworld and also broadcast through France. The Green Knight may be an ancient evocation of spring who had to be slain every winter to renew life, and this strange legendary world is never far away from the knight Gawain, who carries the pentangle – a religious device – on his shield and is known as Mary's Knight. But the author makes him very human, as he does Bercilak de Hautdesert, who at times behaves like a mummer. In extreme tension, he brings these characters into a real life which echoes in modern times.

Most impressive are the descriptions of nature, where the handling of language is masterly. The strange, tortuous journey through the bleak North and Wales to the Green Chapel is so vivid that the chapel itself has been placed by conjecture in the Pennines. The harsh countryside, relieved by the warmth of Hautdesert, is soon abandoned for a mysterious terrain, akin to the world of *The Mabinogion*; and equally effective is the terrible suspense as Gawain lies awake on New Year's Day, waiting for dawn and listening to the gale outside:

> *Though his lids were closed, he was sleeping little.*
> *Every cock that crew recalled him to his tryst. . .*

But apart from this one splendid poem, tucked into its unearned girdle, Arthurian literature in England drones on into the fifteenth century, though it must have had a popular following. In later years the North of England was prominent among regions claiming topographical connections with the Arthurian world, connections which may have been affected by this literature. Meanwhile, it was apparently oblivious to the tumultuous changes breaking over its head – the Black Death, the great social changes lurching out of 'bastard feudalism', the Hundred Years' War, the near-anarchy of the Wars of the Roses.

The literature retained, however, one distinction – the central role allotted to Gawain. Beginning as Arthur's closest ally in Gwalchmai, Gawain in the hands of the

• Sir Tristan harping true love to the fair Iseult; fresco by
William Dyce, 1852, in the House of Lords Robing Room.

• *Left* Morgan le Fay, Arthur's half-sister – in Malory's
stories a sinister enchantress intent on destroying the Round
Table; painting by Frederick Sandys, 1862–3.

French remains a gallant knight, but goes steadily downhill in contrast to Lancelot; he is rejected in the Grail quest. In Malory, he becomes a 'murderer of good knights', redeemed only by his last letter to Lancelot, and by the time he reaches Tennyson, he is one of the worst villains in Arthur's court. This is a miserable fate for a character who, in all his humanity, seems to me to be the best of Arthur's men. And it is gratifying that he remains that in late medieval Northern English writing. On the whole, however, these were years of mediocre works, on which Sir Thomas Malory's masterpiece, *Le Morte d'Arthur*, made an explosive entry.

There is considerable doubt over Malory's identity, with four possible contenders, but most scholars agree on Sir Thomas Malory of Newbold Revel in Warwickshire, who was born about 1410, married around 1440 and had one son who died young. He seems to have spent much of his life in prison, on account of his apparently incorrigible zest for violent robberies, and was jailed seven times between 1450 and 1469. But the cause may have been political: during the Wars of the Roses he might have been framed as a supporter of the duke of York; he may have served under the earl of Warwick at Calais and been with him on Edward IV's sieges of Bamburgh and Alnwick; when Warwick broke with Edward, Malory probably joined the Lancastrians. His final imprisonment was in 1469–70, when his great work was finished. He died in 1471 and was buried in Greyfriars Church not far from Newgate Prison.

This record may seem to contrast with his high ideal of the knightly order, but it is in accord with the worries of his lesser characters, who are concerned to find a good lord and financial security and to see the land well-governed. Just as Geoffrey of Monmouth wrote in a time of civil war, so did Thomas Malory, that other shaper of the English Arthurian consciousness.

One difficulty about Malory's work is that it was printed by Caxton in 1485, which guaranteed it immortality, but Caxton notably reshaped it, finally printing it as an assembly of twenty-one *books*. He gave it the title by which it is known. In 1934 a more authentic text was discovered in Winchester College which revealed the full extent of Caxton's interference; scholars have been much exercised over it ever since. It was, however, the Caxton Malory which reverberated through English history.

One critic compared *Le Morte d'Arthur* to Wells Cathedral: 'Here is a Middle English crypt, there an Anglo-Norman chapel, a late French bit and bits that are pure Malory.' In fact the Middle English crypt forms only the alliterative English epic *Morte D'Arthure* of Book 5, which Malory left unchanged as a 'romance'. This poem in the revived alliterative style shows internal evidence of having been reconstructed from memory; it is modelled on Wace and concentrates on Arthur's Roman wars, but draws for illustration on the campaigns of Edward III and the Black Prince in France. It is written in a powerful Northern idiom, which today has to be translated.

Anglo-Norman had long merged into French and it is 'the late French bits' which form the great majority of Malory's sources, his 'books' and 'tales', transformed by his own magic. Books 1 to 4 are drawn from the *Suite de Merlin* – the more romantic continuation of de Boron – and the surviving fragment of another evidently gigantic French epic, the *Roman du Graal*. Malory shortens and transforms this material into stories of the early years, dominated by Merlin: Arthur's conception, his drawing of the sword from the anvil – 'Whoso pulleth out this sword of this stone and anvil is rightwise king born of all England' – his struggles with rebel kings and his acquiring of Excalibur from the Lady of the Lake. The fine mesh of interlocking stories which Malory creates so superbly includes his own *Balin le Sauvage*, where he adds to the story of the knight who slays and is slain by his own brother and describes the Dolorous Blow which lays a whole country waste. Balin and Balan, together with Kings Ban and Bors, are all old Welsh gods made human, but in general Malory diminishes the supernatural, Morgan la Fay and Merlin, to concentrate on Arthur himself.

Book 5, on Arthur's wars with the Roman Lucius, is modelled more or less directly on the English alliterative *Morte Arthure*, but the routes and battles are drawn from the campaigns of Henry V and Arthur is crowned by the pope. Lancelot is given more prominence, beginning to supplant Gawain as the main hero. Book 6, on Lancelot, is drawn from a highly selective choice from the *Prose Lancelot* of the *Vulgate Cycle*. He now appears as a hero of the Roman wars and goes on to become first knight of the Round Table. He is followed by the book on Gareth, Gawain's brother, which has no known source.

Then come no fewer than five books on Sir Tristram de Lyonesse, which are based on the *Prose Tristan* and comprise over one-third of the whole work. Malory deletes all tragedy from the tale, which forms a chart of Tristan's career to become one of the four best knights in the world; his love for Iseult is an adjunct to his chivalry. Malory invents a return of the lovers to *Joyeuse Garde* to leave them in bliss – though he does not remove the mocking Sir Dinadan. The story becomes another hymn to the knightly order, but it is the least attractive of all his writing.

The remainder of the work, in books 13 to 21, is based on the *Vulgate's Queste* and *Mort Artu*, plus some of the English stanzaic *Le Morte Arthur*. The stories are familiar,

• *Overleaf* Sir Galahad by Arthur Hughes, *c.* 1870,
a Victorian image of the virgin knight venturing through wild
forest on his quest for the Grail.

but they are handled by Malory with increasing confidence. He has no time for the doctrine of grace and eliminates the Cistercian ethos completely; he slaughters the ubiquitous hermits and the themes of religious purification and repentance; and he lacks enthusiasm for the lay saints Perceval and Galahad. It is when knights put personal feelings before anything else that the Round Table collapses. Lancelot's relative success with the Grail is stressed; he rises at the expense of both Gawain and Arthur, and his affair with Guinevere is treated as a matter of poignant regret at unhappy chance. Stripped of the French trimmings, the tragedy of Lancelot in his dual persona becomes almost unbearably stark.

The work then moves into the celebrated end: the premonition of disaster, the last battle begun accidentally by the sword drawn to kill an adder, the memorable scene where Sir Bedevere (Bedwyr comes into his own at last) throws Excalibur into the lake; the death of Arthur. Malory may have intended his greatest set-piece to have been Lancelot's subsequent penitential death, though one suspects he might have preferred Arthur as his hero had his sources permitted him. It is the High Order of Knighthood, personified in all its tragedy by Lancelot, which obsesses him, but it is Arthur – 'Of him all knights may learn to be a knight' – who dominates the final pages and it is Malory's portrait of Arthur rather than of Lancelot which people have remembered ever since. Perhaps, though, he could claim to have combined portraits of both in Arthur's lament as the last crisis breaks: 'and much more I am sorrier for my good knights' loss than for the loss of my fair queen; for queens I might have enough, but such a fellowship of good knights shall never be together in no company'. Queens are ten a penny but good knights are hard to find?

A bare summary cannot do justice to Malory's achievement. In both French and English, he was faced with a huge cobweb of stories. To exalt his High Order of Knighthood, he had to preserve the essence of the epic, but select mercilessly from this vast source of material. He proved brilliantly successful. The foremost Malory scholar, Eugène Vinaver, has indicated some examples, such as Galahad's statement when he sees the final vision of the Grail: 'Lord, I thank Thee, for now I see that that hath been my desire many a day. Now, blessed Lord, would I no longer live, if it might please Thee, Lord.' This, which conveys so much of Galahad's destiny, was a literal translation of some twenty French words from a passage five times as long. Malory had often to single out stories separated by acres of French text and then combine them into a coherent whole.

He had a gift for writing in a terse, pithy manner, with overtones of meaning, which people recognize as somehow 'modern'. It is seen at its best in direct speech. Lancelot, in the final tragedy, kills Gawain's two best-loved brothers:

'Now, fair fellows,' said the king, 'I charge you that no man tell Sir Gawain of the death of his two brethren, for I am sure . . . when Sir Gawain heareth tell that Sir Gareth is dead, he will go nigh out of his mind.'. . . But the knight goes to Gawain who asks him for news of his brothers. . .

'Truly,' said that man, 'Sir Gareth and Sir Gaheris be slain.'

'Jesus defend!' said Sir Gawain. 'For all the world I would not that they were slain, and in especial my good brother Sir Gareth.'

'Sir,' said the man, 'he is slain and that is great pity.'

'Who slew him?' said Sir Gawain.

'Sir,' said the man, 'Launcelot slew them both.'

'That I may not believe,' said Sir Gawain, 'that ever he slew my brother Sir Gareth; for I dare say my brother Gareth loved him better than me, and all his brethren, and the king both. . .'

'Sir,' said this man, 'It is noised that he slew him.'

'Alas,' said Sir Gawain, 'now is my joy gone.' And then he fell down and swooned.

And he and the King wept together for the deaths of Gaheris and Gareth – and of the Round Table.

The power of that straightforward passage, with its anonymous 'the man' telling the dreadful truth, is typical. What Malory did, at the end of the Middle Ages, was to write a 'modern' book. It is characterized by its singleness of purpose and wholeness, the inwardness, of much modern fiction. At a time when the Arthurian cycle was slithering into degeneracy all around, Malory 'gave new life to a dying tradition', at least in the English-speaking world. Thanks to Caxton and his printing press, Malory's work never became mere antiquarianism. It went on, through generations, to win more hearts and minds. Perhaps the conquest which would have pleased Malory most was the nineteenth-century commandeering of his work to be the theme of the Royal Robing Room of the House of Lords.

At the end of his account of Arthur's death, Malory adds:

Yet some men say in many parts of England that King Arthur is not dead, but had by the will of Our Lord into another place; and men say that he shall come again and he shall win the holy cross. I will not say that it shall be so, but rather I will say, here in this world he changed his life. But many men say that there is written upon his tomb this verse:

HIC IACET ARTHURUS, REX QUONDAM REXQUE FUTURUS.

HERE LIES ARTHUR, THE ONCE AND FUTURE KING.

Malory's caution was understandable. In 1485, within days of Caxton's printing of *Le Morte d'Arthur*, King Arthur stepped ashore at Dale in Milford Haven – in the person of Henry Tudor.

• Bedevere throws Excalibur into the lake while the
fatally wounded Arthur awaits his return; from a northern
French manuscript of *c.* 1316.

CHAPTER TEN
ARTHUR·AND BRITISH·EMPIRE

Henry Tudor owed his accession to the English Throne in the first instance to a peculiar historical conjuncture in Wales. The first half of the fourteenth century in Wales had been a period of harsh colonialism. This was disrupted by the Black Death and plagues of the mid-century, which brought about acute social dislocation and raised widespread aspirations with Richard II or sundry Welsh pretenders to the throne being looked to as saviours. Henry IV's usurpation of the English Crown from Richard II in 1399 provoked the rebellion of Owain Glyn Dŵr (Owen Glendower), which lasted for some fifteen years, from 1400, the longest war in the Middle Ages, and mobilized all classes; it ended with the disappearance of Glyn Dŵr, like Arthur.

The revolt had been swathed in the prophecies of Merlin and others, and the sense of expectancy continued through what Welsh historians call the 'spiritual union' with England which followed, through the dissolution of colonialism, the gradual entry of the Welsh into the social life of England and their attempt to escape from the horrors of civil war by pinning their hopes on a saviour, preferably of Welsh descent, from the ranks of the nobility – such as the Mortimers or William Herbert of Pembroke. In the end, their hopes came to focus on Henry Tudor, born in 1457 to the gentry house of Penmynydd of Anglesey.

Henry was the grandson of Owen Tudor, who had been snatched from the Glyn Dŵr revolt into the household of Henry V. Following the King's death in 1422, Owen caught the eye of Henry's widow and married her. King Henry V's son, Henry VI, seems to have been generous in accepting his two half-brothers, Jasper and Edmund, and made them earls of Pembroke and Richmond respectively. Edmund married Margaret Beaufort, who was descended from John of Gaunt, and it was through her that their son, Henry Tudor, acquired his claim to the throne. Edmund died and Henry was brought up by his uncle Jasper; the Lancastrian disaster in 1471 took him away to France, and the poets of the Welsh swung behind him.

In 1485 he sailed from Brittany (in the style of Geoffrey of Monmouth) and landed at Dale, Milford Haven, from where he moved into mid-Wales, rallying Welsh lords from south and north and deliberately courting a Welsh poet in Machynlleth. This rally gave him a respectable army in his challenge to Richard III and at Bosworth field he flew the Red Dragon! Richard lost the Crown and his life in the battle and the Welsh came 'shogging in herds' to Henry's victory *Te Deum* in London, because, reported the ambassador of Venice, they 'may now be said to have recovered their independence, for the most wise and fortunate Henry VII is a Welshman.'

Henry's stress on his Welsh heritage was astute political play-acting. The great Tudor century began in terms of Welsh mythology. He named his first son Arthur (he was to die young), recognized St David's Day and packed the court with minor Welsh officials. London and English society opened up and there was a major migration to the centre of power. The house of Cecil, descended from Dafydd Seisyllt on the borders, was one lasting beneficiary – William Cecil, Lord Burleigh, would become Queen Elizabeth's chief minister – and there were many lesser imitators as the Welsh moved into the new mercantile and naval enterprises of the century.

Henry VII's son, Henry VIII, carried on the tradition. He staged Arthurian pageants at the Field of the Cloth of Gold in 1522 and 1524, and he may have had himself painted into the Round Table at Winchester. In a dramatic move, his minister Thomas Cromwell, who had a Welsh wife, abolished Marcher and Crown lands and organized the whole of Wales into shires, giving it a long-lived class of ruling gentry. This was to make many Welsh resentful of the exclusion of their language from official life, but the immediate effect was to make the Welsh as free as the English.

Henry VIII's break from the Roman Catholic Church and embracing of the Protestant Reformation left the Tudor monarchy particularly vulnerable and Elizabeth's new Protestant Britain had to fight for its life against the Counter-Reformation and its powerful agency, Habsburg Spain. Intellectually and emotionally central to this fight was the assertion of an aboriginally independent and imperial British identity whose roots had to be sought in those ages when Albion was an empire and its Christianity free from Rome. Here, Welsh traditions became inescapable. In fact, the Welsh became junior members of the English realm but senior suppliers of its mythology. Under the Tudors, who fulfilled the belief in the Return of Arthur, England hailed the 'Worthiness of Wales'.

The Tudors spent much time hunting out genealogies which would legitimize their monarchy, being especially keen to trace their descent from Arthur. Antiquarians and historians were encouraged to investigate his history. When Polydore Vergil, an Italian in England on papal business, turned the rationality of the new Italian school of history on Geoffrey of Monmouth in 1534, making slighting comments on Arthurian legends and claiming that when Arthur was allegedly buried at Glastonbury, the abbey had not even been built, the response was deafening. Tudor Renaissance historians rallied passionately to Geoffrey's defence, with new scholars from Wales to the fore – Sir John Price of Brecon and Humphrey Llwyd of Denbigh, a brilliant geographer – along with pillars of the new history based on antiquarian survey, such as John Leland and John Bale, whose work was to climax in William Camden's magnificent *Britannia*. In a Welsh Church which was Welsh for the first time in centuries, not only did scholars produce a Welsh Bible, but Richard Davies, bishop of St David's, and a clutch of Tudor humanists produced a telling argument against the Pope by reaching back into the history of the Celtic Church – 'The Pope came late into Wales and that by the sword of the king of England.'

These humanists, led by Blanche Parry from Welsh Herefordshire, clustered around Elizabeth's court and were joined by numerous seadogs. Everything came to a focus there, as the British-Arthurian cycle reached its climax in learning, poetry, public ritual and propaganda – in Philip Sidney's vision of a Renaissance Protestant order of chivalry in the service of a British empire and in Edmund Spenser's *Faerie Queene*, a rather artificial Arthurian romance modelled on the Italians. Despite the extreme caution of Elizabeth and her chief minister Burleigh, relations with Spain degenerated into open war when the seafaring exploits of Drake, Gilbert and Raleigh precipitated the launch of the Spanish Armada against England in 1588.

Central to the maritime ventures was a remarkable Welshman, Dr John Dee, who was also the thinker behind many of the court masques as well as Philip Sidney's order of chivalry. Born in London of Welsh parents in 1527 – ten years before the celebrated Richard Hakluyt, who was to realize several of Dee's ambitions – he cherished his Welsh roots and the 'British history'. He was a dreamer of dreams of empire and a Christian commonwealth, an admirer of Elizabeth, who cherished him, and it was he who now carried the *History* of Geoffrey of Monmouth, in a new vogue, to unheard of heights.

Like many scholars of the Renaissance, he was a polymath who inhabited a world which was half magic and half science. He became notorious as a sorcerer – a 'caller of devils' – with his metaphysics and mysticism, and his 'angelic conversations' with spirits which were actually scientific principles. Known as the 'Arch Conjurer' of England, he was once imprisoned under Mary for trying to 'enchant' the Queen and when he left for Poland and Prague in 1583 a crowd sacked his library at Mortlake as the den of a black magician. He is said to have inspired both Shakespeare's Prospero and Marlowe's Faust; his house in Prague was known as Dr Faustus's house.

For centuries, people dismissed him as an eccentric and a fraud, but over the last thirty years or so, his reputation has been recovering. In fact, he was one of a small but potent group of thinkers of the late Renaissance who embraced the Occult philosophy, studied the Jewish Kabbala to try to discover the secret language of God and cherished the ideal of a religion which would transcend Catholicism and Protestantism and would find its earthly embodiment in Queen Elizabeth, heiress to the ancient British empire of Arthur. Dee, like the famous Giordano Bruno, the celebrated Italian thinker who was burned at the stake in 1600, might even have served in Walsingham's army of agents – though his Occultism was to finish him in his lifetime.

What he was primarily to Tudor England was a brilliant speculative scientist, a mathematician, geographer and navigator; Elizabeth called him 'hyr philosopher'. One of the founder Fellows of Trinity, Cambridge, in 1546, he moved to Louvain and established friendships with some of the seminal minds in mathematics and geography – Gemma Phrysius, the Flemish Cosmographer to the Emperor; Gerard Mercator the map-maker; the Portuguese Pedro Nunez; and Abraham Ortelius of Antwerp. The lectures of the twenty-three-year-old Dee in Paris were a sensation and he was courted by princes all over Europe. He returned to England, published an augmentation of Robert Recorde's *Grounde of Artes*, a mathematical textbook which ran to twenty-six editions by 1662, and wrote his own seminal preface to the English translation of Euclid. He built up a massive library at Mortlake, mixed with the 'mechaniciens' and was fêted by men in power – the circle of Sir Henry and Philip Sidney and the Dudleys – and taken up by the Queen.

A skilled map-maker, he established himself as the thinker behind many of the exploration and colonization ventures of the English in their search for the north-east and north-west passages to 'Cathay'. He was scientific adviser to the Muscovy Company and the Company of Cathay, corresponding eagerly with ship-masters and navigators, pouring out treatises, maps and instructions in his characteristic blend of crisply practical technological and scientific arguments, imperial dreams, erudition and the Oriental occult. In 1575 began the opening of a great cycle of semi-official, anti-Spanish exploration, colonization and piratical enterprises.

As Martin Frobisher, armed with Dee's advice, launched his expeditions into the north-west and others struggled through the Arctic seas of the north-east, Sir Humphrey Gilbert published his *Discourse* in April 1575, to begin the first serious essay in American colonization. Dee worked carefully through it, recalled an imperial discourse

• Dr John Dee, the remarkable Welsh polymath
who advocated the Queen's return to the triumphs of her ancestor,
King Arthur; anonymous contemporary portrait.

Johannes Dee.
Anglus.
Londinensis.
Æt̃ suæ
67

of his own on Atlantis, as he called America, and during six days in August 1576 wrote the first of four major books calling on Elizabeth to re-establish a great British maritime empire in the northern latitudes, resuming the triumphs of Arthur.

'O Glastonbury! O Glastonbury!' declaimed Dee, 'that Apostle-like Joseph, that triumphant British Arthur!' What Britain needed were a Christian Aristotle and a Christian Alexander; these Dee modestly offered to provide. In his campaign to build a fleet, he could summon up from strictly English precedent only the peaceable King Edgar, who was said to have had four thousand ships. 'And why not Arthurus Brytanis?' – Arthur had been a thorn in Saxon eyes and had defeated them twelve times, whereas Edgar was 'but a mere Saxon'; his progeny qualified for General Empire only because Albion was *now* (Dee underlined the word) the greater part of British Empire. 'But yet,' said Dee, 'there is a little lock of LADY OCCASION, Flickering in the Ayre, by our hands, to catch hold on: whereby we may yet ones more (before all be utterly past and for ever) discretely and valiantly recover and enjoy, if not all our Ancient and due Appurtenances to the Imperiall Brytish Monarchy, yet, at the least, some such Notable Portion hereof.'

This London Welshman seems to have coined the very expression *British Empire* though he used it in a spiritual sense. His first volume of the *General and Rare Memorials Pertayning to the Perfect Arte of Navigation* was devoted to the 'Brytish Monarchie' and its 'Incomparable Islandish Empire'; in it he argued for the creation of a 'Pety Navy Royall' of sixty tall ships, supported by taxation and the mobilization of British resources for imperial expansion. He hinted at the unassailable evidence he was shortly to produce on British claims to northern Atlantic dominion, based on Arthur – for Arthur had enlarged his domains much further, long before the days of Edgar. Dee would reveal to the Queen, herself descended from Arthur, the true foundations of her British state. For if sea power had been the stay of the Athenian state, how much more was this true of the British Empire? 'O Albion, O Britain, O England and I say thrice times over, O Brytan yet again!'. Dee called upon Queen Elizabeth to rebuild a great British maritime empire in the high latitudes, extending from the Orkneys through Iceland and Greenland to the shores of Atlantis, and he graced his book with a beautiful frontispiece, allegorical and partly occult, showing Elizabeth at the helm of an imperial ship, *Europa*, restoring the lost kingdoms of Arthur's British Empire.

Of the two books following up this first volume, a *Hexameron Plat Politicall of the Brytish Monarchie*, with *Tables Gubernatick* for the navigators, is now lost and the second he burned, presumably because it proved theologically dangerous. In his fourth book, the *Great Volume of Famous and Rich Discoveries*, on British projects to the north-east, which he completed in the early summer of 1577, he presented his evidence for an early British empire in the north.

• Queen Elizabeth I at the helm of her imperial ship
Europa restoring the lost kingdoms of Arthur's empire;
frontispiece to John Dee's *General and Rare Memorials
Pertayning to the Perfecte Arte of Navigation*, 1577.

He had two main sources. One was a litany of Arthur's fabulous conquests, which first appeared in print in 1568 in William Lambard's *Archaionomia*. Lambard, a celebrated jurist and author of standard texts on the courts of England, had immersed himself in Saxon documents and translated them into Latin. He was an Arthurian patriot, as were they all, and revelled in the power and sovereignty which the kings of England had 'inherited' from their British predecessors. Speaking of Arthur and using an 'ancient text', he wrote, 'His kingdome was too little for him and his mind was not contented with it.' So he subdued 'all Scantia (now called Norway) and all the Islands beyond Norway, to wit Iceland and Greenland, which are appurtayning to Norway'.

He went on in a sonorous chant, listing all the kingdoms conquered by Arthur, which ranged through the whole of Scandinavia, the Baltic and the Arctic, into Lapland, where he placed the eastern boundary of Arthur's empire. The western frontier stretched to the North Pole and beyond. Among the names was a 'Windland' – identified by some with Vinland of the Icelandic settlements in Newfoundland. (Arthur had clearly greatly extended his conquests since the days of Geoffrey of Monmouth!) Lambard's explanation of the Danish and Norse invasions of England was that the subject Norwaymen had intermarried with the British and, weary of their bony fiords, had come to England to claim their British citizenship!

The roll-call of Arthurian conquests reverberates through the sixteenth century. William Worcestre, an Arthurian antiquarian of the late fifteenth century, who knew of Bristol sailors' attempts to discover the mystery island of Brazil and was familiar with their Icelandic voyages, also knew of the Arthurian conquests from French manuscripts. Lambard duly registers them in Richard Hakluyt's great imperial text, *The Principal Navigations . . . of the English Nation*, and Dee supplements the list with the apocryphal voyages of the Zeno brothers of Venice, an account of which was published in 1558 and which was best known in England from Ramusio's collection of voyages of 1574. The Zeni had peopled the fourteenth-century Arctic with imaginary islands which figured in the great world maps of Mercator and Ortelius, and which Dee allotted to Arthur.

While corresponding with the Flemings about the Arctic regions, Dee was riveted by the information in a letter written to him by Gerard Mercator in April 1577. Mercator said he had drawn his material from the *Itinerary* of the Fleming or Dutchman Jacob Cnoyen, whom Mercator admired, and who himself was quoting an otherwise unknown *Gestae Arthuri* (*Deeds of Arthur*). Both documents have since disappeared. Cnoyen's manuscript, which Mercator had transcribed meticulously word-for-word in Old Dutch and Latin, described the northern lands in terms that were broadly in accord with current geographical notions. Cnoyen referred, however, to the Little People there (Eskimos or *Skraelings*, as the Icelandic settlers in Greenland and Labrador called them, to be followed by Mercator), adding that these people had also been mentioned in the *Deeds of Arthur*. The latter supplied the by then well-known picture of a great range of mountains surrounding the magnetic Pole, cut by multiple channels running through to form the four dread indrawing seas which flowed together into the celebrated Polar whirlpool – the maelstrom.

But at this point there is a break in Cnoyen's manuscript, which has been partially destroyed by fire, and the incomplete text suddenly becomes that of the *Deeds of Arthur*. Arthur abruptly appears. His great army, overrunning Scotland about AD 530, had sailed to conquer the islands, particularly Iceland, and had been warned by four returning ships of the perils of the indrawing seas of the Pole. No fewer than four thousand of Arthur's people were lost there. So, rather than continue, Arthur peopled all the islands between Scotland and Iceland, as well as an island called Grocland on the lip of the indrawing seas, where he found people twenty-three feet tall! In the following year, twelve of Arthur's ships, carrying 1800 men and 400 women, tried to get through into the indrawing seas and reach the Pole. Although half the people were lost, the rest apparently succeeded in getting through. Then the narrative breaks off and Cnoyen abruptly informs his readers that eight of 'these people' had turned up in Bergen in Norway in 1364! One of them was not a native but a fifth-generation descendant of a Fleming, with an astrolabe, who had known an English Minorite who visited the northern lands in 1360 and had written up an account of them.

This information, much of which turned up in Hakluyt's *Principal Navigations*, was characteristically a blend of fantasy and genuine geographical knowledge. The Icelanders who had occupied part of Greenland certainly knew a great deal and their knowledge informs the fifteenth-century maps of the Dane Claudius Claves Swart, the first person to attempt to map these regions. There is nothing implausible about a ship turning up in Bergen in 1364; the Norwegians, disturbed by reports that the Icelanders in Greenland had turned from the Christian religion to the religion of the native peoples of America, had sent Ivar Bardarson there. He returned about 1363 or 1364, having found that the settlement had disappeared.

But who had made these settlers Arthur's people? The Icelanders themselves had an admixture of Celts, mostly Irish, and there may have been some old stories, though there is no evidence. There is a touch of mystery about the seven survivors who turned up in Bergen. Taliesin had cited such a number in the old poem about Annwfn:

> *Three freights of Prydwen went we into it,*
> *Save seven, none came back from Caer Siddi.*

The island of Grocland also caused controversy. Hakluyt believed it to be a double of Greenland, but both Mercator and Ortelius located it as a large heart-shaped island well to the west of Greenland. So did John Dee in his great map of 1580 and it was Dee who was most excited by the new information. 'Gestae Arturi. . .' he noted, 'A rare testimony of great importance to the Brytish title to the Septentrional Regions, Atlantis in particular.' He went on to incorporate the new material, but it also stopped him in his tracks. How could there be survivors of Arthur in the North as late as 1364? Marginal comments on Mercator's letter are full of entertaining remarks: '8 men being of the generation of them which went in King Arthur his tyme to these places discovering . . . I mean in the 25 generations at the least, after King Arthur his tyme allowing longer Ages than now the generall rate is: at between 25 and 30 years to a generation.' These people, he calculated, could not possibly have been Arthur's!

Dee plunged into the British history of Humphrey Llwyd and discovered the potent tale of Madoc, an alleged Welsh prince who was said to have discovered America in 1170, three hundred years before Colombus. At the hands of Dee and a myriad successors this story grew into a legend which was to rival Arthur's, to live for four hundred years and have a direct influence on the history of America. In 1580 Dee presented the Queen with a superbly executed map and a formal 'Title Royal' setting out her claims to northern America, beginning with Madoc. All these Welshmen, grounded in Arthur, were to lodge in what Froude called the 'prose epic' of the English nation – that massive and magnificent compilation, the very voice of British empire, Hakluyt's *Principall Navigations, Voyages, Traffiques and Discoveries of the English Nation* of 1589 and 1598–1600. A revived Arthur, building on Geoffrey of Monmouth and sweeping on to the Pole, Greenland, maybe America, moved to a new climax as a hero of Britain.

But the glory was short-lived. Dee's enterprise was an anti-climax. While Elizabeth was warm to him, her great minister Burleigh was suspicious. Dee had nightmares of Burleigh burning his books. He became paranoid; he would stare at himself in the mirror, 'my skin all overwrought with work like some kind of tuft mockado with crosses blue and red'. He was plagued by the whispering campaign against him as a black magician. In 1583 he took off on his mysterious journey to Poland and Prague and by the time he returned the tide had turned remorselessly against him as an Occult thinker and a dabbler with devils, pilloried by Marlowe. He was banished to an English Siberia in Manchester and died in poverty, to be dismissed as a charlatan for centuries. Wales meanwhile lost its Tudor pre-eminence and slid into the backward province of Poor Taffy. The story of Arthur suffered an abrupt eclipse.

Europe and England plunged into the Wars of Religion, hideous witch-hunts, the English Civil War. This was succeeded by the Scientific Revolution and the rationalism and the maritime expansion of England in the eighteenth century. In these circumstances, Arthurian literature in England followed that of Europe into oblivion.

There were a few stirrings. King James Stuart I of England, though suspicious of Dee and all witchcraft, cherished Arthurian stories and called his realm Great Britain – though that was not to become a reality until the eighteenth century. Ben Jonson wrote the king a couple of Arthurian masques, Milton thought of writing an Arthurian epic for a while, but in the end rejected the idea. In the meantime, Geoffrey of Monmouth's *History* was demolished by the advance of historical scholarship; its last stronghold was Wales, though it was generally acknowledged to hold some truths and its appeal remained real.

Protestant opinion on the whole was resolutely against the Arthurian stories; Roger Ascham wrote a savage attack on Malory, echoing Cervantes: 'open manslaughter and bold bawdry – good stuff for wise men to laugh at – foulest adulterers'. Indeed mockery became a standard response as the legends declined into folktales and chapbooks. Swift and Pope ridiculed them mercilessly and perhaps the last word lay with Fielding in his burlesque *Life and Death of Tom Thumb the Great*, whose tiny hero is ultimately devoured by a red cow.

It seemed that the fate of the Arthurian legends in Britain was following a similar decline to that in Europe, but Malory was still respected – and there was one radical difference. In the nineteenth century, when Britain became for a while the greatest power on earth, Arthur and his men experienced a remarkable and unexpected revival, not least among the people at large. He was celebrated as the first national Hero of the British by the Poet Laureate of Queen Victoria and the Prince Regent and was to grace a Royal Chamber at the heart of the imperial Parliament.

CHAPTER ELEVEN

RESURRECTION

In 1809 the artist and poet William Blake was seized with the ambition to paint for the nation and hang in Westminster Hall and other public places giant, portable frescoes whose colours would be pure and permanent even if the subjects were a hundred feet high. When the Royal Academy and the British Institution rejected his first works, he staged a private exhibition of them at his brother's house in Golden Square; it ran from May to September and was elaborately advertised. Dominating the exhibition was a painting, since lost, which he considered his most important work and was unlike anything else he ever did. Normally his paintings were no larger than two feet six by two; this one was fourteen feet by ten and depicted three life-size figures, modelled on Apollo, Hercules and Pan. It was entitled *The Ancient Britons* and showed the three figures with livid-red pulsing veins, striding over heaps of dead and dying Romans and Britons, while the last Bard sang to his harp and in the mountain background Druid temples were bloodied in the sunset of battle.

The catalogue entry ran: 'In the last battle of King Arthur only three Britons escaped . . . these three marched through the field unsubdued as Gods; and the Sun of Britain set, but shall rise again with tenfold splendour when Arthur shall awake from sleep and resume his dominion over earth and ocean.'

In the advertisement for the exhibition the three Britons were placed, rather obscurely, in a battle against the Roman army and the theme was celebrated in two three-line verses captioned 'from the Welsh Triads':

> *In the last battle that Arthur fought, the most Beautiful was one*
> *That returned, and the most Strong another; with them also returned*
> *The most ugly, and no other beside returned from that bloody Field.*

———✝———

• William Blake's *The Dance of Albion*, an engraving of
c. 1794–6. Blake wrote that 'the stories of Arthur
are the acts of Albion'.

The most Beautiful the Roman warriors trembled before and worshipped:
The most Strong, they melted before him and dissolved in his presence:
The most Ugly they fled with outcries and contortions of their limbs.

This seems to be the first English translation of an authentic Welsh triad of the Middle Ages. Its origins can be found in the first Arthurian romance, *Culhwch ac Olwen*, where there is a reference to three survivors of the battle of Camlan; it recurs in a fifteenth-century set of triads, *Twenty-four Knights of Arthur's Court*, which refers to 'Three Offensive Knights', and in later copies and possible adulterations.

The story was probably passed to Blake through William Owen Pughe, one of a striking group of London Welshmen who came bubbling up out of the Age of Revolution and were dedicated to the revival of the Welsh nation; part of their activities was to reprint old documents, further the myth of Madoc and Atlantic dominion, and proclaim the ancient and noble character of the Druids. The group's leading figure was Edward Williams, better known as Iolo Morganwg, who created a virtually new religion of a purified Druidism and invented the *Gorsedd* or Order of Bards, who were supposedly descended from the deist Druids and who grace the Welsh National Eisteddfod to this day.

Like Blake, these man had been lower-middle-class radicals, but their hopes were now moving from political revolution into some kind of religion. This was particularly true of William Owen Pughe, who probably contacted Blake through William Sharp the engraver. The poet Southey thought Pughe directly responsible for Blake's painting (which he found hideous) and though there is no direct evidence, it seems very likely that Pughe supplied Blake with the material for his 1809 catalogue, which is the work of a Christian poet-prophet struggling to express himself in huge, powerful, often opaque epics. As early as 1794 the Bard as a Welsh Taliesin figure was a powerful force in Blake's poetry:

> *Hear the voice of the Bard!*
> *Who Present, Past and Future, sees;*
> *Whose ears have heard*
> *The Holy Word*
> *That walked among the ancient trees.*

And the frame of his poem *Milton* (1804–8) is similarly built around the Taliesin Bard of Welsh tradition. It explores the nature of over-arching poetic inspiration, similar to the Welsh *Awen* (spirit) which governed the Welsh poets. In the poem, Milton has walked about Eternity a hundred years, returned to the Deep of Earth to redeem her and to report back to the Heavens of Albion. 'Where hadst thou this terrible song?' The Bard replies 'I am Inspired! Poetic Genius is Divine Humanity! . . . So let Milton the awful man, terrific among the Sons of Albion, come into my hand', *here*, where 'the Eternal great Humanity Divine planted his Paradise' . . . for did not those feet in ancient time walk upon these mountains green?

Blake was to despise Druidism as the first organized, hierarchical and hence lying religion and to give the daughters of his fearful Reason – *Urizen*, who was to dominate the poem-cycle – the very colours of Iolo's *Gorsedd* of Welsh Bards. 'Your ancestors derived their origin from Abraham, Heber, Shem and Noah who were Druids,' Blake addressed the Jews in *Jerusalem*; Druid temples (the Patriarchal Pillars) over the whole earth bore witness to this. He was arguing rather like an eighteenth-century Welsh historian, who announced in Welsh, 'Saturn was a Welshman, Jupiter was a Welshman, Mercury was a Welshman'! Blake perceived Britain to have been the seat of the earliest religion, that of the biblical Patriarchs. This degenerated into Druidism which he saw as a failure of man's perception; aspects of the natural order had been elevated into a systemic religion, with a regulatory God which imprisoned man in the prototype of the 'mind-forg'd manacles'.

Blake used Pughe's material of 1809 for his own cosmic purposes. The Fall of Arthur was a symbol for the dissolution of Albion the Eternal Man at the Fall, which was also the Creation. He dissolved into the four components of his being. The Three Britons of his giant painting represented three of the four *Zoas* or human faculties: pathos (*Luvah*), power or sublimity (*Tharmas*) and reason (*Urizen*). The fourth was the ubiquitous *Los* – vision or existence. *Los* was like to the Son of God, Blake says: he was Albion himself. 'The giant Albion was Patriarch of the Atlantic, he is the Atlas of the Greeks . . . the stories of Arthur are the acts of Albion, applied to a prince of the fifth century who conquered Europe and held the empire of the world in the dark ages.'

This breathtaking perception of Arthur as a symbol of humanity, shot through with a mystic vision of aboriginal human unity centred on Albion – Britain – was the most unexpected and rapid reincarnation the Hero of the Britons ever experienced.

Blake's unique vision could have no real sequel. It was a product of his inimitable genius and the interplay between long-established British radicalism and the French Revolution. It thundered in the margins during Britain's generation-long war against Revolutionary France and Napoleon, the period in which Britain, winning supremacy at sea, began to pull away from Europe into world empire. The 'British Nation', remorselessly being created, over the protests of radicals, during the eighteenth century and the French wars (when 'God Save the King' grew from a Tory election song into a British national anthem, rooted in Wales and Scotland almost as fully as in England), ran into extreme social tension in the early nineteenth century before pulling out into the pudding-time of mid-Victorian prosperity. And throughout the period, the new Romanticism bred an intensifying interest in the British past, particularly the remote past, an unexpected consequence of which was the enthronement of King Arthur as the first, national hero of the new 'British'.

The great classical school of history, of which Edward Gibbon was an exemplar, began to be challenged by new writers who started to explore the Middle Ages, which were already being more fully documented by those very historians. But the real impact of the new, intense interest in the British past was on history painting, which became increasingly popular from the 1760s onward. Richard Barber has registered sharply the increasing concern with accuracy in the depiction of people and dress, and the realism that characterized the highly influential work of Joseph Strutt, and has argued convincingly that this in turn had a profound effect on writing. Serious scholarship began to be applied to the poems and plays of the past, exemplified by Bishop Percy's *Reliques of Old English Poetry*, which generated a spate of studies and coincided with the swelling tide of the Gothic Revival in architecture. These were the years of Walter Scott's *Waverley* novels, with their apparently realistic analysis of the past.

On this tide Arthur rode back into public consciousness. Yet, in so far as can be ascertained, although there were three editions of Malory's *Morte d'Arthur* published during 1816 and 1817, there were no other editions before 1858. Malory was to have an effect on Tennyson, but it is possible that the first modern Arthurian literature drew on quite other sources. There was a run of republished medieval English romances of mediocre quality and a few poems, including one by Walter Scott, and most interested readers probably got their first introduction to Arthur from modestly priced editions of George Ellis's *Specimens of Early English Poetry* and a translation of Geoffrey of Monmouth's memorable *British History*. Not until taste shifted towards narrative poems concentrating on historic figures or ideals did the Hero enter his new Kingdom.

All the more remarkable that one of the more instantly recognizable and attractive books to appear in these years was a satire by Thomas Love Peacock, *The Misfortunes of Elphin*, published in 1829, in which he used Arthurian romance to make a humorous assault on the old parliamentary system. A renowned wit, a friend of Shelley and, to a

---

• A painting inspired by Tennyson's first Arthurian poem –
The Lady of Shalott by William Holman Hunt, 1905.

modern reader, an immediately congenial writer, Peacock was attracted to Wales and, married to a 'white Snowdonian antelope', he was a scholar with a very considerable knowledge of old Welsh poetry. In his novel he drew his characters entirely from Welsh legends. A central episode is the abduction of Guinevere by Melwas, king of Somerset, to Glastonbury, which is in the original form of the story and one of the oldest Arthurian tales. Using this framework to pillory the country's old franchise system, he created an original Arthurian story which is one of the best.

A couple of years later, however, *The Lady of Shalott* came from the pen of Alfred Tennyson. He was the man who became 'poetry' to the Victorians – and who was to make Arthur into the greatest hero of nineteenth-century Britain, rooting him in the mind and memory of generations. Tennyson had lived through an unhappy childhood in a riven clerical household and in 1833 suffered deeply at the premature death of Arthur Hallam, with whom he had enjoyed a friendship as close as that of Lancelot and Galahault, and whom he commemorated in *In Memoriam*. He told his son, 'The vision of an ideal Arthur had come upon me when, little more than a boy, I first lighted upon Malory.' Yet *The Lady of Shalott*, his first Arthurian poem, was drawn from an Italian novelette and though the story was based on the Elaine of Malory's Lancelot and Elaine, Tennyson said that in 1832 he had never heard of the Maid of Astolat or Elaine, and that he chose the name Shalott because it had a 'softer sound' than the original Scalott. The poem was dismissed when it first appeared, and the best Tennyson scholars remain uneasy about it, but it has captivated millions (including myself) with its memorable myth in which the wish to face reality and not to face it cracks the mirror.

> *From the bank and from the river*
> *He flash'd into the crystal mirror,*
> *'Tirra lirra', by the river*
> > *Sang Sir Lancelot.*
>
> *She left the web, she left the loom,*
> *She made three paces thro' the room,*
> *She saw the water-lily bloom,*
> *She saw the helmet and the plume,*
> > *She look'd down to Camelot.*
> *Out flew the web and floated wide;*
> *The mirror crack'd from side to side;*
> *'The curse is come upon me', cried*
> > *The Lady of Shalott.*

Within a year of *The Lady of Shalott* Tennyson was drafting the sketch of an epic on King Arthur at the sacred mount of Camelot in the drowned kingdom of Lyonesse, where only the Scilly Isles now remain and where all was hollow below and would one day crumble. Another draft poem in the same year made Arthur symbolize religious faith: as in the Welsh tradition, he had three Guineveres, the first representing primitive Christianity, the second Roman Catholicism and the third, who was to be taken by Mordred, scepticism. Merlin was to symbolize science, Excalibur war, the Lady of the Lake evil and the Round Table liberal institutions. There were other poetic plans, too, but in 1842 he published three more Arthurian poems – *Sir Lancelot and Queen Guinevere, Sir Galahad* and *Morte d'Arthur*. The adverse critical reaction to the last stopped him in his tracks.

Tennyson wrote *Morte d'Arthur* under the immediate impact of Hallam's death and he followed Malory almost religiously.

> *So all day long the noise of battle roll'd*
> *Among the mountains by the winter sea;*
> *Until King Arthur's table, man by man,*
> *Had fallen in Lyonesse about their Lord.*

After beginning by evoking the battle of Camlan, he goes on to describe Bedevere throwing Excalibur to the hand in white samite in the lake and the appearance of the barge with the three queens. The poem is memorable and a version was to reappear in his *Idylls of the King*, but at the time Arthurian stories were little known and the reception put Tennyson off his epic for seventeen years. Perhaps the identification with Hallam was rather too pointed and it did not help that he incorporated a scene set in a university hall where friends dismissed the possibility of such an epic, but the poet, dreaming, has a vision of the coming by barge of the new husband to Queen Victoria, the Prince Regent Albert of Saxe-Coburg, who was known to be a cultivated patron of the arts. Tennyson saw him as

> *King Arthur, like a modern gentleman*
> *Of stateliest port: and all the people cried,*
> *'Arthur is come again: he cannot die.'*

This had decidedly comic overtones and Swinburne wickedly nicknamed the poem *Morte d'Albert*. Though in the event, the Prince Regent was to relieve Tennyson of the burden for many years.

For, in 1834, a great fire attacked the Houses of Parliament, destroying the Commons chamber and badly damaging the Lords. For years Members of Parliament had been discontented with the old huddle of buildings by the Thames and the fire gave the chance to build anew, just when the Reform Act of 1832 had liberated and concentrated the reform energies of a newly enfranchised middle class. Amid emergency political measures and that continuous controversy which heralded the coming of democracy, a commission was appointed to award an architectural prize for a Houses of Parliament design in either Gothic or Elizabethan style. Amid further controversy, Charles Barry won, his assistant being the redoubtable Edward Pugin. So the present cherished Gothic structure began to arise on Thames-bank. Or rather, it didn't! By 1842 Barry was just setting the foundations. In a plethora of irritated committees, a Fine Arts Commission was finally appointed in 1841 to consider the decoration of the interior. This turned out to be a critical appointment. The Commission was moved by the social spirit of the time – the time that created elementary schools, public libraries, art museums – and the walls of the new Palace of Westminster seemed ideal to present to the public a national art which would tell the story of the nation at the very seat of government. The vogue for History Painting was at its peak; Walter Scott's novels and Macaulay's *History of England* were setting the fashion. The Commission was an external body mingling parliamentarians with others of the great and the good. It included Melbourne, Palmerston and Peel, Henry Hallam the historian – father of Tennyson's young friend Arthur – Samuel Rogers the poet and Charles Eastlake its devoted secretary. As chairman, it chose Albert, the Prince Consort.

The choice of Prince Albert, though resident for only a year, was inspired. He was very well educated, had an instinct for the arts, was much travelled and had experience of the history paintings of the Nazarene school of Germans in Italy; indeed he had tried his own hand at painting. His influence on British arts, design and manufacture would find expression in the Great Exhibition of 1851 when Britain paraded its power before a suitably abashed world. The Prince did not get on with Barry and was weak on architecture, but he revelled in painting and for the new Parliament favoured fresco, an ancient wall decoration but one which provoked much controversy, then and since.

In 1845, after public competitions which aroused much enthusiasm, the first fresco commission went to William Dyce of Aberdeen, one of the new Scottish school of history painters who became director of the Government School of Design. And in 1848 Dyce was given the story of King Arthur as the fresco theme for the Royal Robing Room of the House of Lords. The choice of Arthur is a surprise; it can only be assigned to foresight. Though Malory was arousing new interest and Tennyson's *Morte d'Arthur* had appeared, most of the influential Arthurian works did not come out until the

• *Religion*, one of the five Malory-based frescoes which
William Dyce painted for the House of Lords Robing Room,
showing the vision of Sir Galahad, Perceval and Sir Bors
near the end of the Grail quest.

project was well under way. 'The feeling that Arthur was the first of our national heroes,' says one English critic, 'has a notable ancestry,' and he duly cites Edward III, with his Round Table at Windsor, but he then falls back on more recent work in explanation. In fact, it seems clear that the Robing Room of the Lords was itself a major factor in the Arthurian revival.

This room was truly the heart of government at the time – the Lords were then rather more significant than the Commons – and to this day it remains the room where the Sovereign annually assumes the Royal Parliamentary Robes and the Imperial State Crown, before walking in procession through the Royal Gallery, preceded by the Great Officers of State, and entering the Chamber of the House of Lords for the State Opening of Parliament. Nothing could be more redolent of our Gothic constitution.

Certainly Dyce had a terrible Gothic job on his hands. He was delayed by the need to be exact over 'a great quantity of chain mail' and had endless troubles with the painting itself. In the end he was spending so much time on the work that his address was given out by the Royal Academy as the Royal Robing Room, House of Lords. When he died in 1864, sixteen years after his commission, he had completed only four of the intended five large frescoes: 'Courtesy', with Sir Tristan harping to Iseult; 'Mercy', where Sir Gawain, who had cut off a lady's head by misadventure, swears to be merciful and 'never to be against ladies'; 'Religion', the vision of the Grail by Sir Galahad, Sir Perceval and Sir Bors; and 'Generosity', illustrating Lancelot's courtesy when he saves King Arthur after he has been unhorsed by Sir Bors at the siege of *Joyeuse Garde*. The fifth fresco, 'Hospitality', was completed by C. W. Cope and displays Sir Tristan being admitted to the Round Table.

These frescoes, which are notably light on Arthur himself, were based wholly on Malory's *Le Morte d'Arthur*, though one suspects the later Tennyson was having an effect. They are striking but unremarkable. Far different are the eighteen bas-reliefs carved in oak by H. H. Armstead, a sculptor of European reputation. Commissioned in 1866 to supplement Dyce's work, they, too, were derived from Malory and tell the basic story of Arthur through to his removal to Avalon, followed by Galahad's life to his transport to Heaven. Almost weirdly vivid, they have a graphic intensity which prompted a contemporary critic to compare them with the work of Blake. Armstead's world is really the world of the Dark Ages and of Merlin.

To this day, they are greeted by public acclaim, a tribute from a triumphant Britain to Arthur, its first Hero in what is still the symbolic heart of its governance.

The prolific Tennyson had been made Poet Laureate in 1850, largely because of Prince Albert's admiration of *In Memoriam*; he in turn was a dedicated follower of the Prince. No doubt influenced by the activity in the House of Lords, he returned to his Arthurian epic in 1855 and in 1859 published *Enid, Vivien, Elaine* and *Guinevere* as the first instalments of his *Idylls of the King*. They were greeted this time with popular applause, but the poet was hardly at the beginning of his enterprise. He worked on Malory, Layamon, the translation of *The Mabinogion*, on old chronicles, French romances, Celtic folklore. He toured Wales, meditated on the Holy Grail and was influenced by Robert Hawker, a Cornish vicar and the author of *And shall Trelawny die?*.

In December 1861 Prince Albert died prematurely, another Arthur Hallam. Princess Alice wished that Tennyson would 'idealize' her father in verse which he could not literally do, but in 1862, when he visited Queen Victoria at Osborne, the growing

Idylls were reorientated as virtually Laureate work. Arthur began to assume substance, 'an Albertus Redivivus resembling the Consort even in looks'. In this spirit, he published the next instalments in 1869: *The Coming of Arthur, The Holy Grail, Pelleas and Ettarre* and *The Passing of Arthur*.

In the meantime the monarchy had slumped into a crisis; Victoria withdrew into a surly retirement, while English republicanism grew in strength. Tennyson wrote against the trend. In 1871 came the French defeat in the Franco-Prussian War and the Paris Commune; the poet was appalled at 'the red fool-fury of the Seine' and what he saw as the corruption of French literature which had ruined French morale. He incorporated an extraordinary explosion of hatred against it into one of the last of the Arthur sequence, *The Last Tournament* – on the self-inflicted decline of knighthood – which he finished in 1871. Arthur is preparing for the 'Tournament of the Dead Innocence', when one of his 'churls' appears, horribly mutilated. Arthur cries:

> *'My churl, for whom Christ died, what evil beast*
> *Hath drawn his claws athwart thy face? or fiend?*
> *Man was it who marr'd heaven's image in thee thus?'*

The churl replies that it was the Red Knight – 'Some hold he was a table-knight of thine' – who is evil personified and, through the ravished churl, sends Arthur a message:

> *'Tell thou the King and all his liars, that I*
> *Have founded my Round Table in the North,*
> *And whatsoever his own knights have sworn*
> *My knights have sworn to counter to it – and say*
> *My tower is full of harlots, like his court,*
> *But mine are worthier, seeing they profess*
> *To be none other than themselves – and say*
> *My knights are all adulterers, like his own,*
> *But mine are truer, seeing they profess*
> *To be none other; and say his hour is come,*
> *The heathen are upon him, his long lance*
> *Broken and his Excalibur a straw.'*

• *Overleaf* Tapestries woven by William Morris and Co. from designs by Edward Burne-Jones: 'The Summons', 1898–9, calling the Knights of the Round Table to the Quest for the Grail and (below) 'The Attainment: The Vision of the Holy Grail', 1895–6.

And in a dream of Tristram's, Arthur comes to confront the Red Knight – 'Arthur knew the voice' – and let the drunkard kill himself, overbalancing head-heavy into a swamp. . .

> . . . _then the knights, who watch'd him, roar'd_
> _And shouted and leapt down upon the fall'n;_
> _There trampled out his face from being known,_
> _And sank his head in mire, and slimed themselves;_
> _Nor heard the King for their own cries, but sprang_
> _Thro' open doors, and swording right and left_
> _Men, women, on their sodden faces, hurl'd_
> _The tables over and the wines, and slew_
> _Till all the rafters rang with woman-yells,_
> _And all the pavement streamed with massacre:_

And they fired the tower –

> _So all the ways were safe from shore to shore,_
> _But in the heart of Arthur pain was lord._

This nasty, almost sickly paranoid passage is nevertheless an interesting play of opposites. The Red Knight and his degenerate brood might have been spawned by Red Paris, but his stronghold is in 'the North' and he evokes a frightening echo in the disintegrating Round Table. At the heart of the mature Tennyson, as in the mature Yeats, there is a dread, a chill, which threatens his very ideal and which in the completed version of the _Idylls_ he permits to remain.

In the immediate future, the political threat passed. The Prince of Wales contracted typhoid and the upsurge of popular emotion swept anti-royalism away. When Tennyson published almost the final version of the _Idylls_ in 1872, he included a passionately loyal address to the queen, summoning up Albert, and denounced the radicals, hailing England as already possessing 'a slowly-grown and crowned republic'. And when the full _Idylls of the King_ was published in 1885, to quote the redoubtable

---

• _Right_ A Gustav Doré illustration for the story of Geraint and Enid in Tennyson's _Idylls of the King._

• _Pages 202 and 203_ One of the many Victorian and Edwardian paintings inspired by Arthurian poetry, _Lancelot and Guinevere_ by Herbert Draper (1864–1920).

Geoffrey Ashe: 'His colossal prestige and mass readership ensured that the coincidence of events would be fruitful. A nation receptive to royalism again was presented, just at the right moment, with its Laureate's unfolded daydream of Christian monarchy, firmly linked to the queen and her almost canonised husband.'

Tennyson worked hard at the *Idylls*, not least at the old Welsh roots, constantly reshaping them to make Arthur more the centrepiece, the social context more significant. He complained about the heavy-handedness of reviews: 'They have taken my hobby and ridden it too hard . . . there is no single fact or incident in the *Idylls*, however seemingly mystical, which cannot be explained . . . poetry is like shot-silk.' The drift of the *Idylls* is clear. 'The whole,' he said, 'is the dream of man coming into practical life and ruined by one sin . . . it is the history . . . of a whole cycle of generations.' On his eightieth birthday he said: 'My meaning in the *Idylls of the King* was spiritual. I took the legendary stories of the Round Table as illustrations. I intended Arthur to represent the Ideal Soul of Man coming into contact with the warring elements of the flesh.'

Evil is the Saxons and the Waste Land which Arthur has to master. The Eternal making itself real is expressed in an institution: Christian marriage. In a complete break with tradition, respectable wedlock is built into the Round Table – rather like Victoria's court – but is undermined by sensual corruption, symbolized by Guinevere and Lancelot, and by spiritual deception: the Grail inspires spiritual strivings of the wrong sort (too Catholic?). Religious monarchy is the ideal, but glory gives way to tragedy and finally the fabric collapses. Yet there is hope of a Return; Arthur is immortal and offers a deathless model.

The popularity of Tennyson's work is difficult to overstress. It was perhaps the most successful Arthurian poem ever written, read by literally millions. It put the British reading public in possession of Arthur as interpreted by Tennyson, and made a particular conquest in painting, engraving, the arts in general. The celebrated photographer Julia Margaret Cameron made two volumes of photographs, one wholly devoted to the *Idylls*; friends posed for parts, her husband was Arthur. Gustave Doré's large volumes illustrating Tennyson were among the most popular editions.

Tennyson's faults are patent and though his poetry is no longer generally to our taste, it is full of memorable moments. My own favourite is the account of Bedivere after Arthur, on his barge with his queens, has become 'one black dot against the verge of dawn, And on the mere the wailing died away . . .'

• A photograph by Julia Margaret Cameron depicting
Tennyson's lines 'So like a shatter'd column lay the King'
from 'The Passing of Arthur' in *Idylls of the King*.

Then loudly cried the bold Sir Bedivere:
'Ah! my Lord Arthur, whither shall I go?
Where shall I hide my forehead and my eyes?
For now I see the true old times are dead,
When every morning brought a noble chance,
And every chance brought out a noble knight. . .
But now the whole Round Table is dissolved
Which was an image of the mighty world,
And I, the last, go forth companionless,
And the days darken round me, and the years,
Among new men, strange faces, other minds.'

Other major writers and artists were moved by the same themes. William Morris, who had read Malory at an early age, responded at once to Tennyson's early lyrics. In 1854 his associate Edward Burne-Jones told a friend to learn Tennyson's *Sir Galahad* by heart before joining the chivalric order which he and William Morris proposed to found. Morris was the poet among them and his handful of lyrics, published in a collection of 1858, were subtle studies of mood and character, culminating in his 'Defence of Guinevere':

And every morn I scarce could pray at all,
For Launcelot's red-gold hair would play,
Instead of sunlight, on the painted wall,
Mingled with dreams of what the priest did say . . .

His poems were full of colour and dominated by a sense that, as one character says, 'my life went wrong.' But Morris broke with his fellow pre-Raphaelites and with Tennyson's Arthur. A committed socialist, he moved away from the aristocratic world to English peasants and Germanic heroes.

His pre-Raphaelite colleagues continued, like Morris, to nurture medievalism, but they concentrated on an exploration of emotion in contrast to idyllic settings. Their major achievement was painting. In a striking series of frescoes for the Oxford Union in 1857–58, Dante Gabriel Rossetti, like Morris, showed a feeling for the tragic, notably in his *Failure of Sir Launcelot to Achieve the Grail*, while his oil paintings and his

• *Queen Guinevere* by William Morris, 1858. Morris founded with Edward Burne-Jones a chivalric order inspired by Tennyson's poems.

watercolours, like Morris's poetry, concentrate on the tragic moment, as in *Galahad at the Ruined Chapel*. Edward Burne-Jones, on the other hand, preferred the spiritual side and returned constantly to the theme of the Holy Grail. He designed a splendid series of tapestries on the Grail quest which were manufactured by Morris and Co.

Public taste was by now firmly wedded to narrative poetry and there was one gap in the legends, left by Malory's and Tennyson's uneasiness with the original love story of Tristan and Iseult. Matthew Arnold was moved by a single article in the *Revue de Paris* to work on it, following up with a reading of the 1817 edition of Malory. His story is original, beginning at Tristram's death-bed and working through flashbacks, and has striking touches, but it is charged with a highly ambivalent attitude to love itself:

> And yet, I swear, it angers me to see
> How this fool passion gulls men potently;
> Being, in truth, but a diseased unrest,
> And an unnatural overheat at best.

'Fool passion' there was in plenty in the work of Algernon Swinburne, an English Gottfried, whose personal declamations of his passionate poems, jumping up and down on a sofa, tended to the comic. His poetry has its greatness. He read widely, claiming that Wagner's opera was a major influence. He presented a series of set-pieces and concentrated utterly on what he saw as the essence of Tristan – primal passion – as in the lovers' last kiss:

> . . . and her head
> Bowed, as to reach the spring that slakes all drouth;
> And their four lips became one silent mouth.

As in the earliest tales, Swinburne makes Tristan a seafarer, and the sea looms over everything; the love potion is drunk during a storm and in *Iseult at Tintagel* the lone lover looks at their life:

> And all their past came wailing in the wind,
> And all their future thundered in the sea.

Swinburne, who saw himself as an anti-Tennyson, was deliberately provocative, but he highlights crippling weaknesses in the Poet Laureate. To eliminate the very stuff of the love-stories of the 'Matter of Britain', to make Arthur a blameless king, to skirt around the meaning of Guinevere and Tristan, to insist on the married love of the knights and confront it with the caricature of the Red Knight – all this might win the praise of Mr Gladstone and make the poet universally acceptable in the best circles, but it removed one vital aspect of reality from the cycle.

So did his single-minded dedication to the monarchy, to the memory of Prince Albert. Geoffrey Ashe makes a powerful case for the prosecution. Arthur's Britain, at the hands of Tennyson, played an appreciable part in reviving the glamour of the monarchy, long in default, by fostering that peculiar British mentality which sees medieval ritual and feudal monarchy co-existing with democracy – an attitude of mind under threat only in our own day. 'No continental monarchy found a Tennyson.' In the long run, it led to a dead end. It could only decline into 'children's books, romantic little societies, the gift-shops and pastiche Hall of Chivalry at Tintagel'.

This is true. The extent of Tennyson's achievement cannot, however, be gainsaid. He captivated millions in his time. Most people's perception of Arthur was filtered through him. Some of his passages are independent of time and there is some sense in him of a striving back towards British roots, towards a reality which evades much of the literature. In a sense, with Tennyson, one long tradition of Arthurian writing comes to an end. The British public were put in possession of their patrimony and, charged with the memories of it, they entered the testing time of the twentieth century, still with an echo in the mind of

> . . . *that gray king, whose name, a ghost,*
> *Streams like a cloud, man-shaped, from mountain peak*
> *And cleaves to cairn and cromlech still.*

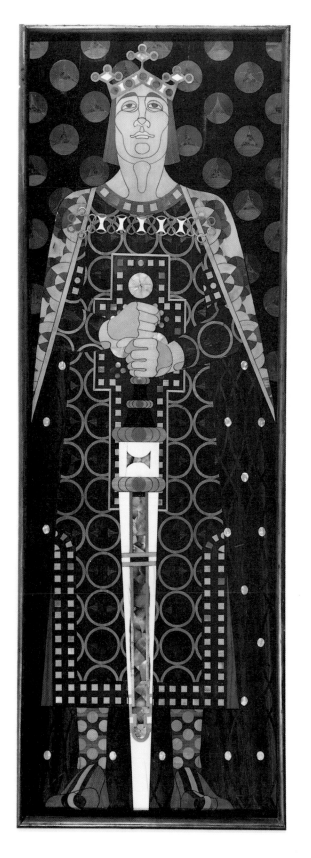

CHAPTER TWELVE
... AND·FUTURE·KING?

How has Arthur fared since Tennyson, among 'new men, strange faces, other minds'? There has been a veritable explosion in Arthurian studies, a torrent of books, ranging from scholarly work to the wildest speculation. Arthurian societies jostle international Arthurian congresses and Glastonbury festivals. Alternative religions and histories find multiple expression through the Hero. The legends, sometimes disguised, filter through comic books, cartoons, films, video games, theatrical experiences.

Richard Barber, a penetrating analyst of Arthurian writing, calculates that when the first edition of his major study, *King Arthur: Hero and Legend*, appeared in 1961, the International Arthurian Society had issued twelve volumes of its annual listing of scholarship on Arthur, including some 2500 items; in 1986, at the time of the current edition, there were another twenty-two volumes listing some 11 000 further books, articles and reviews. As for work that could not be described as scholarly, the reader has difficulty finding his feet, let alone his head.

Yet I feel a certain sense of doom. The major interest of most non-scholarly work – and of some scholarly work, too – lies in the authors rather than the subject. This may always have been true, but now the very diffusion of the legends and the acceleration, multiplication, transformation of their interpretations threaten a kind of dissolution.

Most of the writers have been British. Richard Barber, ever hawk-eyed for Arthurian writing, has drawn our attention to several French and German writers and composers of the last century and this, and to an American, E. A. Robinson, whose Pulitzer Prize winning poetry between 1917 and 1927 seems to have been unjustly neglected. And there is of course Wagner, who based his operas on serious research. But, in essence, the phenomenon has been insular. Arthur in our own day had been a peculiarly British hero.

• King Arthur and Sir Lancelot depicted in marquetry panels
designed by Josef Engelhart in Vienna in 1904.

Drama offers an index to one visible shift – towards a historical Arthur derived from the increasing volume of scholarship. Arthur Symons's *Tristan and Iseult* of 1917 was a powerful treatment of love, with Iseult the dominating figure; and in 1923 there appeared Laurence Binyon's *Arthur*, though it does not realize its hero. Thomas Hardy's play, *The Famous Tragedy of the Queen of Cornwall* (1923), is a curious attempt to tell the story of Tristan and Iseult (the latter killing Mark) in terms of the fifth century, complete with archaic language and Greek choruses; it finds it hard to escape from Hardy's own Wessex. These plays, however odd, remain embedded in the tradition established in the nineteenth century.

Moving ahead, however, to 1955 and *The Long Sunset* of R. C. Sherriff (of *Journey's End*), Arthur, placed early in the fifth century, becomes an ambiguous barbarian warlord to whom, with Gawain, some imperial Roman power has been transferred. Though not very successful, it at least registers the advance in historical knowledge.

In 1972 *The Island of the Mighty* by John Arden and Margaretta D'Arcy was performed at the Aldwych theatre by the Royal Shakespeare Company. An impressive production, it was based on historical evidence, dealt with Arthur, Merlin, Taliesin and others, and developed into a polemic against British imperialism in Ireland. The piece became famous because Arden and D'Arcy quarrelled with the producer and cast, were ejected from rehearsals and promptly picketed the stage door!

That people can observe advances in historical knowledge and still build a new structure of imagination on them is clear from several of the newer theatrical companies. For example, *Brith Gof*, a Welsh touring company of international repute, presented in 1993–94 an 'experience', with audience participation and multi-media techniques, which was apparently based on Malory and centred on Arthur's last days. The future, with its use of television, 'virtual reality' techniques and interactive modes, seems to offer endless variety, at least superficially – though how much difference such technology can make to the underlying themes, apart from short circuiting them altogether, is a moot point.

The historical drive has been less clear in poetry. T. S. Eliot's *The Waste Land* was based on Jessie Weston's theories of an underlying pagan or semi-pagan presence and made use of Arthurian themes without the personnel, while John Masefield's *Midsummer Night* (1927) made unusual use of Welsh sources, but is only partially successful. There are two powerful poetic essays. Charles Williams's *Taliessin through Logres* (with two s's in Taliesin!) and *The Region of the Summer Stars* are extensions of Tennyson and use the analogue of a female body for the Roman and Byzantine empires with, beyond Logres, the 'sea-wood' of Broceliande, Carbonek the Grail castle and Sarras, home of the Grail. Against this background, the legend is played out and ends tragically. But the poetry is so intensely religious and so obscure in its vocabulary (it needed a commentary by C. S. Lewis) that it remains a specialist's choice. Much the same is true of the work of David Jones, the Welsh poet and painter, whose many, heavily annotated references to Welsh Arthurian tradition and Malory in *In Parenthesis* (1937) and *The Anathemata* (1952) demand impossible knowledge of the general reader.

The most successful and genial Arthurian work of our day has without a doubt been that of T. H. White. A retired teacher with a profound knowledge of animals and the outdoors, and a dislike of the twentieth century, White was a strange man with a weird and wonderful sense of humour. His first book, *The Sword in the Stone* (1938), has an excited, youthful feeling and remains understandably popular. After twenty more years of work and trouble with publishers, including the forced deletion of a diatribe against war, in 1958 he published several of his books as a tetralogy, *The Once and Future King*, which was a best-seller. It had the dubious distinction of serving as model for the musical and then the film, *Camelot* (Richard Barber suggests it was better served by Walt Disney's cute cartoon treatment).

White went back to Malory, but inverted the legend. The whole Middle Ages is present at the same time; actual monarchs appear as fictitious shadows of Arthur, who himself is no 'distressed Briton hopping about in a suit of woad', he is a Plantagenet with Saxon serfs; the Celts are his enemies! White was uneasy with Guinevere and the Holy Grail, but within this compass, his imagination and humour are given free play. Arthur grows from the boy Wart into the king, tutored by Merlyn (with a y), who is something of a self-portrait. Merlyn goes on being a key figure. He has a gift for remembering the future while forgetting the past – he is liable to talk about Mafeking and top-hats – and his multiple time-scale becomes thematic. In White's hands, Malory's characters acquire fresh life. All the books are enlivened by a sense of humour: the Saracen knight Palomides speaks babu English and as for the Round Table:

> 'You could never sit a hundred and fifty knights at a round table. Let me see . . .'
>
> Merlyn, who hardly ever interfered in the arguments now, but sat with his hands folded on his stomach and beamed, helped Kay out of the difficulty.
>
> 'It would need to be about fifty yards across,' he said. 'You do it by $2\pi r$.'

– which catches precisely the tone of Geoffrey of Monmouth's Merlin.

And the Round Table is in the end shattered because 'Mordred is using guns'. 'Now that the guns have come,' said Arthur, 'the Table is over.'

The most moving passage comes in *The Candle in the Wind*, where an ailing Arthur, in a tent, converses with a page boy, 'fresh and decent', Tom of Newbold Revel – who is in fact Sir Thomas Malory!

Arthur Put it like this. There was a king once, called Arthur. That is me. When he came to the throne of England, he found that all the kings and barons were fighting against each other like madmen and, as they could afford to fight in expensive suits of armour, there was practically nothing which could stop them from doing what they pleased. They did a lot of bad things, because they lived by force. Now this king had an idea and the idea was that force ought to be used, if it were used at all, on behalf of justice, not on its own account. Follow this, young boy. He thought that if he could get his barons fighting for truth, and to help weak people and to redress wrongs, then their fighting might not be such a bad thing after all. So he gathered together all the true and kindly people he knew and he dressed them in armour and taught them this idea and sat them down at a Round Table and King Arthur loved his Table with all his heart.
Page I think it was a good idea, my lord.
Arthur It was and it was not. God knows . . . things went wrong. The Table split into factions, a bitter war began, and all were killed. . . My idea of these knights was a sort of candle. . . I have carried it for many years with a hand to shield it from the wind. I am giving you the candle now – you won't let it out.
Page It will burn.

Geoffrey Ashe sees *The Once and Future King* as possibly a farewell appearance of Arthur's 'visionary kingdom'. He may be right. He says even White's denial of the historical reality marks a transition; the Fact is coming into its own – and here he is without doubt correct.

The volume of scholarly study of both the historical Arthur and his legend reached such a pitch by 1959 that Roger Sherman Loomis, himself a prolific and creative writer on Arthur, helped by Professors Jean Frappier and Eugene Vinaver, edited the first of the 'landmark books', *Arthurian Literature in the Middle Ages*, to which thirty-four scholars from all over Europe and the USA contributed. This work has become

• An Edwardian idealized image of the beautiful young warrior king – *King Arthur* by Charles Ernest Butler, 1903.

something of a bible. Supplemented by international congresses and other symposia, its first modernization has appeared in *The Arthur of the Welsh*, edited in 1991 by Rachel Bromwich, A. O. H. Jarman and Brynley F. Roberts. Books such as these have added a whole new dimension to our understanding (and removed some from it, too!). This book itself would be impossible without them. The process will no doubt go on – though one takes leave to doubt how much our understanding will benefit.

Scores more books have appeared, arguing from some historical evidence or other for some identification or other with persons or places. Accompanying this has been an effort to map all those places which claim an Arthurian connection. In the illustrated *A Travellers' Guide to the Kingdoms of Arthur* (1983) by Neil Fairbairn, the south of England claims sixteen sites, Brittany seventeen, the north of England and Scotland thirty-four, the south-west fifty-one and Wales fifty-four.

In some of these books, the authors seem hell-bent on slaking their own thirst for a hero-figure rather than anything else. This seems true of Nikolai Tolstoy's *The Quest for Merlin* (1985), which is firmly grounded in historical evidence up to the point where it takes off into an obsessive quest, which apparently tries to pinpoint an individual to one grotto in Scotland! Even in one of the better attempts to identify Arthur, Graham Phillips and Martin Keatman's *King Arthur: The True Story* (1992), a fine enquiry into the evidence, which singles out Powys as Arthur's probable centre – an opinion with which I have considerable sympathy – goes on to place a man and a dynasty, and identify places, in a process which loses at least this reader. I am reminded of the two gentlemen who sold up everything they had to finance their campaign to convince the world that Arthur was buried in Glamorgan – and conceived a violent hatred of the historical profession in its failure!

Then there are the works of fiction based on historical research, such as Alfred Duggan's *Conscience of the King* (1951), which sees Arthur through the eyes of the West Saxon dynasty as the man who used heavy cavalry and leads into Duggan's discussion of the British failure to maintain the horse-breed. Or Meriel Trevor's *The Last of Britain* (1956), set among the Britons immediately after Arthur's disappearance, which has been criticized by Geoffrey Ashe for making the world-weary inhabitants of Bath and Gloucester insufficiently 'Celtic', indistinguishable from any other world-weary inhabitants of the late Roman Empire; I think, however, that by that time most of the Romans in Britain were in fact Britons!

In 1980 the American Marion Bradley brought out *The Mists of Avalon*, a feminist version of the legend in which women are the central figures. Guinevere is once again Gwenhwyfar, as in the original Welsh; a female angel shows her the Holy Grail. And the conclusion is unavoidable:

No, she thought . . . Arthur was wrong. You cannot call down God to serve your own purposes this way . . . And then she wondered – What is wrong with me, that I am thinking to criticize Arthur or even the bishop for what they did? Yet then with new strength she thought – By God, yes! They are not God, they are only men, and their purposes are not sacred.

Earlier, in 1963, Rosemary Sutcliff's *Sword at Sunset* was perhaps the best of the history-based fiction. It has been praised by both Richard Barber and Geoffrey Ashe and in fact Sutcliff follows the precise trajectory of the thought of Geoffrey Ashe. For Geoffrey Ashe towers over the field of both historical scholarship and historically based fiction. An admirable man, he believes in a historical Arthur (his latest candidate being Riothamus, king of the Bretons) and he has presided indefatigably over archaeological digs, festivals, society meetings and television presentations, enrolling historians and archaeologists in the cause. A historian who is sceptically aware of the kind of speculations historians normally shun – and ready to jettison them when necessary – he is something of a hero to the present writer and all his many books can be recommended, in particular *The Quest for Arthur's Britain* (1968), which he edited and in large part wrote, with the help of archaeologists Leslie Alcock, C. A. Ralegh Radford and Philip Rahtz. Leslie Alcock himself, in his *Arthur's Britain* (1971), makes splendid reading.

A historian may be forgiven for favouring his own kind! But I do not know what I or my colleagues would make of the current wave of 'alternative' approaches to history, medicine, culture and society, which are centred on Glastonbury and are focused as much on the Druids and Merlin as on Arthur. Behind them lies a notion of 'hidden ideas' in the legend cycle, which has produced non-Christian work advocating a green, feminist and pagan alternative. Some of its adherents have engaged in pitched battles with the police at Stonehenge over 'our heritage'.

In fact, this trend is a reminder of those old Bronze Age Gods of the Britons who figure in the Arthurian legends as semi-magical persons in Arthur's entourage or as the people he and his men encounter – that whole tissue of Maimed Kings and their Waste Land, the Challenges at Springs, the Annual Kings and their annual replacements, Sarras, the Green Knights. This world was opened up by Jessie Weston's *From Ritual to Romance* and has recently been reinforced by John Darrah's *The Real Camelot* (1981). The latter is a very powerful book, rigorously argued, perhaps over-rigorously – it has a gruesome picture of an assembly of castrated kings waiting to die in west Wales! – but I think it argues a defensible case. The strange, half-remembered semi-pagan characters were one cause of the peculiar appeal of the Arthurian legends. Might they not represent the earliest memories of the human race in Western Europe?

These considerations cannot apply to Arthur himself or his close companions. Arthur was a Christian. If he existed at all, as I think he did, he emerged as a hero of the Britons at the beginning of their four-hundred-year-long struggle for freedom against the Saxons and was enshrined in the literature of the Welsh. He thus found himself launched into one of the most spectacular odysseys Europe has ever known. Perhaps we should be content with that and the myriad interpretations it has engendered?

But the journey goes on, into realms that I at any rate cannot conceive. It may result in an Arthur who is fundamentally unrecognizable. I prefer to say farewell – and welcome to him now, in those haunting words of Tennyson's Bedivere, who was once the old Welsh hero Bedwyr, come into his own at last:

> *Ah! my Lord Arthur, whither shall I go?*
> *Where shall I hide my forehead and my eyes?*
> *For now I see the true old times are dead,*
> *When every morning brought a noble chance,*
> *And every chance brought out a noble knight. . .*
> *But now the whole Round Table is dissolved*
> *Which was an image of the mighty world,*
> *And I, the last, go forth companionless,*
> *And the days darken round me, and the years,*
> *Among new men, strange faces, other minds.*

BIBLIOGRAPHY

Original Arthurian literature available in translation, listed here in chronological order.
* = readable

*Gildas's 'The Ruin of Britain', ed. and trans. by Michael Winterbottom (Phillimore & Co., London, 1978).
*British History and The Welsh Annals, trans. by John Morris (Phillimore & Co., 1980).
*The Mabinogion, trans. and intro. by Gwyn Jones and Thomas Jones (J. M. Dent, Everyman's Library, London, 1949; reprint 1976). For the Welsh Arthurian tales, Culhwch and Olwen and The Dream of Rhonabwy – two of the four independent native tales; The Lady of the Fountain, Peredur Son of Efrawg, and Gereint Son of Erbin – the three romances; and the Four Branches of the Mabinogi.
Trioedd Ynys Prydein: The Welsh Triads, ed., trans. and commentary by Rachel Bromwich (University of Wales Press, Cardiff, 2nd edn 1978). For those with a stomach for hard scholarship.
*Geoffrey of Monmouth, The History of the Kings of Britain: Historia Regum Britanniae, ed. and trans. by Lewis Thorpe (Penguin Classics, Harmondsworth; reprint 1982).
*Wace, Roman de Brut and Layamon, Brut from Arthurian Chronicles, trans. by Eugene Mason (J. M. Dent, Everyman, London, 1976).
*Chrétien de Troyes, Arthurian Romances, ed. and trans. by D. D. R. Owen (J. M. Dent, Everyman's Library, London; reprint 1991). For Eric and Enide, Lancelot, and Yvain and Perceval.
*Beroul, The Romance of Tristan, trans. by Alan S. Fedrick (Penguin Classics, Harmondsworth, 1970).
*Wolfram von Eschenbach, Parzival, trans. by A. T. Hatto (Penguin Classics, Harmondsworth, 1980).
*Gottfried von Strassburg, Tristan, trans. by A. T. Hatto (Penguin Classics, Harmondsworth, 1960).
The Vulgate Version of the Arthurian Romances, ed. and partly trans. by H. O. Sommer (reprint AMS Press, New York, 1979). 8 vols, gigantic, for reference only.
*The Quest for the Holy Grail (from the Vulgate Cycle), ed. and trans. by P. M. Matrasso (Penguin Classics, Harmondsworth, 1969).
*The Death of King Arthur (from the Vulgate Cycle), ed. and trans. by James Cable (Penguin Classics, Harmondsworth, 1971).
*Sir Gawain and the Green Knight, ed. and trans. by Brian Stone (Penguin Classics, Harmondsworth; reprint 1974).
*Sir Thomas Malory, Le Morte d'Arthur, trans. by Janet Cowen, intro. by John Lawlor, 2 vols (Penguin Classics, Harmondsworth, 1969).
The Works of Sir Thomas Malory, ed. by Eugène Vinaver, Oxford Standard Authors (Clarendon Press, Oxford, 1990). A standard reference work.

Dr John Dee is quoted at length in two of my books. Gwyn A. Williams, *Madoc: The Making of a Myth* (Oxford, reprint 1987) and 'Welsh wizard and British empire' in *The Welsh in their History* (Croom Helm, London, 1982). Dee's own *General and Rare Memorials Pertayning to the Perfecte Arte of Navigation* (London, 1577) is in print, but in the British Library. See also, in general, Frances Dee in her many books, particularly *The Occult Philosophy in the Elizabethan Age* (Routledge & Kegan Paul, London, 1979).

*William Blake is covered in David V. Erdman, *The Poetry and Prose of William Blake* (New York, 1965) and his *Blake: Prophet against Empire* (Princeton University Press, revised ed., 1977). The Arthur section here is from an unpublished talk of mine at Oxford.

*Works of Art in the House of Lords, ed. by Maurice Bond; intro. by John Charlton; detailed description of the works of art and the rooms they are in by Jeremy Maule (HMSO, London, 1980).

*Alfred Tennyson is covered in *The Poems of Tennyson*, ed. by Christopher Ricks (Longman, London, 1969). There is a pungent treatment in Geoffrey Ashe, *The Quest for Arthur's Britain* (see below).

Other nineteenth- and twentieth-century writers are mentioned in chapters 11 and 12.

Scholarly, ultra and more liberal:

*Leslie Alcock, *Arthur's Britain: History and Archaeology AD 367–634* (Allen Lane, London, 1971).

*Richard Barber, *Ring Arthur: Hero and Legend* (The Boydell Press, Suffolk; reprint 1986). A generous and thorough treatment of the whole of Arthurian history and literature by a prolific Arthurian scholar. It appeared in earlier editions under the names of *Arthur of Albion* (1961) and *King Arthur in Legend and History* (1973). See also, by the same author, *The Arthurian Legends; an Illustrated Anthology* (The Boydell Press, Suffolk; reprint 1987), and *The Figure of Arthur* (Longman, London, 1972).

*John Darrah, *The Real Camelot: Paganism and the Arthurian Romances* (Thames & Hudson, London, 1981). Rigorous and challenging, probably drives the case too far, but should be read.

Arthurian Literature in the Middle Ages, ed. by R. S. Loomis (Clarendon Press, Oxford, 1959). Thirty-four scholars of international repute, covering Britain and Europe. Fundamental, not easy. R. S. Loomis is also the author of many other celebrated works, e.g. *Celtic Myth and Arthurian Romance* (Columbia, 1927) and *Wales and the Arthurian Legend* (University of Wales Press, Cardiff, 1956).

The Arthur of the Welsh, ed. by Rachel Bromwich, A. O. H. Jarman, Brynley F. Roberts (University of Wales Press, Cardiff, 1991). The first serious modernization of Loomis's volume, with a great deal more up-to-date material on Wales, Brittany and related material. Essential, if difficult.

*The Quest for Arthur's Britain, ed. by Geoffrey Ashe, with Leslie Alcock, C. A. Ralegh Radford, Philip Rahtz (Paladin, London; reprint 1973). An Informative book, edited and much of it written by a remarkable man. See many other works by him, especially *King Arthur's Avalon* (Fontana, London; reprint, 1990); *The Discovery of King Arthur* (Debrett's Peerage Ltd, London, 1985) and many others.

Some interesting books:

Geoffrey Ashe, _A Guidebook to Arthurian Britain_ (Longman, London, 1980).

Neil Fairbairn, _A Travellers' Guide to the Kingdoms of Arthur_, with photographs by Michael Cyprien (Evans Brothers, London, 1983).

*Graeme Fife, _Arthur the King: the Themes behind the Legends_ (BBC Books, London, 1990). Racy, unorthodox and entertaining, full of robust reflection on many issues.

*John Morris, _The Age of Arthur_, 3 vols (Phillimore & Co., London, 1977). Committed to the thesis that Arthur was an Emperor. Not in any way accepted, but fascinating reading.

*Graham Phillips and Martin Keatman, _King Arthur: The True Story_ (Random House, Arrow, London, 1992–3). One of the best of the multitudinous 'detective stories'; the general identification I tend to agree with, but I find the final conclusions hard to take.

*Nikolai Tolstoy, _The Quest for Merlin_ (Hamish Hamilton, London, 1985). Fascinating and very thorough, becomes imaginative.

Many other books will crop up in the course of reading. Make your own way!

INDEX